PROBLEMS OF RUSSIAN ROMANTICISM

Problems of Russian Romanticism

Edited by
ROBERT REID
Lecturer in Slavonic Studies
Queen's University, Belfast

Gower

PG
3015.5
.R6
P68
1986

Published by

Gower Publishing Company Limited,
Gower House,
Croft Road,
Aldershot,
Hants GU11 3HR
England

Gower Publishing Company,
Old Post Road,
Brookfield,
Vermont 05036
U.S.A.

British Library Cataloguing in Publication Data

Problems of Russian Romanticism.
   1. Russian literature——19th century——
History and criticism   2. Romanticism
   I. Reid, Robert, *1948–*   II. Series
891.709'003   PG3012

ISBN: 0 566 05029 3

Printed in Great Britain by Blackmore Press, Longmead, Shaftesbury, Dorset

Contents

Editor's preface

The literature of the romantic age has perennially attracted the widest spectrum of critical interest because each succeeding generation has perceived in it (generally with justification) the archetypes of its own 'modern' literary forms. For the Russians romanticism is of unique importance because under its influence their literature developed much of its national character. The six Russian writers dealt with in this volume reflect the wide and varied range of this influence during its most potent phase — the first half of the nineteenth century. The greatest writers of this period — Pushkin, Gogol and Lermontov — were deeply affected by romanticism, but its impact on their works is highly personalised and generally unideological. By contrast, Marlinsky, Odoyevsky and Venevitinov, lesser known but significant figures in the history of Russian romanticism, subscribed to a more programmatic view of romantic art, which they developed along revolutionary or philosophical lines. The present work aims not only to offer a representative picture of the complex world of nineteenth-century Russian romanticism, but also to furnish some insight into Russian romantic aesthetics, both past and present: its ideological controversies and its relation to contemporary western theories of romanticism.

As editor, I should like to thank the other five contributors for their patience and co-operation in the compilation of this work.

Robert Reid
Belgrade 1986

The contributors

A. D. P. Briggs
Senior Lecturer in Russian Studies, University of Bristol

Neil Cornwell
Senior Lecturer in Slavonic Studies, Queen's University, Belfast

Neil B. Landsman
Lecturer, School of Languages and Area Studies, Portsmouth Polytechnic

T. E. Little
formerly Lecturer in Russian Studies, University of Hull. Now at Holy Cross College, Mosgiel, New Zealand.

A. B. McMillin
Professor of Russian, University of Liverpool

Robert Reid
Lecturer in Slavonic Studies, Queen's University, Belfast

1 Russian theories of romanticism

ROBERT REID

The age of romanticism, coinciding as it did in Russia with the emergence of a distinct national literary tradition, has been a subject of abiding fascination for both pre- and post-revolutionary Russian literary historians and theorists. For much of the Soviet period, it is true, the terms in which it could be written about were severely circumscribed, but since the late 1950s an increasing freedom of approach has been evident in the number and variety of theoretical treatments of romanticism; indeed, as L. G. Leighton has noted, discussion of the subject has at times taken a form reminiscent of the Lovejoy—Wellek—Peckham debates of some forty years ago.[1] On the whole, however, theory and controversy have been dominated by criteria unique to the history of Soviet aesthetics and by such topics as the nature of revolutionary romanticism and the relation of romanticism to socialist realism.

The originality of thought on romanticism which now makes itself felt in Soviet letters is the product of a determined struggle against an earlier aesthetic dogmatism, traces of which still survive. So while there have indeed been Soviet Lovejoys mistrustful of 'definitive definitions' of romanticism, the experience of which this mistrust is born is something altogether different from the reprise of Dupuis and Cotonet which was Lovejoy's starting point.[2] Soviet theorists have produced accounts of romanticism which have no obvious counterparts in the West, but, equally, some of the more recent trends in Anglo-American romanticism studies typified by M. H. Abrams, Irving Massey and others, in which romantic thought and methodology are accorded more than mere historical relevance, have as yet found no reflection in Soviet

1

literature on romanticism, though they might be readily applied to it.[3]

My aim in this chapter is twofold: firstly to examine the views on nineteenth-century romanticism of such prominent Soviet critics as U. R. Fokht, G. N. Pospelov, I. F. Volkov, Yu. V. Mann and so on, and to discuss their methodology; secondly to look at features of the work of Russian aestheticians from the 1820s and 1830s in the hope of providing a profitable juxtaposition with the foregoing. The full extension of nineteenth-century definitions of romanticism has been amply documented elsewhere;[4] here the intention is to point to some early theoretical insights which, romantic in character and inspiration, have, it is felt, something positive to offer to a contemporary discussion of romanticism.

In a recent work, A. P. El'yashevich, reviewing the progress of Soviet thought on romanticism over the last two decades, ventured a dichotomy between 'dominant' theories which seek to define romanticism in terms of a single pervasive characteristic and theories of 'structure' which seek to build up an aggregate (*sovokupnost'*) of characteristics in order to arrive at a synthetic definition.[5] He noted a further division in the dominant theories between those of the Timofeyev school, who see romanticism and realism as two timeless modes of creativity, and those like Volkov and, to some extent, Fokht who identify romanticism with artistic subjectivity. El'yashevich's classification is certainly useful in itself but also because it illustrates a principle which seems to pervade thought on romanticism at every level, including the artistic, namely exclusive dualism. Philip Hobsbaum's term 'the romantic dichotomy' sounds applicable enough to this principle, but in practice he limits it to 'the dichotomy between mind and body, education and emotion, knowledge and intuition'.[6] Nobody familiar with critical theories of romanticism could fail to recognise the bicellular reproduction of synonyms characteristic of this dichotomy when in danger of definition. For the question is, at what point in the chain of synonyms can it safely be said that a given pair have no more in common with their predecessors than the fact of being either dichotomous or at least mutually exclusive? Hearing, for instance, that 'education/emotion' is substantially the same dichotomy as 'mind/body' expressed in a more social context, may I then continue the chain with discipline/chaos; society/anarchy; conservative/revolutionary, and so on?

The problem is that the romantic dichotomy is no respecter of disciplinary divisions. The purely aesthetic classic/romantic becomes the more historicised archaist/innovator of Tynyanov or the thoroughly politicised reactionary/progressive once beloved of Soviet criticism.[7] Or it may be transformed into the immemorial philosophical rivalry of

Aristotle and Plato popular with Sheviryov and some of the earlier Russian writers on romanticism. Likewise realism may be equated with empiricism or materialism, and romanticism with idealism. In western criticism, while such dichotomous views of romanticism might be thought sweeping, the protean ease with which they manifest themselves in spheres as diverse as philosophy, art and social and political thought would not in itself be problematical. Wellek's three-way definition of romanticism makes room for philosophical and historical, as well as purely artistic, categories.[8] Northrop Frye, recalling Kant's advice to Fichte, suggests that the latter and Schelling were really literary, rather than philosophical, minds.[9] It is of course true, as Morse Peckham suggests, that some historical phenomena, notably social movements have ceased to be thought of as specifically romantic phenomena.[10] On the other hand Howard Mumford Jones is able to see the French, though not the American, Revolution in terms of romantic aspirations.[11] Moreover recent trends in romantic scholarship, which Peter Thorslev attributes to the 'belated influence of . . . Sartre, Heidegger, and others' and the 'resurgence of interest in things Hegelian', have only served to strengthen that approach to romanticism which regards it as a philosophical as much as a literary phenomenon.[12]

Here the Soviet and western approaches to romanticism radically part company. The modern Soviet approaches to romanticism, though they had begun to surface some years earlier, find their sanction in the literary debates which took place in the Institute of World Literature in 1957. There two previous official views of romanticism, one more extreme than the other, were laid to rest. The first was that which had been propounded by the theorists of the Russian Association of Proletarian Writers (RAPP) during the late 1920s and early 1930s. Seeking to protect the young and vulnerable growth of the new proletarian literature, they set up what was, for romanticism, a ruinous equation between art and philosophy. One of RAPP's theoreticians, L. Averbakh, stated it as follows: 'Materialism and idealism mean not only a particular attitude and world view . . . they are also different ways of writing'.[13] A. Fadeyev put it even more starkly: 'We distinguish realism and romanticism as methods more or less consistent with materialism and idealism in artistic creativity'.[14] This was the nadir for romanticism in the history of Soviet criticism. Wholly identified with a 'false' philosophy and with the social basis of that philosophy, the bourgeoisie, romanticism was merely the literary formulation of the doomed participant in a dialectic supposedly taking place on every level of reality.

The result of this view of literature was to set up the dichotomy *par excellence* in the history of romantic criticism: realism/anti-realism. Apart from the glaring absence of romanticism which this dichotomy enforced, later critics noted the typological ineptitude of the formula:

anti-realism was a receptacle into which all ideologically unacceptable genres, schools and movements were thrown, whether classical, romantic or symbolist, whether or not related by anything more than their disgrace. A second critical objection to this and subsequent dichotomies was that it was based on evaluation (*otsenka*) rather than scientific method, on the supposition that one literary school is, for a non-literary reason, superior to another. The shift in this view, which began in 1932 and culminated with the Writers' Congress two years later, was characterised chiefly by the concession that there was such a phenomenon as revolutionary romanticism which could and perhaps should become an active participant in the realistic method. Romanticism was accordingly resurrected only to be sliced in two by a new and more protean dichotomy.

The establishment of this 'two romanticisms' methodology is principally attributable to the influence of Gorky, though, as V. I. Kuleshov points out, it was not unknown to Belinsky and the early romantics.[15] Gorky himself modified its terminology at least once, calling it, when first formulated as early as 1909, individualistic romanticism/collectivist romanticism, and later, in 1928, the more well-known passive romanticism/active romanticism.[16] From this initial pair have developed what Kuleshov calls 'a long chain of variants' and he lists as synonyms for passive — reactionary, conservative and regressive; and for active — progressive, advanced and, one might add, revolutionary.[17] While this dichotomy (and its variants) was a considerable improvement on its predecessor it has been largely subject to the same criticisms. A. N. Sokolov asked trenchantly whether there was any point in speaking of romanticism at all if it were so clearly composed of incompatible elements.[18] Kuleshov, whose interests lie with the Slavophiles in particular, argues that they were no less 'active' or more 'passive' than the revolutionary Decembrists and in support of this argument quotes what appears to be an agitational song from the unlikely pen of K. Aksakov.[19] Apart from these methodological objections, it is also true to say that this modified approach to romanticism was far from conferring on the latter the autonomous historical and artistic status which it deserved. When I. Gronsky declared in October 1932, 'We are for romanticism', he certainly did not mean romanticism *per se*. He was for 'socialist, revolutionary romanticism'.[20] Romanticism was accorded the status of an inferior and often suspect variant of realism and it was incumbent upon literary historians to show in effect that nineteenth-century Russian romantics had been doing their best to be progressive and that works like Lermontov's *Demon* or *Mtsyri* were really works of realistic intent, limited however by the unfortunate circumstances of the writer's socio-cultural outlook and place in history.

4

Above all Gorky's active/passive dichotomy with its many variants was still based on essentially non-aesthetic criteria. One could speak of romanticism but only in terms which reflected essentially socio-historical oppositions. It is scarcely surprising that when the attack on this traditional view began in the 1950s it was directed particularly to rupturing once for all the tenacious alliance between artistic and philosophical or sociological criteria in approaches to romanticism. In part, this also implied attacks on dichotomous classifications for such reasons as were detailed above. The alliance gave way but the dichotomy proved more persistent. B. G. Reizov's 'romanticisms', so reminiscent of Lovejoy's plurality, enjoyed a brief flowering of enthusiasm in 1957 but also attracted retorts from A. N. Sokolov identical even in terminology with those of Wellek's to Lovejoy.[21] However L. I. Timofeyev in the same year reformulated the old dichotomy of realism/anti-realism in the more civilised form of realism/romanticism where neither element is understood either philosophically or sociologically but simply as a timeless method of artistic creation. Claiming support in the works of Belinsky, Timofeyev conceives romanticism as the transformative principle in art. The romantic artist, according to Timofeyev, stresses 'his aesthetic evaluations of reality . . . either rejecting or affirming one or other aspect of it'.[22]   The realist, by contrast, tries to represent reality 'in such forms . . . as may be observed in life itself, more exactly, within the bounds of the social causality of the age'.

Timofeyev's dichotomy of art still finds support in Soviet scholarship. Its chief virtue is the status it affords to romanticism: 'Romanticism does not basically contradict realism. As Belinsky rightly said, they both move towards the single aim of generalising the life process'. Thus the difference between the romantic and realistic outlooks is seen largely as a matter of stress. However, even given the most favourable conditions of comparison with realism, romanticism tends to be slighted by the juxtaposition, if only by implication. 'Within the bounds of the social causality of the age' has a certain scientific authority to it which, in the Soviet tradition, belongs to realism as of right. I. F. Volkov also noted the methodological weakness of Timofeyev's 'arbitrary' formulation of romanticism, pointing out that the transformative principle which Timofeyev regards as the principal characteristic of romanticism is by no means unique to romanticism but may also be found in 'sentimentalism, expressionism and intellectualism'.[23] This weakness arises, of course, from the essentially non-historical basis of Timofeyev's definitions. True, he does speak of the necessity of distinguishing 'romanticism in the wide sense of the word' (that is, his primary definition) from the 'narrow sense' of an artistic method associated with the romantic epoch, but many critics would now dispute whether the 'wide sense of the word' is romanticism at all and, as we shall see, have invented a better terminology to cope with this distinction.

Soviet romanticism scholarship since the 1950s has thus been characterised by a widespread questioning of the old dichotomous views, whether of romanticism itself or of literary creativity as a whole, and by a rejection of the absolute equation between romanticism and idealism. Literary history has been a major catalyst in this process, particularly the work of such critics as G. A. Gukovsky who in effect stressed the autonomy of the romantic period, which in its uniqueness could not and should not be judged as inferior to the age of realism.[24] Historicism, always strong in the Russian literary tradition, does not however always yield objectivity or harmonise opinions. Shevyryov, who in 1835 urged 'thinking history' as an antidote to Russia's cultural inexperience, declared, 'Life is always new, but knowledge of the past is already one half of experience'.[25] Equally we may invert the proposition: knowledge of the past may be half of experience, but life itself is always new. The hint of caution which thus emerges is surely what Henri Peyre has in mind when he writes that: 'it is always plausible to modernise the past . . . and (not without a certain *naïveté*) to pay it the compliment of having resembled ourselves'.[26] Thus those who wish to argue for the autonomy of romanticism as an artistic movement may agree with K. N. Grigoryan that there is no need for 'the picture of a literature's internal development exactly to coincide with the history of socio-political and philosophical thought'.[27] But those who wish to argue precisely such a coincidence will agree with Volkov's equation between a particular set of unstable social conditions and the emergence of the romantic consciousness in Europe.[28] Others still may wish to stress with A. M. Gurevich the different form taken by that consciousness in Russia where 'the personality never felt itself so insulated, isolated and cut off from the whole as in the West' and romanticism coexisted with Enlightenment ideas.[29] The history of romanticism, far from offering a single objective view of the phenomenon, must inevitably become an adjunct to individual critics' definitions or understandings of that phenomenon. It is hard to agree with A. A. Gadzhiyev's division of Soviet romantic criticism into the 'typological' *and* the 'historical'.[30] It is rare to find the latter approach without some element of the former implied, though the reverse is not necessarily true and there is, therefore, some validity to S. Ye. Shatalov's call for 'the unifying, merging and fusing of two methodologies or approaches: the typological and the concrete historical'.[31] On the whole, however, it is less meaningful to contrast a historical approach to romanticism with a specific aesthetic methodology than to examine different approaches to methodology itself and this, one feels, is the value of El'yashevich's classification, mentioned above, in which romantic critical theory divides into two approaches: the 'dominant' and the 'structural'.

It is not altogether clear why El'yashevich uses the term 'structure' in this context rather than the commoner term 'typology' which is clearly what he means by it. Typology is now a major preoccupation of Soviet romantic scholarship and among its major proponents are Sokolov, Kuleshov, I. Neupokoyeva and G. N. Pospelov. It is *par excellence* a scientific approach intent on an aggregation and classification of the manifold variants of romanticism which so dispirited Lovejoy, and it is pursued, as Neupokoyeva likes to put it, both 'vertically' and 'horizontally', that is, taking account of both historical and national variations in romantic form.[32] It hotly maintains, particularly against criticisms such as Reizov's, that there is a general phenomenon to be dealt with in the study of romanticism. Sokolov asks challengingly:

> If in many literatures, there has arisen a phenomenon with which it has become normal to associate the appellation of romanticism, then inevitably questions arise: what is common to romantic movements which have sprung up in different countries? What is the unified essence of romanticism in view of the variety of its national forms? How do general and particular relate in romanticism?[33]

The need to come to terms with the essence of romanticism or with its general meaning as an *a priori* makes typology rather different from a conventional science despite the scientific spirit of its approach. As Kuleshov says:

> The typology of romanticism cannot be established in a purely empirical manner. It is an aggregate theoretical influence which transfers the study of the general and particular in romanticism on to the comparative plane and on to a new and higher level.[34]

Typologists expend much effort in pointing to the inadequacy of former attempts at defining or classifying romanticism. This applies as much to the cruder dichotomies already mentioned as to the schematic divisions of earlier Russian romanticism scholars like P. N. Sakulin and I. I. Zamotin, whose three- or four-way classifications of romanticism (for instance Zamotin's individualism/nationalism/universalism) are felt to be insufficiently flexible.[35] Indeed it might not be an exaggeration to describe typology as an approach to romanticism which affirms a commonsense belief in the phenomenon of that name, eschews definitions *pro tem.* and devotes itself to a detailed study of the differences and similarities between various forms of romanticism in the hope that ultimately a natural definition will emerge.

For other theorists, however, the fact that romanticism is generally viewed as a single phenomenon (Reizov's pluralism finding little support) is sufficient reason to attempt a definition of that elusive general character or essence in which the typologists believe without however becoming mired in the particularities of typology. These theorists represent the 'dominant' approach in El'yashevich's terminology. He includes Timofeyev in this category too, but, as I hope has been made clear, Timofeyev still represents the dichotomous approach to romanticism despite his modifications to it and so displays a methodology quite distinct from the typologists on the one hand and theorists, such as U. R. Fokht and Volkov, who seek to associate romanticism with one salient feature. As El'yashevich rightly points out, the key to both these critics' approaches to romanticism is subjectivism but there is also considerable divergence between them in the value they put on the latter.

Clearly subjectivism would come very high in a list of essential characterisations of romanticism. As a phenomenon it is not peculiar to romanticism, but considering romantic subjectivism in specific socio-historic terms, it is possible to see it as the unifying principle within a diversity of political, philosophical and artistic movements and as the common feature within each movement. Volkov represents this view very thoroughly and attempts to show that the common feature in all romantic literature is the 'human individual both as object and subject of creativity'.[36] The advantages of Volkov's approach are its breadth and catholicity. Romantic subjectivity or the cult of the individual applies to the egoistic philosophy of Fichte and the politics of Napoleon, and underlies F. Schlegel's theory of romantic irony and the phenomenon of dualism in romantic literature.[37] Volkov's insistence on taking subjectivity into account as an essential ingredient of any romantic phenomenon enables him to pin down certain intellectual stances which are typically, though not exclusively, romantic, such as, for instance, two-world dualism (dvoyemiriye). Volkov points out that, though (to risk a calque from Russian) the 'discosmos' was familiar to medieval man as heaven/earth and to Renaissance and Enlightenment man as the discrepancy between real and utopian human society, romantic man's reception of it differed from his predecessors' precisely in the subjective terms in which he conceived it.[38] The subjective element is sufficiently strong in Volkov's opinion to justify calling the romantic version of this descrepancy a 'tricosmos' for there is in it not merely the opposition between a world rejected and an ideal world sought, but a third 'inner' world of the subject which explains and motivates the seeking and rejecting.

Impressive though Volkov's subjectivism is, it is still based on a rather crude equation between romanticism and socio-historical conditions and on the still unfortunately widespread supposition that the behaviour of historical figures is explicable by the fact that, unlike ourselves, they were ignorant of the real socio-economic laws of human existence:

8

The romantics saw that these [trade and monetary] relations separate people and alienate man from society, but they were as yet unaware that it was precisely on the basis of the universal dominance of trade and monetary relations that the strongest and most distinct social units — the bourgeoisie and proletariat — were enabled to form themselves and to lead through their struggle to the establishment of a single socialist union of individuals, peoples, nations and governments.[39]

From an insistence on the same equation comes perhaps a tendency to speak of romantic creativity in terms almost indistinguishable from realism:

So, when the romantic creates his artistic world from the tangible reality contemporary to him, he reproduces [that reality's] human characters as concrete and historical, as the proper characters of human individuals living in the given concrete historical reality.[40]

For a treatment of romantic subjectivity which does not base itself on such non-literary criteria we must turn to U. R. Fokht's theory of the intuitive impulse in romantic creativity.

Fokht prefaces his ideas with the following highly significant observation: 'An understanding of art as one of the modes of ideologically reflecting reality demands the clarification of the gnoseological premises of any artistic method'.[41] Fokht's approach, then, is epistemological: he is interested in exactly how reality becomes idea in the artistic process and is willing to define that process accordingly. Thus realism is based on and characterised by 'observation, study, generalisation and typification of objective reality' and originated at the Renaissance.[42] Romanticism, by contrast, is distinguished by an 'intuitive perception of reality'. In this epistemological emphasis, Fokht comes close to identifying a single basis for both artistic and philosophical modes of perceiving reality, but this is far from the deleterious identification of art and philosophy already touched on in the context of earlier Soviet aesthetic theory; indeed it is much nearer to the views held by some of the nineteenth-century Russian romantics themselves on the nature of the artistic process.

Fokht is careful to circumscribe his use of 'intuitivism' in context. It is not, he insists, the epistemological theory of the same name which posits direct knowledge of the object as the only form of perception.[43] He is also at pains to point out the role of the intuitive 'leap' as a necessary initial stage in all branches of science (the role of the experimental process being to verify the said leap).[44] His most significant circumscription however is that which pertains to the particular gnoseological climate in which intuition is most likely to replace a more rational mode of knowledge. The condition which most favours it is the writer's dissatisfaction with reality whether for 'moral (Zhukovsky), social (Ryleyev), or psychological (Fet)' reasons.[45] In view of such dissatisfaction on the part of its proponents it is not surprising that 'romanticism concentrates wholly on the desirable and the possible'.[46] This concentration is based largely on intuition in the absence of more rational means of realising desiderata. To this extent Fokht's intuition coincides partly with the traditional concept of romantic imagination, bridled however in as much as it is still a response to objective reality.

The intuitive approach of the romantic is vividly illustrated in Fokht's comparison of three autumnal nature descriptions by Pushkin, Nekrasov and Tyutchev respectively. The first two poets offer a 'selection of objective details' with the aim of realistically conveying the landscape.[47] Tyutchev, predictably enough, achieves something rather different: 'an intuitive penetration into reality with its concealed dynamism and contradictoriness'.[48] For Tyutchev: 'the pictorial details become a means for expressing the author's understanding, not only of autumn but of reality in general'. Fokht goes on to classify intuition according to a modification of the criteria noted above: psychological (Zhukovsky, Fet), philosophical (Odoyevsky, Tyutchev), social (Ryleyev).[49] These classifications are, naturally enough, also his classifications of romanticism itself.

The intuitive approach to romanticism is not only methodologically sound but it also infuses into critical theory something of the refreshing flavour of original romantic practice. Fokht however also insists on rationalising intuition into a submissive position on psychological authority:

> Attentiveness to the possible, striving to express an ideal and an intuitive perception of life facilitate the emotional fervour so characteristic of romanticism. This arises from the very nature of emotion itself: 'emotion is induced by an insufficiency of information necessary for the achievement of an aim. Replacing and compensating this insufficiency, it [emotion] provides for the continuation of action and facilitates the search for new information...'[50]

Strangely enough, in support of his view of the romantic's intuitive penetration into the truth of things, Fokht introduces a quotation from G. D. Gachev which suggests, in contradiction to the above, that romantics did not care much for 'information' even when it was available: they 'did not respect facts or the appearance of things: the latter, they considered, could only distort the truth and by weighing down the artist prevent him from getting at it'.[51] Finally we may legitimately ask whether the romantic's appropriation of the intuitive mode of perception arises from some cause quite other than his moral or social disaffection. Arthur K. Moore, writing of substantially the same phenomenon under the title of 'oracular expression', sees its origins in quite different terms:

> Romanticism fabricated a poet of vast oracular powers largely from superstitious notions and suspicious philosophies which the Renaissance has gathered up somewhat by chance with the rational part of the Graeco-Roman legacy.[52]

Admittedly Moore is dealing with the extremer aspects of romantic intuition but the implication that the latter is connected with the survival or revival of ancient notions of the bardic role is perhaps no less valid an explanation of it than notions of gnoseological inadequacy. After all, such inadequacy does not necessarily produce an intuitive response: it may produce a Bacon as easily as a Pascal.

The relation of art to philosophy, of artistic consciousness to epistemology, are indeed crucial to the subjectivist approach to romanticism. It may well be argued that the creative process has its own laws which may run parallel to but are not determined by prevalent philosophies or ideologies. On the other hand A. M. Mikeshin, noting that romanticism first made its appearance in the literary arts, has some justification in claiming that: 'literature, by comparison with architecture, sculpture, painting and, particularly, music, is the most "ideological" form of art' and 'like no other concentrates and condenses the ideology, psychology, ethics and aesthetics of its epoch' and is consequently the most 'spiritually synthetic' of all the arts.[53] These observations typify not so much a Soviet as a Russian view of the peculiar functions of literature, traditional since the 1830s. It is a view which lends itself to *a priori* theorising about the relationship of literature and literary movements to philosophy and history, a tendency present not only in Soviet criticism but, as we shall see, in the aesthetic theories of the early romantics. It would be wrong however to conclude a review of major Soviet approaches to romanticism without mentioning two names which do not fit readily into the categories we have been dealing with.

Ye. A. Maymin and Yu. V. Mann represent what might be termed the 'pragmatic' approach to Russian romanticism in that they do not preface their considerable studies of the subject with preconceptions about methodology: what methodology they have derives naturally from the particular aims of their works. Partly, one feels, this approach grows out of an exasperation with typological and classificational techniques; as Maymin says, 'It is simply impossible to embrace and name everything. Nor should a [methodological] scheme strive to do this. It can only determine the principal tendencies of the phenomenon'.[54] Maymin actually works on a modification of Fokht's classifications of romanticism and it 'has, above all, a practical character'. Contemplative romanticism is represented by Zhukovsky, civic and revolutionary by

Ryleyev and philosophical by Venevitinov, Tyutchev and Odoyevsky. Pushkin and Lermontov are seen as having a romanticism of 'synthetic' character, that is, a particular combination of the aforementioned classes with, in addition, 'irrepeatable' characteristics of their own.

Mann distinguishes his approach to romanticism as follows: 'Our investigation differs from general works on Russian romanticism . . . in leaving aside the problems relating to the creative history of works and their mutual influence etc., etc., and concentrates instead on aspects of artistic structure'.[55] Mann objects to Sokolov's system because he does not think that the mere aggregation of classifications is any material improvement on theories which attempt to subsume romanticism under a single definition; both methods offer only 'summary or impressionistic valuations' whereas the structural approach seeks to analyse the true substance of romantic works in themselves.[56] Mann concentrates in particular on 'artistic conflict' or 'opposition' in his analysis of romantic works. This opposition arises, according to Mann, from a simple creative axiom: 'a property of poetic utterance in general, whereby, in affirming one thing, it *ipso facto* denies another and vice versa'.[57] Such oppositions are found in central character/others; historical/contemporary; rural/urban; native/civilised, and so on. Inevitably there is a dialectical flavour to such a critical approach. The progress of literature is seen, in part at least, in terms of the intensification, abatement and solution of such conflicts. This approach to romanticism has affinities with that of H. G. Schenk's concentration on the 'contradictoriness, dissonance and inner conflict of the Romantic mind'[58] which leads him to pursue his subject in terms of similar oppositions admittedly from a less structural perspective than Mann: progress/disenchantment; forebodings/nostalgia for the past; nihilism/yearning for faith, and so on. Mann can be said to achieve a genuine approach to romanticism with the advantage that it grows out of an in-depth investigation of romantic works themselves rather than from theoretical generalisation. In particular his treatment of the romantic dichotomy in its various forms is achieved largely within an artistic framework and without recourse to the socio-political criteria frequently encountered in earlier Soviet romanticism scholarship.

It is surely no accident that during the twenties of this century both P. N. Sakulin in Russia and Lovejoy in America voiced their dissatisfaction with the plethora of contradictory definitions of romanticism.[59] No doubt, theirs was a timely cry of exasperation at the coral-like growth of definitions which had been proceeding steadily for the last century. But Lovejoy's denial of the unity of romanticism is by no means the only reaction to the bewildering complexity of definitions.

It may be argued that since accretion is a process it must be subject to some law. El'yashevich, for instance, sees this process as 'the rise, development, pre-eminence and fall of scientific hypotheses' and calls it a 'dramatic and majestic chapter in the history of any science'.[60] Hypotheses, even when they have been 'discarded by life' do not sink without trace and have served the purpose of 'showing a particular side' of the object of study, or, presumably, if they were false, of facilitating the emergence of the true hypothesis. A similar view of intellectual progress is held in the West by Albert Hofstadter who holds that 'forms are built to let the essential purpose advance and . . . advance can be continued only by the renewed destruction of these forms'.[61] Hofstadter calls this process the 'dialectic that is involved in all forward-looking life'. However, it is far from self-evident that hypotheses are subject to the sort of ordered obsolescence implied by El'yashevich, for in the case of romanticism contemporary definitions are by no means always better equipped to explain the phenomenon than those of a century and a half ago, and besides this, rejected corner stones are constantly being picked up and built back into the masonry.

But there is another aspect to Lovejoy-ism: it is directed as much against the word romanticism as against the accumulation of definitions. The word has both 'congenital and acquired ambiguities' which makes it untrustworthy. The result is that:

> When certain of these Romanticisms have in truth significant elements in common, they are not necessarily the same elements in any two cases. Romanticism A may have one characteristic presupposition or impulse, X, which it shares with Romanticism B, another characteristic, Y, which it shares with Romanticism C, to which X is wholly foreign.[62]

This mistrust of the name romanticism, called by its critics nominalism, is strikingly similar to some of the things Wittgenstein was saying about verbal exactitude some twenty years later:

> Consider for example the proceedings we call 'games'. . . . What is common to them all? — Don't say: 'There *must* be something in common, or they would not be called "games"' — but *look* and *see* whether there is anything common to all. — For if you look at them you will not see something that is common to *all*, but similarities, relationships, and a whole series of them at that.[63]

Wittgenstein examined groups of games and noted that in any group you may find 'many correspondences' with another group but 'many common features drop out and others appear'. The difference, however, between Wittgenstein and Lovejoy lies in the former's attitude to 'vagueness'. For Wittgenstein a word like 'game' lacks 'boundaries'. It is at best a system of family relationships which eludes further definition. But this lack of definition is not necessarily a deficiency in the application of any word: 'Is it even an advantage to replace an indistinct picture by a sharp one? Isn't the indistinct one often exactly what we need?'[64]

The awareness that some concepts *are* blurred and the awareness that they may *need* to be blurred are the very alpha and omega of Russian romanticism scholarship. Vyazemsky's elusive house-sprite and Belinsky's 'enigmatic subject', traditional prefaces to the challenging tasks of definition, may indeed have to be accepted for what they are, adequate definitional premises in themselves.[65] Maymin, for instance, cannot see the advantage in setting up or attempting to set up an exhaustive definition of romanticism, particularly in view of the fact that literary terminology is, of its nature, conditional and relativistic.[66]

Something of the Wittgensteinian spirit is undoubtedly present in modern Soviet romanticism scholarship. G. N. Pospelov, for example, speaks of a 'homonym tree' of romanticism which has grown up with the years.[67] It has a basic 'sense-trunk' and branches representing the proliferating theories. The critic's task is to note the disposition of the branches without however being able to unravel all the history of its growth. This is a nice image, not least because it revives the spirit of organicism in which many of the romantics themselves approached art. It is also an epitome of the aims and methods of the typological approach to romanticism, which is scientific in spirit, mistrustful of *a priori* theorising and hopeful of eventual definition. Its scientific character is in marked contrast to the old dichotomous treatments of romanticism which it replaced: realism/anti-realism; passive/active romanticism. Dichotomy of course is not an ideal basis for classification since inevitably 'one side of a dichotomy is always characterised negatively, by the non-possession of the attribute which characterises the other side; and there is therefore no positive notion which we can develop in the subdivision of this side'.[68] Even terms like 'passive' are really disguised negatives signifying, for instance, in this case, the absence of activity, or, in the case of 'reactionary', the absence of progress. The sole advantage of dichotomy and the reason for its erstwhile predominance is its suitability for expressing categorical value judgments.

In contrast to such crudeness of approach, typology reverts to the classic mode of definition *per genus et per differentiam*. This explains the stress placed by Sokolov, Kuleshov and others on investigating both the 'general' and 'particular' features of romanticism. However, as Kuleshov notes, 'It is a most difficult problem to show the specific functioning of this "general" which may contain elements disparate in scale and meaning'.[69] Nevertheless a number of rules now seem to have emerged, which convincingly circumscribe the general field of research signified by the word romanticism. The most important of these is the widely accepted distinction between romanticism and *romantika*. The origin of the distinction is traceable to A. I. Beletsky, who, writing in 1927, formulated the axiom that: 'an artistic style . . . is usually connected to corresponding moods and is determined by a corresponding world-view: but the opposite need not apply: an idealistic mood need not demand for its expression a romantic style'.[70] What Beletsky referred to as an 'idealistic mood' is now called *romantika* by perhaps the majority of Soviet writers on Russian romanticism. It is indeed a most useful concept because, by distinguishing the romantic impulse from true romantic style in a work of art, it helps to explain the phenomenon of what is sometimes called romanticism *ante litteram*: the presence of quasi-romantic features in the works of Homer, Shakespeare and other literary figures who pre-date the romantic period proper. *Romantika* also enables one to speak of a common impulse underlying both romantic art and other philosophical and social phenomena contemporary with it, without however having to style the latter 'romantic' too.

Pospelov introduces a further concept which parallels the functions of *romantika* and which offers, in particular, a decent way out for the negative side of the old realism/anti-realism dichotomy. Pospelov's 'normativism' is essentially a positive formulation of anti-realism, shorn of course of its pejorative implications. By contrast with those in a realistic work, characters in a normative work 'act in conformity to the abstract conceptions of the writer'.[71] Thus a normative work is controlled principally by an arbitrary scheme of its writer and while, therefore, romantic works could be placed in the normative category they would by no means exhaust it, for it would also encompass works of sentimentalist, utopian and allegorical character, and so on. It is significant that the old negative category of 'not-realism' converts into the useful category of normativism, chiefly because romanticism has now been accorded rightful autonomy within that category. The opposition with realism however remains unaffected.

Finally mention must be made of Fokht's distinction between movements (*techeniya*) and schools (*napravleniya*) as a means of clarifying an understanding of romanticism.[72] Like romanticism/*romantika* it is a non-reversible implicative: all schools are movements, but the reverse is not necessarily so. Movements pre-date schools, which are, in effect, the self-conscious formulation or programming of movements. Such equations as these, in which the essential features of romanticism are distinguished from the non-essential and the general from the particular, are the characteristics of typological methodology and are perhaps its principal contribution to the study of romanticism. The chief drawback of such a system is its tendency towards a scholastic disinvolvement from the spirit of romanticism itself, despite a professed belief in the same. Romanticism becomes instead an objectified specimen for study and a historically distanced one at that. Alien to it for the most part are the sort of subjectivism (in its respectable sense) and dualistic criteria which characterised the theories of the romantics themselves and which find some reflection, as we have seen, in the work of Fokht and Mann.

It was suggested above that dichotomy is of nugatory value in the sort of critical idiom to which Soviet criticism formerly applied it. Yet its existential validity is indisputable. Not-self, for instance, may be an unpromising category from the point of view of the empirical scientist, but for the poet or philosopher who posits it as an ontological opposition to self it is a compelling axiom. A single subject may have an infinitude of predicates or not-subjects but the differentiation between subject and predicate remains the indisputable basis for proposition. Mann, as noted earlier, suggests that the affirmation of any one thing must inevitably posit its opposite and it is the very partiality of the romantic affirmation, its subjectivity, which generates the traditional romantic dichotomies of self/not-self; individual/society, etc. Romantic definitions are, as John B. Halsted rightly says, heuristic.[73] So too are the various formulations of the romantic dichotomy. Those who wish to see some eternal principle in it will call it, with H. J. K. Grierson, the systole and diastole of man's history.[74] Those who wish to regard the matter in psychological terms may support Bohdan Urbankowski's Darwinian division of romantics into weak and strong, according to whether they did or did not surrender in the struggle between self and world.[75] The same opposition may even be converted into philosophical terms if we care to use William James's division of philosophers into two types: the tender-minded and tough, which, not surprisingly, coincides with the distinction between idealist and materialist.[76]

As for romantic aestheticians themselves, however, they preferred to express the dichotomy in terms of emphasis rather than of downright opposition. It is an emphasis closer in nature to the selectivity of visual focus and perhaps for this reason graphic image and metaphor abound in their representations of intellectual and aesthetic processes. V. F. Odoyevsky, for instance, expressing the relation between idea (which in the Schellingian tradition he equates with philosophical truth) and form (which he regards principally as an artistic prerogative), represents the former by the fixed centre of a circle and the latter by the infinitude of points on the periphery.[77] This diagram may be taken to represent other such allotropic oppositions as truth/originality; one/many; the contemplator of truth/the interpretative artist.[78] Essential to them all is the organic view that the whole reconciles the parts and that duality is merely a particular and subordinate aspect of unity.

The most striking aspect of Odoyevsky's aesthetic views in particular is his use of musical parallelism to illustrate both aesthetic and philosophical perception. The idea or circle-centre now becomes the harmonious chord in which a plurality of notes sound as one. By contrast the form or expression of the idea is the temporal extension of these notes into the consecutiveness of melody. Harmony and melody thus represent the 'intensive and expansive' aspects of any phenomenon.[79] I. Ya. Kronenberg uses almost identical terms with the same intention, adopting the image of a great river filled by many tributaries 'from opposite countries of the world' which unite and combine in a single current.[80] This is his illustration of the synthetic function of a work of art which has the power of reconciling and uniting a diversity of conflicting human passions in a single theme. Shevyryov also saw the function of art in terms of healing and reconciling the heterogeneity of the objective world. Aesthetic effect in its sublimest form is a transcendent unity although the phenomena which produce it may be various and contradictory: 'In this single feeling all sublime objects agree despite the different forms of it'.[81]

Apart from its parallels with such modern critical concepts as structural polyphony, Odoyevsky's harmony/melody has its relevance to the analysis of the lyro-epic genre of romantic poetry. For plot, or the epic element, conceived as temporal extension, and the lyric, conceived as supra- or a-temporality, are commonly regarded as to some degree under mutual tension or in opposition within a lyro-epic work. There would indeed be justification in regarding this a-temporality as a harmonious simultaneity of what are, on analysis, separate temporal notes capable of melodic (epic) extension. Such an extension does indeed take place in any critical exegesis of a lyric work which explores the consecutiveness of the creative process by which this 'intensive' work is produced. The same critical exegesis works in reverse when applied to a work of epic structure; now the 'expansiveness' of plot is gathered back into such intensive a-temporal formulations as the *theme* or *idea* of the work of which this expansiveness is the formal expression.

By contrast with Odoyevsky, Marlinsky distinguishes truth itself from the means of acquiring it, of which there are two: the inner imaginative and the outer empirical, the world as it could be and the world as it is.[82] The world as it could be, with its inner source, is the origin of romanticism and the world as it is, by inference, is the source of classicism. Marlinsky also has an interesting exposition of the three possible relationships of form to idea in art: firstly, both exactly balanced — the case, supposedly, in ancient classical art; secondly, form prevailing over idea resulting in the empty formalism of neo-classicism; finally in romanticism, idea prevailing over form, a situation which Marlinsky illustrates metaphorically: romantic art is like an overflowing cup or like gunpowder blowing a gun apart; or it is like sap within a tree, converting itself into a multiplicity of forms — leaves, bark, blossom, and so on.[83] Marlinsky further represents the exigencies of idea and form as a stream winding between the banks of what is and what might be; and invention, the principal inspiration of poetry, he regards as the result of the merging of the inner and outer sources of cognition, the imagination and observation.

Clearly then, for Marlinsky romanticism is distinguished by the adaptive problems faced by form in embodying an idea which is a virtual projection rather than a concrete image of reality. In the individual romantic work this may result in the sundering of formal constraint under the explosive power of idea. On the level of genre, it must inevitably result in a multiplicity of forms which, however, as the arboreal image uniquely shows, are harmoniously related through the whole despite their individuality. The same organic symbol of the tree is used less spectacularly by Kronenberg to image the growth of a single work of art from a single idea.[84] Undoubtedly though it is of most interest as an example of an organicist typology of romanticism whereby, given the premise that art is in some sense a living form, or at least one which mirrors life, the variants of a given expressional mode or genre such as romanticism are not merely to be contrasted with one another as though unconnected but are to be related to one another via their mutual relation to the whole. As we have seen, Pospelov employs something quite close to this idea, without however pursuing fully its implications in his classificatory method.

There is, moreover, an organicist view of the history of artistic ideas. Odoyevsky, for instance, sees influence in terms of the seeds of one cultural age coming up in the next, the implication being that the same age does not both originate (sow) and benefit from (reap) a given idea.[85] Sredniy-Kamashev takes an opposite view: culture he sees as primarily associated with peoples who individually enrich cultural progress by taking their own intellectual and artistic development to a certain level of perfection, but no further.[86] Such was the case with Graeco-Roman classicism. The new style, romanticism, developed in another place and time — Christian western Europe. However, in keeping with the microcosmic and anthropinistic view of the world common to many romantics, Nadezhdin sees the history of cultural change as imaged by the human face on which the successive ages of the owner stamp their dominant traits as a cumulative process.[87] The implications of this idea for literary historians are plain enough, concerning as they do the vexed question of continuity and change in literature. Clearly it is at odds with the *preodoleniye* (overcoming) notion of the succession of literary methods which is often applied to romanticism and realism. Stress is laid instead on the essential unity which underlies the accidental though dramatic changes wrought by time. It is an approach which would lend itself in particular to the study of romanticism in the context of a given national literature.

Axiomatic to certain theoretical views on the development of literature was the relationship of art to criticism. Both Shevyryov and Kronenberg suggest that art must of its nature historically precede criticism and therefore the legislation which springs from criticism is an abstraction from earlier unreflective art forms.[88] In this connection Plato and Aristotle recur as exemplars of the two aesthetic moments, the creative and the critical. Plato, understandably, is an admired figure. For Sredniy-Kamashev he is the perfect poet-philosopher in whom idea and fantasy fuse.[89] Venevitinov, however, is unusual in airing the sensitive problem of Plato's hostile attitude to the poet in *The Republic*.[90] The poet, it seems, is only of use in intuiting the ideal state, at a stage when, reverting to Fokht's theory, there is insufficient information to enable it to be founded. Venevitinov's *Anaxagoras: A Dialogue of Plato* is also interesting as an example of the dialogic form so often favoured by romantic aestheticians. It is used by Vyazemsky and Shevyryov, without the overt Platonic overtones.[91] The appeal of the mode is clear: it is the perfect illustration of the harmony of opposites, truth emerging out of opposition and ignorance.

The principal limitation of early Russian romantic aesthetics is its insistence, understandable enough, on defining romanticism in terms of its opposition to classicism. From the modern point of view, of course, it lacks historical perspective and indeed there is always a critical superiority in mere latterness. In the context of critical retrospection one can agree with Mann's adaptation of Wellek and Warren's notion that a masterpiece from a given period surpasses in quality the contemporary aesthetic theories which first tried to cope with it.[92] On the other hand one may argue that Marlinsky's equation between Christianity and romanticism, once a widespread notion, is not so much an invalid view of romanticism as a now not very fashionable one.[93] As for organicism, it is difficult to tell from W. K. Wimsatt's interesting article on the subject whether we are to understand it as dead or living as a critical approach, but it is possible to believe that its insights can still enrich contemporary methodology.[94] Finally, as we noted earlier, it should not be surprising that when literary theories come under analytical scrutiny they are found to mirror structural features of the literary objects they were invented to represent conceptually. Perhaps this helps to justify them.

At any rate the two principal Soviet approaches to romanticism, the dominant-subjective and the typological-empirical, bear a striking affinity to Marlinsky's imagination/empiricism, Nadezhdin's centripetal/centrifugal, Kronenberg's intension/extension and Odoyevsky's centre/periphery. As El'yashevich notes, the two methods need each other: the dominant to justify itself by typological evidence and the typological to prove that it is not a congeries of unrelated artistic forms, but has some essential romantic identity as a unifying feature.[95] Both agree on the integrity of the romantic phenomenon but are disagreed as to the theoretical mode of expressing it. This too is a feature of romantic creativity at large, which above all is suspicious of the verbal expression of ideas, of the conversion of the one into the many. Tyutchev's thoughts on the subject are well enough known. Ryleyev, too, held that commonly words and not ideas underlie critical disputes.[96] Odoyevsky was particularly forthright in maintaining that 'the incomplete and untruthful exists only in expressions'.[97] His less pessimistic corollary to this statement is that, in order to grasp the idea behind words, to reconstitute the one from the many, 'one must supplement in expressions that which is insufficient in them for the clarification of knowledge'. Likewise, in the midst of an aesthetic discourse, Sredniy-Kamashev begs his readers 'not to attach themselves to words but to penetrate their meaning, for words are only signs'.[98]

There is indeed something to be said for an intuitive approach to romanticism, not only in Fokht's sense of the word, but in Sredniy-Kamashev's spirit of sceptical penetration into the substance behind the theoretical arguments. For the dominant and typological approaches are not simply contrasting methods of dealing with a subject; taken together they are in part a simulacrum, in part a product of the focalised partiality of thought which creates the dyads of idea and form, unity and multiplicity, self and other, and which constitutes the hypostasis of romantic consciousness.

Notes

1. L. G. Leighton, *Russian Romanticism: Two Essays*, The Hague, 1975, p. 5.
2. Arthur O. Lovejoy, 'On the Discrimination of Romanticisms' (*Proceedings of the Modern Languages Association*, XXXIX, 2, 1924, p. 229).
3. M. H. Abrams, *Natural Supernaturalism*, London, 1971; Irving Massey, *The Uncreating Word*, Bloomington, 1970.
4. In such works as Rudolf Neuhäuser, *The Romantic Age in Russian Literature*, Munich, 1975, and for the history of the word 'romantic' in Russian literature: Sigrid McLaughlin, 'Russia: Romaničeskij – Romantičeskij – Romantizm', in *'Romantic' and its Cognates: The European History of a Word*, ed. Hans Eichner, Manchester, 1972, pp. 418–73.
5. Ark. El'yashevich, *Yedinstvo tseli – mnogoobraziye poiskov*, Leningrad, 1980, pp. 363ff.
6. Philip Hobsbaum, 'The Romantic Dichotomy' (*British Journal of Aesthetics*, XVI, 1976, p. 45).
7. Yuriy N. Tynyanov, *Arkhaisty i novatory*, Leningrad, 1929, repr. Munich, 1967.
8. R. Wellek, 'The Concept of "Romanticism" in Literary History' (*Comparative Literature*, I, 1, 1949, pp. 1–23, 147–72).
9. Northrop Frye, 'The Drunken Boat: The Revolutionary Element in Romanticism', in *Romanticism Reconsidered*, ed. Northrop Frye, New York, 1963, pp. 1–2.
10. Morse Peckham, 'Romanticism and Behaviour' (*Philosophical Exchange*, I, Summer 1974, p. 65).
11. Howard Mumford Jones, *Revolution and Romanticism*, Cambridge, Mass., 1974, p. 12.
12. Peter Thorslev, 'Romanticism and the Literary Consciousness' (*Journal of the History of Ideas*, XXXVI, Summer 1975, p. 564).
13. L. Averbakh, *O zadachakh proletarskoy literatury*, Moscow-Leningrad, 1928, p. 104, quoted in Ark. El'yashevich, op. cit., p. 283.
14. A. Fadeyev, *Na literaturnom postu*, 21–2, 1929, pp. 6–7, quoted in Ark. El'yashevich, op. cit., p. 288.
15. V. I. Kuleshov, 'Tipologiya russkogo romantizma', in *Romantizm v slavyanskikh literaturakh*, ed. Kuleshov, Moscow, 1973, p. 22.
16. The first formulation was in Gorky's Capri lectures of 1908–9; the second in 'O tom, kak ya uchilsya pisat'' (M. Gor'kiy, *O literature*, Moscow, 1953, pp. 307–34).
17. V. I. Kuleshov, loc. cit.
18. A. N. Sokolov, 'K sporam o romantizme', in *Problemy romantizma*, ed. U. R. Fokht, Moscow, 1967, p. 17 (hereafter *Problemy*).
19. V. I. Kuleshov, op. cit., p. 16. See also his *Slavyanofily i russkaya literatura*, Moscow, 1976, for observations on Slavophile romanticism, esp. pp. 78ff.
20. I. Gronsky: transcript of a speech made at the First Plenum of the Organising Committee of the SSP, quoted in Ark. El'yashevich, op. cit., p. 299.
21. B. G. Reizov, 'O literaturnykh napravleniyakh' (*Voprosy literatury*, I, 1957, pp. 94ff); A. N. Sokolov, op. cit., p. 11. In particular both Sokolov (p. 11) and Wellek ('Romanticism Re-examined', in *Romanticism Reconsidered*,

op. cit., p. 106) use the term 'nominalism' for their opponents' theories, since both Reizov and Lovejoy maintain that the different forms of 'romanticism' have only the name in common.

22. L. I. Timofeyev, *Osnovy teorii literatury*, 5th edn, Moscow, 1976, p. 105. The subsequent quotations from Timofeyev are from pp. 104—5.

23. I. F. Volkov, 'Osnovnyye problemy izucheniya romantizma', in *K istorii russkogo romantizma*, ed. Yu. V. Mann, et al., Moscow, 1973, p. 7.

24. G. A. Gukovsky, *Pushkin i russkiye romantiki*, Moscow, 1965, pp. 15ff.

25. S. P. Shevyryov, 'Istoriya poezii', 1835, in *Russkiye esteticheskiye traktaty pervoy treti XX veka*, Moscow, 1974, II, p. 419 (hereafter *Traktaty*).

26. Henri Peyre, *Qu'est-ce que le Romantisme?*, Paris, 1971, p. 9.

27. K. N. Grigoryan, 'Sud'by romantizma v russkoy literature', in *Russkiy romantizm*, ed. Grigoryan, Moscow, 1978, p. 5.

28. I. F. Volkov, op. cit., pp. 15ff.

29. A. M. Gurevich, 'O tipologicheskikh osobennostyakh russkogo romantizma', in *K istorii russkogo romantizma*, ed. Yu. V. Mann, et al., Moscow, 1973, pp. 512, 511.

30. A. A. Gadzhiyev, 'Romantizm kak yavleniye tipologicheskoye' (*Uchonyye zapiski Kazanskogo gos. universiteta*, CXXIX, 7, 1969, p. 25).

31. S. Ye. Shatalov, Introduction to *Istoriya romantizma v russkoy literature: Vozniknoveniye i utverzhdeniye romantizma v russkoy literature* (1790—1825), ed. A. S. Kurilov, Moscow, 1979, p. 10.

32. I. Neupokoyeva, 'General Features of European Romanticism and the Originality of its National Paths', in *European Romanticism*, ed. I. Soter and Neupokoyeva, Budapest, 1977, p. 27.

33. A. N. Sokolov, op. cit., p. 11.

34. V. I. Kuleshov, op. cit., p. 6.

35. I. I. Zamotin, *Romanticheskiy idealizm v russkom obshchestve i literature 20-30kh godov XIX stoletiya*, St Petersburg, 1907, passim; P. N. Sakulin, *Russkaya literatura*, Moscow, 1926, I, pp. 351ff.

36. I. F. Volkov, op. cit., p. 9.

37. Ibid., pp. 16, 17, 23, 25, for the respective topics.

38. Ibid., p. 25.

39. Ibid., p. 15.

40. Ibid., p. 20.

41. U. R. Fokht, 'Nekotoryye voprosy teorii romantizma (zamechaniya i gipotezy)', in *Problemy*, pp. 77—8.

42. Ibid., p. 78.

43. Ibid., p. 79. Fokht dismisses the affinity too easily: see Robert Reid, 'Russian Intuitivism' (*Irish Slavonic Studies*, I, 1980, pp. 43—59, esp. p. 46).

44. Loc. cit.

45. Ibid., p. 83.

46. Ibid., p. 84.

47. Ibid., p. 81; *Yevgeniy Onegin*, IV, pp. 38—9; Nekrasov's *Zheleznaya doroga* (1864).

48. Ibid., p. 82; Tyutchev's 'Yest' v oseni pervonachal'noy . . .' (1857).

49. Ibid., p. 91.

50. Ibid., p. 84. Fokht quotes from P. V. Simonov, 'Chto takoye emotsia?' (*Nauka i zhizn'*, 3, 1965, p. 57).

51. Ibid., p. 85; G. D. Gachev, 'Razvitiye obraznogo soznaniya v literature', in *Teoriya literatury*, Moscow, 1962, p. 248.

52. Arthur K. Moore, 'The Instruments of Oracular Expression' (*Diogenes*, LXXXIII, 1973, p. 1).

53. A. M. Mikeshin, 'Problema istoricheskikh sudeb russkogo romantizma v sovremennom literaturovedenii', in *Iz istorii russkogo romantizma*, vyp. 1, ed. N.A. Gulyaev, et al., Kemerovo, 1971, p. 7.

54. Ye. A. Maymin, *O russkom romantizme*, Moscow, 1975, p. 23, for this and subsequent Maymin references unless otherwise stated.

55. Yu. V. Mann, *Poetika russkogo romantizma*, Moscow, 1976, p. 4.

56. Ibid., pp. 12, 13.

57. Ibid., p. 19.

58. H. G. Schenk, *The Mind of the European Romantics*, London, 1966, p. xxii.

59. Arthur O. Lovejoy, op. cit., passim; P. N. Sakulin, *Teoriya literaturnykh stiley*, Moscow, 1928, p. 14.

60. Ark. El'yashevich, op. cit., p. 240, for this and subsequent El'yashevich references unless further stated.

61. Albert Hofstadter, 'The Aesthetic Impulse' (*Journal of Aesthetics and Art Criticism*, XXXII, Winter 1973, p. 172), and for subsequent quotation.

62. Arthur O. Lovejoy, op. cit., pp. 236—7.

63. Ludwig Wittgenstein, *Philosophical Investigations*, tr. G. E. M. Anscombe, 3rd edn, New York, 1968, p. 31.

> Betrachte z.B. einmal die Vorgänge, die wir 'Spiele' nennen. . . Was ist allen diesen gemeinsam? — Sag nicht: 'Es *muss* ihnen etwas gemeinsam sein, sonst hiessen sie nicht "Spiele"' — sondern *schau*, ob ihnen allen etwas gemeinsam ist. — Denn, wenn du sie anschaust, wirst du zwar nicht etwas sehen, was *allen* gemeinsam wäre, aber du wirst Ähnlichkeiten, Verwandtschaften, sehen, und zwar eine ganze Reihe.

64. Ibid., p. 34.

65. An apocryphal utterance by Vyazemsky to Zhukovsky: 'Romanticism is like a house-sprite: there is a conviction that it exists, but where are its tracks, how can it be defined, how can you put your finger on it?' Quoted in Ark. El'yashevich, op. cit., p. 236; V. G. Belinsky, *Polnoye sobraniye sochineniy*, ed. N. F. Bel'chikov, et al., Moscow, 1954, VII, p. 144.

66. Ye. A. Maymin, op. cit., p. 4.

67. G. N. Pospelov, 'Chto zhe takoye romantizm?' in *Problemy*, p. 42.

68. H. W. B. Joseph, *An Introduction to Logic*, Oxford, 1906, p. 107.

69. V. I. Kuleshov, op. cit., p. 6.

70. A. I. Beletsky, 'Ocherednyye voprosy izucheniya russkogo romantizma', in *Russkiy romantizm*, Leningrad, 1927, p. 6.

71. G. N. Pospelov, op. cit., p. 72.

72. U. R. Fokht, op. cit., p. 63.

73. John B. Halsted, ed., *Romanticism*, London, 1969, p. 1.

74. H. J. C. Grierson, *Classical and Romantic*, Cambridge, 1923, pp. 5—6. It is of course true that Grierson was using this phrase in the context of the classical/romantic opposition. This in no way invalidates its applicability to the 'romantic dichotomy' in context; indeed, classical/romantic, corresponding to constraint/freedom and objectivity/subjectivity must represent one of the

earliest and most vital formulations of the dichotomy. It is interesting to compare Grierson's aortic image (in which contraction equates with classicism and expansion with romanticism) with those of Marlinsky discussed below.

75. Bohdan Urbankowski, 'Revaluation of Romanticism' (*Dialectics and Humanism*, 1, 1978, p. 63).

76. William James, *Pragmatism: A New Name for some Old Ways of Thinking*, London, 1908, p. 12.

77. V. F. Odoyevsky, 'Opyt teorii izyashchnykh iskusstv s osobennym primeneniyem onoy k muzyke', 1825, in *Traktaty*, p. 160.

78. Ibid., p. 161.

79. Ibid., p. 166.

80. I. Ya. Kronenberg, *Aforizmy*, 1825, in *Traktaty*, p. 291.

81. S. P. Shevyryov, 'Razgovor o vozmozhnosti nayti yedinyy zakon dlya izyashchnogo', 1827, in *Traktaty*, p. 513.

82. A. A. Bestuzhev-Marlinsky, 'O romantizme', in *Traktaty*, p. 583.

83. Ibid., p. 584; subsequent Marlinsky references are from this page.

84. I. Ya. Kronenberg, loc. cit.

85. V. F. Odoyevsky, op. cit., pp. 162—3.

86. I. N. Sredniy-Kamashev, 'Neskol'ko zamechaniy na rassuzhdeniye g. Nadezhdina "O proiskhozhdenii, svoystvakh i sud'be poezii tak nazyvayemoy romanticheskoy"', 1830, in *Traktaty*, p. 414.

87. N. I. Nadezhdin, 'O sovremennom napravlenii izyashchnykh iskusstv', 1833, in *Traktaty*, p. 418.

88. S. P. Shevyryov, 'Teoriya poezii', 1836, in *Traktaty*, p. 525; I. Ya. Kronenberg, 'Istoricheskiy vzglyad na estetiku', 1830, in *Traktaty*, p. 297.

89. I. N. Sredniy-Kamashev, 'O razlichnykh mneniyakh ob izyashchnom', 1829, in *Traktaty*, pp. 372 ff.

90. D. V. Venevitinov, 'Anaksagor: beseda Platona', 1830, in *Traktaty*, pp. 193—4.

91. P. A. Vyazemsky, 'Vmesto predisloviya k "Bakhchisarayskomu fontanu"', 1824, in *Traktaty*, pp. 148—54; S. P. Shevyryov, 'Razgovor o vozmozhnosti . . .', in *Traktaty*, pp. 508—16.

92. Yu. V. Mann, op. cit., p. 5.

93. A. A. Bestuzhev-Marlinsky, 'O romane N. P. Polevogo, "Klyatva pri grobe gospodnem"', 1833, in Rudolf Neuhäuser, op. cit., p. 99.

94. W. K. Wimsatt, 'Organic Form: Some Questions about a Metaphor', in *Romanticism: Vistas, Instances, Continuities*, ed. David Thorburn and Geoffrey Hartman, Ithaca, 1973, pp. 13—37.

95. Ark. El'yashevich, op. cit., p. 381.

96. K. F. Ryleyev, 'Neskol'ko mysley o poezii', 1825, in *Traktaty*, p. 586.

97. V. F. Odoyevsky, 'Sushcheye ili nesushchestvuyushcheye', c. 1825, in *Traktaty*, p. 170, for this and the subsequent quotation.

98. I. N. Sredniy-Kamashev, 'Neskol'ko zamechaniy . . .', in *Traktaty*, p. 412.

2 Fallibility and perfection in the works of Alexander Pushkin

A. D. P. BRIGGS

I

There is every reason to associate the name of Alexander Pushkin with the artistic movement known as European romanticism. This movement, notoriously difficult to circumscribe either by general definition or by dates, arose from a dissatisfaction with the traditional constraints imposed by classical and neo-classical art, assisted as these were by the widespread devotion to rationalism which characterised eighteenth-century European sensibility. An impulse towards greater freedom, originality and imagination, by no means limited to the arts alone, gathered momentum and soon spread itself among the literate people of many countries, exciting men's and women's minds by its new possibilities. Each European literature, jealous of its individuality and ashamed of the bad name soon to be acquired by the movement because of excesses resulting from overindulgence in the newly acquired freedoms, is now reluctant to admit that it was ever host to romanticism in anything like a pure form. Russian literature denies this as volubly as any, though it remains true that approximately between 1820 and 1840 first the poetry and then the prose of that nation underwent a process of renewal which, although indigenous in its expression, nevertheless owed much to the general spirit of romanticism and to Byron and Shakespeare in particular. These two decades, the heyday of romanticism in Russia, marked precisely the period of Pushkin's maturity, from the publication of *Ruslan and Lyudmila* when he was twenty, to his death by duelling — early in 1837. This is the first reason why he and the movement are linked together.

The second reason is that Pushkin was conscious of the new literary spirit and, as well as adapting it to suit his own purposes, he made a number of statements about the theory of romanticism. On the whole these comments do not yield many clues to an understanding of either the European literary scene or Pushkin's own achievement. Sometimes they encompass too much to be useful, as when he states that 'the Romantic school . . . is marked by the absence of all rules but not the absence of art'[1] or when he asks 'What forms of poetry are to be assigned to the Romantic school?' and gives his own answer: 'All those which were not known to the Ancients and those whose earlier forms have suffered change or been replaced by others'.[2] Elsewhere he is inclined to reject literary historicism altogether: 'in literature I am a sceptic . . . and . . . to me all its sects are equal, each exhibiting both good and bad sides'.[3] On another occasion he refers to the misuse of literary jargon as follows: 'Our journalists use the words "Classic" and "Romantic" as a term of general abuse like old women who refer to dissolute young men as "freemasons" or "Voltaireans" without knowing anything about Voltaire or freemasonry'.[4]

The first two of these comments were issued before Hugo's *Préface de Cromwell* (1827) and the last two before *Hernani* and the ensuing battle (1830). Heine's *Die Romantische Schule* appeared in 1836, only months before Pushkin's death. It is clear that Pushkin was still part of an unfolding process and we should not be surprised that his views on the overall movement do not provide us with penetrating insights into the relationship which existed between it and himself.[5] A useful summary of his attitude is provided by John Bayley:

> If the label 'romantic' meant anything for Pushkin, it could be applied in any age to a work which obeyed no rules but its own . . . the proper sense of romanticism was for him a literary technique, not a movement of the soul.[6]

If Pushkin's recorded opinions on romanticism are rather disappointing — the more so because of his acute perceptions on other literary topics — his manipulation of the possibilities opened up by the movement is quite the reverse. The third reason for considering Pushkin in relation to contemporary developments in European literature is the strongest. He is definable by his *de facto* treatment of the new liberties. Our understanding of this poet is sharpened by an awareness of what he did with romanticism and what he did not do, where he subscribed to its new traditions and where he departed from them, how he was betrayed by its false promises and how, more frequently, he resisted its blandishments. A study of Pushkin and romanticism will benefit the former more than the latter, by sharpening the definition of his exceptional literary quality. This quality is more variable than we are often led to believe, Pushkin having been guilty of more errors and lapses than are commonly acknowledged. These underadvertised shortcomings sometimes have their origin in his misuse or overuse of the energies newly released by romanticism. The purpose of this chapter is to draw attention to a number of these imperfections and to take issue with those who seek to ignore or to disguise them. This may sound like the debasement of a great artist but the reverse is intended. Pushkin still has difficulty in gaining acceptance by world opinion as a literary master, despite the increase in attention paid to him over the last two decades. His genius lacks the commanding universality and consistency of Shakespeare; it cannot be neatly packaged and exported like that of Cervantes. It is not all that long since a distinguished reviewer expressed with some acuity the doubts and impatience which assail the foreign reader of Pushkin. His reference to 'Pushkin's notorious and unhappy pre-eminence as the least translatable of poets' was followed by the direct question, 'Is it all, perhaps, a confidence trick?'[7] Although much has been written on Pushkin since the time of that review the doubts linger on. They will not be dispelled by too great an insistence on the unchanging high quality of Pushkin's writing. Some indication of his shortcomings administered with due emphasis on the small proportion of his work for which they are accountable, should actually serve to enhance the poet's stature. Firstly, this might help to diminish the unduly reverential attitude so frequently adopted in his company, to which he never aspired and which he would have ridiculed out of existence. Secondly, it should project into greater prominence that small group of his works, including *Yevgeniy Onegin, The Bronze Horseman (Medniy vsadnik),* perhaps *The Queen of Spades (Pikovaya dama)* and certainly a couple of dozen lyric poems, which are properly described as unqualified masterpieces.

II

A commonplace in Pushkin criticism is the idea that his inborn, and carefully nurtured, classical instinct enabled him to avoid the worst temptations and pitfalls of romanticism. The idea is so obvious and has been so widely expressed that by now it amounts to a literary axiom. 'His style . . ., scarcely touched by Romanticism, is . . . classically perfect';[8] '. . . a poet as naturally classical as Pushkin in an epoch fashionably and self-consciously romantic';[9] 'for all his flirtations with Romanticism, he remained true to his literary education of Classicism';[10] 'the deep-lying . . . roots of Pushkin's style . . . are French and classical';[11] '. . . Pushkin had finally broken with a false Romanticism which had never suited his classical spirit';[12] '. . . pure, disinterested, classic art';[13] 'Russia's qualified successor of the antique world';[14] '. . . poetry of classical precision and firmness';[15] 'this sense of balance and proportion

. . . reminds the reader of Greek art when he reads Pushkin and gives us the impression that the poet is a classic, however much he may have employed the stock-in-trade of Romanticism'.[16] Such is the general view and there is little to be set against its underlying truth. All the same this collective judgement oversimplifies what is, in fact, rather a complicated question and, worse than that, it has led to an assessment of Pushkin which is too uniform and which sometimes refuses to see mistakes and deficiencies where they really do exist.

It is not quite true to say that Pushkin was 'scarcely touched' by romanticism or that his susceptibility to its temptations may be dismissed as mere 'flirtation'. Some of his deviations went deep, lasted long, and resulted in a number of works wholly or partly infected with what are commonly accepted as being among the more noxious romantic bacilli, exaggeration, oversimplification, excesses of passion and ambition, and so on. One of Pushkin's early poems, *The Black Shawl* (*Chornaya shal'*, 1820), provides an arresting example of the mediocrity into which he was occasionally seduced by the new possibilities laid out so enticingly by European romanticism, and which he would one day transcend with triumph and consistency. Based on a Moldavian folk song, it recounts the murder of an unfaithful girl and her lover. The teller of the tale catches the two of them *in flagrante delicto*. The killing is described in the lurid terms which have come to be associated with the excesses of passion to which unrestrained romanticism was prone to lead and which scarcely typify the Pushkin whom we accept as the fountain-head of modern Russian literature:

> I entered the chamber in that remote place;
> The false maid was in an Armenian's embrace.

> My head swam, and then . . . to my dagger's refrain
> In mid-kiss the blackguard was taken and slain.

> I stamped on the man's headless body and stayed,
> Pale-faced and unspeaking, my eyes on the maid . . .
>
> (*Pol. sob.*, I, p. 278)

There is always a market for this sort of thing and the piece came rapidly to enjoy popular success. One of Pushkin's contemporaries, Vladimir Gorchakov, speaks of its early popularity with General Orlov in Kishinev.[17] Musical versions embellished fashionable drawing rooms.[18] There are several to choose from, solo songs and duets, a cantata, even a one-act pantomime-ballet.[19] In later years it fell from grace and this poem is now largely disowned. Mirsky described it as 'one of the crudest and least distinctly Pushkinian things he ever wrote'[20] and Nabokov as 'some indifferent couplets in amphibrachic tetrameter',[21] though more recently Bayley has implied that we should accept *The Black Shawl* as an efficient and equable exploitation of contemporary taste.[22] In fact although the poem does possess two easy virtues, an agreeable euphony and folkloric simplicity, these properties would not have been beyond the powers of any amateur poetaster of the period. Conversely, to the twentieth-century eye and ear it seems meretricious; its former glory has faded into an outworn fabric made up from sensational and sentimental material. It can be read nowadays only with indulgent amusement.

With *The Black Shawl* Pushkin seems to have fallen into a romantic pitfall. He did not do this often. It has been pointed out on many occasions that an array of safety devices normally protected him from such dangers. A perceptive essay by A. Slonimsky[23] gives some examples of how this is done. *The Prisoner* (*Uznik*, 1822) seems rather similar to *The Black Shawl* (especially in its use of the same rare metre) but fends off the attack from romanticism by 'features of realism' and 'compressed thinking' expressed in 'strictly logical forms'. Another poem, *To the Sea* (*K moryu*, 1824), on the other hand, culminates in a eulogy addressed to Napoleon and Byron, in which the praise is restrained and qualified; Slonimsky describes how further material on Napoleon was excised by the poet because of the danger to the balance of the poem and its main theme of valediction. Here we see Pushkin applying his much-advertised instinct for restraint and understatement. The sea in this poem is allowed a dual role; it becomes a symbol of freedom, but, before that, it is clearly a representation of the real sea, observed and experienced by Pushkin and recreated with every available poetic device. Bayley expresses the opinion that in this poem, 'The place becomes instant and intimate to us through sound',[24] and he extends the same idea to a poem written within a few days of *The Black Shawl*, 'The orb of day has died' ('Pogaslo dnevnoye svetilo', 1820), which by means of its 'acoustic opulence' recalls Horace's *Oceano Nox*.[25] Many other examples could be advanced from the earlier poems of Pushkin to show that he was usually capable either of drawing back from the worst temptations extended by romanticism, or of turning necessity to advantage by applying romantic techniques such as opulent sound effects to a relevant purpose.

Occasional lapses into unrestrained romanticism, with their attendant risibility, are, however, not restricted to the earliest of Pushkin's works. *The Fountain of Bakhchisaray* (*Bakhchisarayskiy fontan*) contains an example of romantic heroics embarrassing in its purity. Girey, left distraught following the death of the one he has loved and lost, is sometimes revisited by a recollection of her, even on the battlefield. When this occurs he freezes into immobility, even in mid-swipe:

Often he lifts his sword, arm flailing,
But then, poised, motionless he stays
And glares round with demented gaze
And terror-stricken air; then, paling,
He whispers words that no one hears
And yields to scalding, streaming tears.

(Pol. sob., II, pp. 333—4)

These lines alone, located towards the end of a poem by no means devoid of some of Pushkin's finer qualities, invalidate the whole piece. However successful the translation of them, it would never be possible to present them to a foreigner as part of the achievement of a literary master regarded in his own country as the equivalent of a Shakespeare, a Dante or a Cervantes.

These two brief examples come from Pushkin's early work. It is clear, however, that the romantic propensity towards overindulgence did not desert Pushkin along with his youth. Let us move forward to the period of his *Little Tragedies* (*Malen'kiye tragedii*, 1830). These are mature works and they are held in high esteem. Janko Lavrin describes them as being 'amongst the most condensed things Pushkin ever wrote'.[26] Bayley's claim is that they 'show most clearly a language realising the full potential of its simplest words'.[27] Richard Hare believed that they 'rise to the high level of his best work'.[28] There are four of them, all written during the celebrated Autumn period when Pushkin was incarcerated in Boldino by an outbreak of cholera: *The Miserly Knight* (*Skupoy ritsar'*), *Mozart and Salieri*, *The Stone Guest* (*Kamenniy gost'*), *The Feast during the Plague* (*Pir vo vremya chumy*). There is little doubt in the minds of the critics that *The Stone Guest* is not only the best of them, it is one of the finest works ever penned by the poet. E. J. Simmons describes it as 'in every respect . . . a masterpiece in miniature';[29] G. O. Vinokur as considered by many authorities 'the most accomplished of all his works';[30] Lavrin as 'an admirable masterpiece';[31] Oliver Elton as 'a miniature masterpiece'.[32] The French critical school does not dissent. Charles Corbet believes it to be '. . . la plus intéressante, la plus vivante de ses "petites tragédies"',[33] and André Meynieux sets it down as 'une oeuvre singulière et même insolite en Russie'.[34] If anything the acclaim directed at *The Stone Guest* has increased rather than declined. Mirsky states with full confidence that 'it shares with *The Bronze Horseman* the right to be regarded as Pushkin's masterpiece . . . it has no equal'.[35] Elsewhere he claims that '*The Stone Guest* is admirable and perfect *from whatever standpoint it be viewed*'.[36] One of the most recent comments on this work belongs to John Bayley, who says, 'the idea of the dramatic sketch . . . is elevated to the status of a master genre, culminating in *The Stone Guest*, a climax of perfection . . .'.[37]

Against these repeated claims, some of which amount to a suggestion that this is not merely an exquisite masterpiece but actually the finest work written by perhaps the finest literary artist ever to use the Russian language, it might be useful to consider by way of an example an extract taken from just before the middle of this dramatic sketch. Don Juan has entered Laura's room unexpectedly, interrupting a conversation between her and Don Carlos. Within seconds the two men have fought an impromptu duel with swords, Don Carlos has been killed, and Laura and Don Juan, reunited after a long separation, have discussed both the murder and the circumstances of Juan's return to Madrid. Now they embrace each other, and the following dialogue ensues:

> *Laura*:   My dear friend! . . .
> Wait! Not before the dead! . . . Where can we put him?
>
> *Don Juan*: Oh, leave him there. Ere dawn tomorrow morning
> I'll carry him away beneath my cloak
> And lay him at the crossroads.
>
> *Laura*:   But take care
> That no one sees you.
>
> (*Pol. sob.*, III, p. 316)

Even this brief extract is enough to indicate something of the melodramatic content of *The Stone Guest*. It is not atypical. In the very first speech of the playlet Don Juan describes what he is about to do: fly down the familiar streets of Madrid with his moustaches hidden under his cape and his brows covered by the brim of his hat. The ending is the one familiar to students of the Don Juan legend; the Don is visited by the stone statue of the Commander whom he has killed and is taken down to Hell by him. Into this colourful material a number of ideas have been introduced by some critics apparently in justification of the extravagant praise so often extended to *The Stone Guest*. The suggestion is that these melodramatic characters should, after all, be taken seriously. Don Juan is no odious betrayer of women and slayer of rivals; he proves capable of real love and is raised to the stature of a tragic hero overtaken by Nemesis at the very moment when he discovers true affection. In fact there is no evidence that his 'love' for Doña Anna, although expressed to her with great passion, differs from that which he has experienced so often before. It has even been imagined, erroneously, that the difference between Doña Anna and her predecessors is marked by her sinking down to Hell along with Juan;[38] in fact the final words 'they disappear' apply, in the traditional manner, only to the statue and his male victim.

The action and the characterisation of this playlet, from which Pushkin's well-known sense of everyday reality seems conspicuously absent, seem weak enough to disqualify *The Stone Guest* from any claim to absolute excellence. It is the poetry in the piece which must account for the way in which it has captivated so many minds. Don Juan comparing frigid northern women with sultry southern beauties and then recalling Doña Inez; the celebrated balcony scene between Laura and Don Carlos which includes her description of the beauty of the evening — there are one or two passages like these in which Pushkin's remarkable talents come into play. It is significant that in these brief moments the poet rediscovers some of those qualities which, under most circumstances, protect him against the dangers of romanticism. These are, briefly, a sense of style and structure (partly dependent on antithesis: contrasts between northern and southern women, the northern and southern climate); an instinct for brevity and understatement (the passages being short and unassertive); the insinuation of down-to-earth, everyday details, real and relevant ones rather than stock properties (smells of lemon and bay, the call of the night-watch); and the sophisticated manipulation of poetic sounds, providing both euphony and suggestiveness without overwhelming the listener.

The Stone Guest does possess poetic strength, but it seems to have been misapplied. Pushkin has made one of his rather rare literary miscalculations. He has taken hold of an old legend encrusted with fascinating preoccupations only too dear to the human heart. Sexuality, immortality, retribution for unethical conduct, humour and local colour, together with the magnificent idea of supernatural intervention by means of an animated statue, are all packed together into this small vessel. It is interesting to note that in all the hundreds of versions of this legend (even in Molière's *Dom Juan*), the mixture has proved too rich; there is not an unalloyed masterpiece among them — with the sole exception of *Don Giovanni*, in which it is clear that the triumph has everything to do with the wit and elegance of Da Ponte and the musical genius of Mozart, and nothing to do with the actual story. Pushkin has compounded the difficulties by choosing an even more condensed form than usual, the playlet, and it does not succeed. The result is not catastrophic failure but excessive saturation. The poetess Anna Akhmatova, intending to praise the work, refers to its *golovokruzhitel'nyy lakonizm*,[39] itself a nicely condensed phrase which means 'style so concise as to make the reader dizzy'; in fact she defines precisely the way in which the work goes wrong. So much is pressed upon the characters in so short a space that the actions they are required to perform, and the speeches they are required to pronounce, are telescoped together. Verisimilitude is the first casualty and misplaced humour the first undesirable intruder. Romantic theatricality is suggested by the familiar paraphernalia — moustaches, duels, corpses and graveyards. One of the faults easily diagnosed in many an outright failure of romantic literature is overambition, the attempt to include too much and solve too many problems at one stroke. In his own inimitable way Pushkin seems to be guilty of this in *The Stone Guest*. This alone is sufficiently disappointing; the misfortune is compounded every time someone attempts to present this work as one of his very finest.

An intriguing idea is that if Pushkin had chosen to spin out this material into a full-length play, or modernise and adapt it into a *poema*, it might have merited the suggested comparison with *The Bronze Horseman* which, as things stand, is inappropriate. This kind of speculation is normally fruitless but here the question of form is important. Liberation from the rules and regulations imposed upon earlier writers was one of the attractions offered by romanticism and Pushkin was not slow to avail himself of the new possibilities. One of his greatest triumphs, *Yevgeniy Onegin*, depends for its success partly on unusual properties of form; it is a novel yet it is written in verse and the stanza employed is an imaginative, malleable adaptation of the sonnet. This is one of the most glorious hybrids that literature has ever produced. However, there is no guarantee that the combination of traditional forms into new ones will always succeed. Pushkin's *Little Tragedies* are not suited to the stage, on which their unreality would obtrude even more strongly. Their more captivating qualities are poetic rather than theatrical; the soliloquies by Salieri (*Mozart and Salieri*) and the Baron (*The Miserly Knight*) include some of the poet's finest lines. There is a case for suggesting that Pushkin's playlets in verse are ill-conceived; the constituent forms do not mix and the result this time is a misshapen and ultimately sterile creation.

Pushkin's most important work for the theatre, *Boris Godunov*, was written half a decade earlier than *The Stone Guest*. In the case of this play the faults have been widely advertised, even to the extent of being overemphasised. They do have a strong connection with the romantic movement in the person of the one dramatist, William Shakespeare, whose universality and apparent disregard for the niceties of form held a great appeal to the artistic innovators of the period. Heinrich Heine summed up the appeal of Shakespeare by suggesting that 'with Protestant clearness [he] smiles over into our modern era'.[40] *Boris Godunov* was written under the smiling influence of Shakespeare whose history plays are recalled in many ways, by the theme of usurpation, the preoccupation with the author's national past and the serious attempt to portray reality rather than present stylised characters and situations. Pushkin's play has been widely discussed and the general conclusion is a negative one. It is held that, although a number of the scenes are beautifully wrought individual entities, they do not coalesce to form a unified work of art. If the centrifugal qualities of the play have been exaggerated this is perhaps for a good reason. It has been argued elsewhere[41] that there is greater unity to *Boris Godunov* than meets the eye and that this has been lost to view because of a deliberate step taken by Pushkin to disguise the shape of his play. It is in fact a five-act Shakespearean historical tragedy and was probably designed as such but Pushkin removed the divisions into acts and scenes, possibly in order to distance himself from Shakespeare whom he seemed to have been following too closely. For the same reason he took the otherwise strange decision to saddle his iambic pentameters with rigid observance of the second-foot caesura and constant end-stopping of his lines, two inhibiting features which result in a hobbled kind of poetry, far removed from the free-flowing blank verse of, for instance, the *Little Tragedies*. The miracle is that this play nevertheless includes several scenes of indisputably high literary and dramatic quality, it is anything but unstageable (though it is, in fact, rarely produced) and it includes, in Pimen's famous monologue, some of the (deservedly) best known verses in the treasure-house of Russian poetry. *Boris Godunov* is a complex phenomenon about which much remains to be said and written. For our present purposes it demonstrates again Pushkin's willingness to be drawn in directions favoured by other writers in the romantic period, his propensity for misjudgment and error and his tendency, when he is going wrong, to do so in his own manner rather than simply fall into a trap traditionally set for romantic writers.

III

Even in the period of his full maturity from 1830 until his death, Pushkin remained susceptible to lapses which, like some of those described above, not only have connections with romanticism but also remain underacknowledged. The tendency to overlook, disregard or misrepresent these shortcomings may be explicable in terms of what has been described as 'Pushkinolatry'. The phrase belongs to John Bayley, in this reference to *The Tales of Belkin* (*Povesti Belkina*): 'it was only when Pushkinolatry was well under way that they came to be treated with the same reverence as the rest of his work'.[42]

The Tales of Belkin is one such imperfect work, though it is true also that several critics have expressed misgivings as to its overall quality. Another, which has received substantial acclaim and less in the way of negative reservations, is *The Captain's Daughter* (*Kapitanskaya dochka*). It seems improbable that a serious literary commentator should express the opinion that Stendhal's *Scarlet and Black* is 'much overrated', dismiss Balzac in a passing remark as 'essentially mediocre' and then, in the same work, go on to describe *The Captain's Daughter* as a 'charming short novel' and 'an admirable novella', but this was achieved by Vladimir Nabokov.[43] More extreme pronouncements belong to the Soviet critic N. L. Stepanov who asserts that '*The Captain's Daughter* occupies a prime position in world literature',[44] and to Anna H. Semeonoff who suggests that 'in respect of its historical interest, as well as of its literary quality, [it] is one of the finest short novels of its kind'.[45] Judgements like these seem unduly biased in Pushkin's favour and likely to puzzle outsiders approaching his work for the first time, particularly since we are now speaking of the prose, which loses less in translation. On the other hand Pushkin's story *The Queen of Spades*, often described as one of the finest tales in the whole of Russian literature and itself hovering throughout near to the excesses of Gothic melodrama, may be said to justify the generous treatment accorded it. What are the differences between these three works? Which of them has a genuine claim to fame extendable beyond national confines into popularity on a world scale? To what extent is romanticism responsible for the shortcomings of Pushkin's best-known prose?

The Tales of Belkin (1830) and *The Queen of Spades* (1833) invite comparison in the present context because of the trappings of romanticism with which they are so strikingly decorated. Each of the five *Tales* contains a plot, characters, situations or attitudes which are outlandish; they are oversimplified or exaggerated to accord with the contemporary taste for the fantastic and the sentimental. For instance, the main character of *The Shot* (*Vystrel*), Silvio, is presented in these terms: 'His sombre pallor, the sparkle in his eyes and the thick smoke issuing from his mouth gave him a truly diabolical air' (*Pol. sob.*, IV, p. 50). Two other tales, *The Snowstorm* (*Metel'*) and *Mistress into Maid* (*Baryshnya-krest'yanka*), are rather silly love stories based upon disguise, misunderstanding and coincidence. The one story which possesses some subtlety of character and situation, and the only one with an ending in which sadness predominates, is *The Postmaster* (*Stantsionnyi smotritel'*), and even this tale contains a good deal of raw sentimentality, including an abduction, a pathetic parent left behind, his rejection and subsequent death followed by valedictory visits to the cemetery by his daughter and then the narrator. As for *The Coffin-Maker* (*Grobovshchik*), it contains a passage which begins,

> The room was full of corpses. Moonlight, shining in through the windows, lit up their faces all yellow and blue, their sunken mouths, their dim, half-closed eyes and protruding noses . . . Adrian was horrified to recognise them as people who had been buried by his own efforts . . . (*Pol. sob.*, IV, p. 71).

But what of *The Queen of Spades*? This story too deals with the supernatural; magic joins forces with murder and the outcome of it all is madness. Both works are well stocked with romantic preoccupations and methods; is there really any difference between them?

The difference, which is substantial, hides ironically within another shared similarity: the intention of both works to neutralise by parody the excesses of literature in the romantic period. This purpose is, in both cases, overtly expressed. *The Snowstorm*, for instance, includes a now celebrated assertion that 'Mariya Gavrilovna had been raised on French novels and was therefore in love' (*Pol. sob.*, IV, p. 57); later on she is referred to as 'a veritable heroine of a novel' (*Pol. sob.*, IV, p. 64). Similarly, a well-known exchange near the beginning of *The Queen of Spades* reminds us of the awfulness of recent popular literature. The Countess is speaking to her grandson:

> 'Paul . . . send me some sort of new novel, but, please, not one of those that are being written nowadays.'
>
> 'How do you mean, grand'maman?'
>
> 'I mean a novel that doesn't have the hero strangling his father or his mother and doesn't have any drowned bodies. Drowned bodies terrify me!'
>
> (*Pol. sob.*, IV, p. 197)

These amount to clear statements — though the point is obvious enough without them — that the writer is not wholly serious. Part of his purpose is to ridicule people who take literature too seriously, people with execrable literary taste and the writers who pander to them. This is a common practice for Pushkin who is at his best when toying with the literary illusion while simultaneously exploiting it to the full. A great deal of his work hovers tantalisingly between virtuosic fulfilment of chosen literary possibilities and a genial mockery of them. The best example of this is provided by the novel *Yevgeniy Onegin* which develops its story and examines the process, doing so at one and the same time in a light-hearted and off-hand manner worthy of its distinguished predecessor *Tristram Shandy*. Ever since the Russian formalist critic Viktor Shklovsky exposed this method more than half a century ago,[46] it has become increasingly clear that the attitude extends well beyond that novel. It is now possible for John Bayley to state without risk of exaggeration, 'The question and quality of parody is never far away in Pushkin . . .'.[47]

The question is, what lies beyond the parody? This is where *The Tales of Belkin* and *The Queen of Spades* part company. In the former the parody seems to have got out of hand. Again it is Bayley who expresses this cogently when he says that these stories 'escape into a dramatic limbo in which elements of parody appear and vanish without the apparent consent or intention of the compiler'.[48] As they do so they cannot avoid acquiring a resemblance to their despised targets which is too close for comfort. Furthermore, with the possible and partial exception of *The Postmaster*, they exclude extraneous material which might be held to possess greater value than mere parody, itself an excellent art-form but not one by means of which an artist can rise to the greatest heights. *The Tales of Belkin* are slender pieces. There is no denying their neatness. Perhaps for their style alone they even deserve to be called 'compact novels'[49] or 'the first stories of permanent artistic value in the Russian language'[50] though there is in such statements a sense of straining literary charity as far as it will go and of doing so in the knowledge that their author produced masterpieces on other occasions. The original readers and reviewers did not have that advantage since the *Tales* were not published under Pushkin's name. If one tries to imagine the now impossible task of reading and criticising these stories *ab ovo*, with no knowledge of the author's identity, it is hard to be too harsh on the contemporary critic who wrote of them:

> There is not the slightest point to any of these stories. You read them: they are nice, they run along harmoniously, but when you have finished nothing remains in your memory but a vague notion of the plot.[51]

Attempts to read more into *The Tales of Belkin* are fraught with danger, though they have been made. Mirsky dismissed them by accepting *The Tales* as masterpieces though 'not because of the deep hidden meanings which imaginative criticism has of late discovered in them'.[52] He would have been unimpressed by the most recent attempt which, setting aside literary considerations, sees this work as an elaborate code, furnished with reverberating clues and used by Pushkin to give voice to otherwise inexpressible political ideas.[53]

The Queen of Spades is different. The story does have a mischievous inclination towards parody. Pushkin used it to ridicule what one critic lists succinctly as 'the popular romantic themes of ghosts, the superman, madness and genius, unrequited love, demonic interference, the triumph of virtue, the midnight tryst, and so forth'.[54] Nevertheless all of this is played down. The accompanying explanations preserve verisimilitude until the very end. Complex ideas provide the story with sophisticated meanings beyond the scope of *The Tales of Belkin* — the illusory concept of human freedom, the contrary awareness of our rough-hewn ends being shaped by an outside destiny, the hidden power of human sexuality.[55] Meanwhile a feeling of the passage of time remains strong as the action alternates between two distinct ages, a sense of place is secured by the most judicious arrangement of detail, while the characterisation, although sketchy in the usual manner of Pushkin, is persuasively conducted in a series of differentiated portraits, each in its own way claiming attention or sympathy and justifying the assertion by Henry Gifford that '*The Queen of Spades* can be said to reveal much psychological finesse . . .'[56] All the time profound ironies, based particularly on a series of non-events or failures to achieve close objectives, are working on the reader's consciousness with a wry humour. Furthermore the qualities of this story are accessible to foreign readers. Its poetic language may be untranslatable, but its elegant structures, narrative interest and teasing questions of morality and psychology are all transmutable into other media. At the end of it all, and only on mature reflection, an awareness is gained of the delicacy of this operation. Pushkin has brushed against the grotesque, sailed near to melodrama, approached sensationalism, dallied with prurience and sentimentality, but at no time has he been guilty of an indiscretion. If *The Queen of Spades* has parodied the cheap tale of the supernatural it has done so in the most effective way, by demonstrating how a good one should be written.

We must not now be tempted to look for parody in every corner of the poet's work. Parody cannot rescue *The Black Shawl, The Fountain of Bakhchisaray, The Stone Guest* or *Boris Godunov* from whatever faults they possess. Nor has it any determining presence in Pushkin's historical story, *The Captain's Daughter*. This is another rather slender piece of writing, somewhat overvalued by general critical opinion, and important more for its historical role in Russian literature than its intrinsic artistic merit. *The Captain's Daughter* does not pretend to be a historical novel; it is properly described as a *povest'*, or novella, a title which should lead us to expect rather sketchier material than, for instance, Scott's *Waverley* (1814), Stendhal's *Scarlet and Black* (1830) or that outright masterpiece of historical fiction in the first third of the nineteenth century, Manzoni's *The Betrothed* (1827). For literary rather than historiographical reasons Pushkin's modest story ought to be excluded from comparison with these more substantial works, let alone with Tolstoy's. The deficiency which makes this so is precisely the opposite of the shortcoming identified as detracting from the merits of *The Stone Guest*. Whereas the latter is too densely packed with a surfeit of material, *The Captain's Daughter*, on the contrary, supports too rarefied an atmosphere. Pushkin has applied to it his famous formula, 'Precision and brevity — these are the two virtues of prose',[57] as if it were appropriate to all forms of prose at all times, which is not the case. It is no accident that all the best known and most successful literary—historical works (as well as most of the lesser known and less successful ones) are long. Length and leisure are fundamental requirements of this genre in order to build up convincing historical pictures as well as rounded literary characters. It was a mistake for Pushkin to believe that because precision and brevity had served him well on so many occasions before, in verse as in prose, these same qualities were needed to produce a good literary—historical romance. From this mistake arise both the minor irritations and the larger shortcomings of *The Captain's Daughter*. The minor irritations may not matter a great deal though one or two examples are worth citing. It would have been useful for us to have had more details of the processes by which young Grinyov fell in love with Masha; when this occurs and a proposal is made in Chapter 5, it seems premature and scarcely justified by the thinly described previous encounters. In the same way we thirst for details of the agony Grinyov must have experienced on the eve of his duel (Chapter 4), of the tactical thinking behind the apparently foolish sortie from the fortress which led to its easy capture (Chapter 5) and of the surprising decision (in Chapter 12) by Pugachov to spare the grovelling Shvabrin, caught out in his infamous treatment of Masha, which was expressed in the unconvincing sentence, 'I shall spare you this once, but don't you forget that the next time you commit any offence this one will also be remembered against you' (*Pol. sob.*, IV, p. 306). Most historical novels, if anything, lay on the detail too thickly, but in *The Captain's Daughter* we have a right to complain of short measure.

The same deficiency amounts to a major flaw when applied to Pushkin's depiction of character. It is true that, by some mysterious process worked by a fine artist, the major characters Grinyov, Savelich and Pugachov manage to appropriate sufficient detailed attention to establish themselves convincingly. The trouble occurs with the two characters who play parts of real significance but who do not appear often enough, or stay long enough in the forefront of our consciousness, to create the appearance of anything more than a simple personality presented to us in a single dimension and are thus divorced from our general impression of what human nature is like. Masha and Shvabrin are characters from melodrama, the one a vulnerable and swooning heroine, the other a villain in everything he does. Not that everyone would agree with this statement. John Bayley, for instance, anticipates such criticism by stating the very opposite. According to this critic not only has Masha 'none of the artificial detachment of a Scott heroine' but 'Shvabrin's fictional villainy is convincingly established', and 'Certainly there is nothing of the stage villain in Pushkin's economical sketch of Shvabrin's nature'.[58] If the certainty implied in this last sentence (which forms part of a footnote) is well grounded one wonders why the contrary suspicion need be denied at all. In any case it is hard to see how such a charitable estimation of these two characters is to be justified. On almost every appearance Masha can be relied upon to blush, weep, swoon or hide away and we are not told of much else that she does. Similarly almost all Shvabrin's actions resound with caddishness; they tend to be qualified by expressions such as 'with sincere malice and feigned mockery' (*Pol. sob.*, IV, p. 287), 'in his bitterness' (p. 302), 'His face . . . expressive of sombre malice' (p. 309), 'vile' (p. 313), 'with a malign smile' (p. 317) and (in the omitted chapter) 'his face [expressing] malice and pain' (p. 327). In the character of Shvabrin Pushkin stands condemned by his own high standards. In an often-quoted comparison drawn between the characters of Shakespeare, who enjoy a rich complexity which is recognisably human, and those of Molière, who are so oversimplified that they carry over their monomaniacal characteristics into the simplest of everyday actions, Pushkin accuses the latter as follows: 'Molière's Miser is miserly — and that is all . . . Molière's Hypocrite trails after his patron's wife — hypocritically; takes on the care of an estate — hypocritically; asks for a glass of water — hypocritically'.[59] It may be that Shvabrin is not so bad as this. Perhaps he performs ordinary functions not like a villain but like an ordinary person; but if he does Pushkin has not seen fit to fill out this part of his personality. These two characters do have an air of oversimplification. As such they lend weight to the general feeling of discomfort which builds up throughout *The Captain's Daughter*, a feeling that we are being hustled too rapidly through complex events and are allowed only cursory glances at important issues and characters. Pushkin seems to have fallen into another literary pitfall; precision and brevity are not the two virtues of prose if you wish to create a masterpiece in the genre of historical fiction.

IV

The direction of this chapter so far has been negative. Error and weakness have been paraded in an attempt to demonstrate that Pushkin was by no means immune from all the dangerous side effects which accompanied the new ideas ushered into European literature by romanticism. Much remains to be said on the positive side. In the first place there are unedifying aspects of romanticism in which Pushkin displayed no interest whatever. Although a lover of country life he never indulged in the worship of nature; the pathetic fallacy is absent from his work. Although superstitious and fascinated by the workings of destiny he shows no tendency towards transcendentalism, abstract philosophising, religious mysticism or any vague sense of idealism. There is some toying with the supernatural in his writings but this is dealt with satirically or in a lightly suggestive manner. He keeps a tight rein on emotion and sensation, and although some of his work is pessimistic he has no taste for lachrymose melancholy. In matters of form he was a sensible experimentalist, pushing existing possibilities towards their outer limits and combining them into new strands of potential, rather than trying to dazzle the onlooker with revolutionary pyrotechnics. Despite all that we have said he was protected by instinct and training against excess. Thus a large proportion of the ocean-tide of romanticism washed over him to little effect.

Secondly, even when emulating an admired romantic model, he relied on his innate classical spirit to reduce the risk of self-betrayal. This is seen at its clearest in his attitude to Byron. The 'Byronic' period lasts for four or five years (1820–4); it is unByronic to begin with, remote from Byron at its end and soon overtaken by a series of achievements of an entirely different order. There are two clear examples. If *Yevgeniy Onegin* began vaguely as an imitation of Byron's *Don Juan* it adopted even at the outset a more disciplined form and went on to develop over the years into a fully-fledged novel, elegant in design, filled with true-to-life characters and dialogue, raising serious moral issues and setting new standards in literature and language. Equally remarkable is Pushkin's development in the field of the narrative poem where his relationship with romanticism is most clearly demonstrated. Four southern narratives belong to the Byronic period: *The Caucasian Captive* (*Kavkazkiy plennik*, 1820–1), *The Robber Brothers* (*Brat'ya razboyniki*, 1821), *The Fountain of Bakhchisaray* (1822) and *The Gypsies* (*Tsygany*, 1824). The borrowings from European romanticism are obvious, particularly in the remote and exotic settings, among Circassian tribesmen, in a Crimean harem centuries ago, in a camp of outcasts beyond the Volga and among a band of gypsies wandering the plains of Bessarabia. Vagueness of motivation and characterisation, emphasis on local colour, stereotyped speech, cliché-ridden ideas of the corruption of civilisation as opposed to the purity of nature and those who live close to her — these, and other habitual romantic mannerisms, hover ominously in the air. However, they are kept largely at bay even at the outset and as Pushkin matures they are dissipated, powerfully and forever. Even at this early stage Pushkin's descriptions of the extraordinary surroundings are restricted to an almost scientific deposition of relevant detail. His restraint is demonstrable in a number of ways. Sheer length is significant. Where Byron luxuriates in his use of language and allows most of his narrative poems to ramble on well beyond a thousand lines (in the case of *Childe Harold's Pilgrimage* well beyond four thousand) Pushkin starts with 777 lines in *The Caucasian Captive* and sees to it that every narrative poem afterwards gets shorter still. Interestingly enough, both poets produced at least one poem which is exceptional in this respect: Byron's *The Prisoner of Chillon* limits itself to 392 lines and much is gained in the process, whereas

Pushkin loses a good deal when he allows *Poltava* (which is really two stories in one and they would have been better kept apart) to escape and run away to almost 1500 lines. To this we must add the fact that Byron normally uses a longer line than Pushkin, which is the case also when we compare *Don Juan*'s 16000 lines with *Yevgeniy Onegin*'s less than 6000. By such simple figures are garrulity and laconism brought face to face. Overindulgence and restraint are demonstrable by reference to a single quotation from the end of Byron's *The Giaour*,

> . . . the generous tear
> This glazing eye could never shed.
> Then lay me with the humblest dead,
> And, save the cross above my head,
> Be neither name nor emblem spread,
> By prying stranger to be read,
> Or stay the passing pilgrim's tread.

Pushkin at his lowest ebb could never have brought himself, for any reason, to rhyme six successive lines with the same sound. The very idea is offensive to him, a tawdry display of the easiest of the poet's skills. The whole span of Pushkin's dozen narrative poems consists of six or seven thousand lines of verse admirably rhymed in patterns which, without attracting obvious attention, vary the tone and support the meanings with efficiency and subtlety. Only on four or five occasions will this company extend temporary membership even to a *triple* rhyme, and on each occasion there is good reason for its entry. In *Count Nulin* (*Graf Nulin*) the device is used twice to humorous effect. Pushkin's forbearance in limiting the use of this firework (which is allowed only one appearance in the rollicking *Gavriiliada*) does him the greatest credit.

The Gypsies, already shortened to 569 lines, represents a great step away from Byron. Compared with *The Caucasian Captive* it is compressed, variform, imaginative and altogether more interesting, with real issues of human psychology and morality for us to ponder. Nevertheless the treatment of the main theme, freedom, is heavy-handed, the words *volya*, *vol'nyy* and *svoboda* cropping up with tedious regularity, and some of the language is stilted. There are too many unnecessary archaisms and poeticisms; this is the last narrative in which anyone will be allowed to say, 'Leave, children, your couch of bliss' (*Pol. sob.*, II, p. 345), instead of 'It is time to get up'. The poem stands out as a classic example of transitional work but there can be no doubting that it contains some excellent passages. Two of them are to be found where they count most, at the beginning and the end. Like a film director the poet zooms down and in from a long-distance aerial shot of the wandering gypsies and then approaches their camp from a curiously oblique angle by drawing attention to their glittering camp fires as seen from outside, through the waggon-wheels. Within moments we are whisked into the midst of one family and the story is under way. This is imaginative narration of a high order. It is matched by the zooming up and away at the conclusion of the poem as we leave Aleko's solitary waggon in the middle of the steppe, equating him, in one of Pushkin's sparingly used metaphors, with a wounded crane who cannot fly south with the rest of the flock.

An awareness of the limitations of these earlier poems enhances admiration for his mature ones. *Count Nulin* (1825) and *The Bronze Horseman* (1833) produce a double sense of wonderment, first that they sound so perfect, with every poetic means exactly attuned to the desired ends, and second that so much is included in so small a compass. Not a syllable seems to be wasted or wrongly deployed. It is significant that neither of them contains a wisp or a whiff of anything associated with Byronism or romanticism. Not that *Nulin* is in the same class as *The Bronze Horseman*. It began as a direct parody of Shakespeare's *The Rape of Lucrece* and an amused look at the workings of chance events in human history. One appetising moment of parody remains; Nulin blunders through the darkness in his gaily coloured dressing-gown, knocking things over as he goes, and fails in his clumsy attempt at seduction; this is an amusing simulation of Tarquin's stallion-like progress through the castle and all-too-successful raping of Lucrece. Besides this the poem is full of sheer narrative interest and an infectious spirit of play. Pushkin casts an acute eye over the rural scene, epitomising in his finest manner as he goes. We are treated to the most elegant and delicate piece of satire, ranging wide, informative and devoid of acrimony. It is all told at a brisk pace and an unusually amusing twist is reserved for the last line. There is nothing amounting to a palpable flaw in this excellent poem, not even that of triviality; we are occasionally reminded, albeit through the tiniest hints, of social and family problems, awkward psychological truths and even ethical dilemmas. The main aim and achievement, however, centre around the unique pleasure of good story-telling which is what sets the poem below *The Bronze Horseman*.

The multifarious claims made in substantiation of the importance of *The Bronze Horseman* have been drawn together into one bold assertion, that it is nothing less than 'the most remarkable of nineteenth-century poems'.[60] This is not a judgment made in haste. It would indeed be difficult to discover a poem written in that period which combines so many qualities, attempts so much without sounding a false note, and does so in such a short space. A detailed examination of the poem has been undertaken elsewhere, and will be again and again.[61]

Even in summary form the qualities are impressive. Pushkin's manipulation of the resources of the Russian language, in at least three different styles, has been acknowledged as a remarkable example of instinctive musicality directed by a discriminating intelligence. The uncomplicated but moving story, and the ideas which accompany it, work themselves out in a complex system of hidden structures and cross-references which impart a sense of cohesion. The appearance of harmony and unity provides a flavour of paradox in view of the contrapuntal and antithetical methods by which the poem's arguments are presented. In modulating between these arguments, from theme to theme and between events concerning the protagonists, Peter, Yevgeniy, the city of St Petersburg and the river Neva, Pushkin shows that instinct for brevity, measurement and proportion with which his name is often equated and which is nowhere better exemplified. The seriousness of the poem, although uncharacteristic, is its greatest attribute; apart from some passing remarks on Yevgeniy as he is introduced and a little jibe at Count Khvostov, a contemporary poetaster, Pushkin dispels the accustomed atmosphere of flippancy or cynicism. No ponderous exertion of will appears to have been necessary for him to raise in the reader's mind a whole series of interesting ideas, some of them philosophical issues which, before this poem, had seemed to be beyond the poet's intellectual range. These concern issues of local, that is to say, Russian, significance, to do with the shaping and ordering of her society, past, present and future, a broader consideration of political questions such as the benefits and shortcomings of autocracy and democracy, a sad acknowledgement of the fragility of individuals, communities and even large institutions when they get in the way of the glacial movements of history and, overriding all of these ideas, a fearful reminder of the elemental powers belonging to the natural universe beside which humankind appears like a puny and short-lived irrelevancy. This latter notion, implicit throughout *The Bronze Horseman* and emphasised at the beginning and the end of the poem, shows how remote Pushkin has become, now at his most serious and significant, from the attitudes of the natural world adopted by European romanticism in general. All of these qualities are brought together in less than five hundred lines of memorable Russian verse.

V

The quality of Pushkin's achievement is to some extent measurable in negative terms. What he stopped doing, when he changed course, what he omitted — these non-existent attributes can contribute to an appreciation of his success. It is important to acknowledge that he did make wrong decisions, fall into error and produce some mediocre works. He sometimes allowed himself, in the broad sweep of his interests, to assimilate too much of the European romantic spirit. We have made an attempt to describe what went wrong in some of the flawed works which resulted, to trace Pushkin's movement away from misjudgment, and to isolate certain works of indisputable quality. Russians will argue that, even at his worst, Pushkin remains a great literary master. This is because his poetry *sounds* so perfect. Essentially minor works, like *The Caucasian Captive* and *The Fountain of Bakhchisaray*, are filled with a music so pleasing that it is easier to believe in their quality than to think of their immaturity. The beguiling euphony of all Pushkin's work, as well as being his hallmark and signal achievement, has been responsible for some misjudgment. To take an extreme example, his 'concord of sweet sounds' must surely be responsible for a pronouncement on Pushkin made by his most reliable critic in the English language which otherwise sounds idiosyncratic. 'The longer one lives,' Prince Mirsky confides, 'the more one is inclined to regard *King Saltan* as *the masterpiece of Russian poetry*.'[62] Happy memories of a Russian childhood, mingling with the recollection of the lovely music of this otherwise empty fairy tale, seem momentarily to have turned even Mirsky away from good sense. If we are to listen only to melody we shall repeat yesterday's mistakes by continuing to believe that some of Pushkin's works are better than they really are and that almost all the poet's *oeuvre* belongs to the category of surpassing excellence. This wrong supposition will continue to bemuse the non-Russian world and hinder rather than advance the spread of the poet's reputation.

In the last analysis, although Pushkin, as a contemporary of European romanticism, was deeply impressed by the new ideas liberated by the movement, he was neither dependent on it nor, in his best works, much affected by it. Some of Europe's finest artists who were active in the same period have also been subjected to close scrutiny in an attempt to determine how far they may be described as classical and how far romantic. Recent works have spoken as follows, for instance, about Goya (1746–1828) and Beethoven (1770–1827): the former 'is such an individual artist, and so much a genius that perhaps we should not think of him as part of a movement, still less the exponent of a fashion',[63] and the latter 'simply did not speak the language of the romantics. He had started in the classic tradition and ended up a composer beyond time and space, using a language he himself had forged'.[64] For all his aberrations these remarks apply exactly to the achievement of Alexander Pushkin.

Notes

1. 'Draft note on Tragedy' (1825), in Tatiana Wolff, *Pushkin on literature*, London, 1971, p. 130.
2. 'Draft on Classical and Romantic poetry' (1825), ibid., p. 126.
3. 'Draft article on Boris Godunov' (1828), ibid., p. 221.
4. 'Literatura u nas sushchestvuyet, no kritiki yeshcho net' (prob. 1830), in A. S. Pushkin, *Polnoye sobraniye Sochineniy v shesti tomakh*, ed. M. A. Tsyavlovsky, Moscow-Leningrad, 1936, V, p. 303 (hereafter *Pol. sob.*).
5. This subject is explored in detail in John Mersereau Jr's article, 'Pushkin's Concept of Romanticism' (*Studies in Romanticism*, III, 1, 1963, pp. 24—41), which ends however with the following sentence: 'We can hardly reproach Pushkin for failing to provide a viable interpretation of romanticism when, in fact, a century and a quarter after his death the phenomenon is still seeking its ultimate definition'.
6. John Bayley, Introduction to A. Pushkin, *Eugene Onegin*, tr. Charles Johnston, Harmondsworth, 1979, p. 15.
7. Donald Davie, 'Pushkin Plain', a review of *Pushkin: Selected Verse* (ed. John Fennell), *Guardian*, 20 March 1964.
8. Marc Slonim, *The Epic of Russian Literature*, Oxford, 1964, p. 90.
9. John Bayley, *Pushkin: a Comparative Commentary*, Cambridge, 1971, p. 91.
10. Joe Andrew, *Writers and Society during the Rise of Russian Realism*, London, 1980, p. 13.
11. Prince D. S. Mirsky, *Pushkin*, London, 1926, p. 22.
12. John Fennell (ed.), *Pushkin*, Harmondsworth, 1964, p. xii.
13. Oliver Elton, *Verse from Pushkin and Others*, London, 1935, p. 8.
14. Col. G. V. Golokhvastoff, 'Poushkin, his place in letters', in *Pushkin: The Man and the Artist*, New York, 1937, p. 211.
15. Edmund Wilson, 'In honour of Pushkin', in *The Triple Thinkers*, Harmondsworth, 1962, p. 44.
16. Maurice Baring, *Landmarks in Russian Literature*, London, 1960, p. 193.
17. David Magarshack, *Pushkin: a Biography*, London, 1967, p. 107.
18. See, for instance, Henri Troyat, *Pushkin*, tr. N. Amphoux, London, 1974, p. 326.
19. Details of the musical versions are given in N. Vinokur and R. A. Kagan, *Pushkin v muzyke: spravochnik*, Moscow, 1974, p. 160.
20. D. S. Mirsky, op. cit., p. 75.
21. A. Pushkin, *Eugene Onegin*, tr. with commentary by Vladimir Nabokov, New York, 1964, III, p. 155.
22. Bayley, *Pushkin*, pp. 86—7.
23. A. Slonimsky, *Masterstvo Pushkina*, Moscow, 1963, pp. 46—51.
24. Bayley, *Pushkin*, p. 87.
25. Ibid., p. 88.
26. Janko Lavrin, *Pushkin and Russian Literature*, London, 1947, p. 161.
27. Bayley, *Pushkin*, p. 206.
28. Richard Hare, *Russian Literature from Pushkin to the Present Day*, London, 1947, p. 37.
29. E. J. Simmons, *Pushkin*, New York, 1964, p. 328.

30. G. O. Vinokur, 'Pushkin as a Playwright', in D. J. Richards and C. R. S. Cockrell, *Russian Views of Pushkin*, Oxford, 1976, p. 203.
31. Lavrin, op. cit., p. 174.
32. Oliver Elton, op. cit., Introduction, p. 11.
33. Charles Corbet, 'L'originalité du *Convive de Pierre* de Pouchkine' (*Revue de la littérature comparée*, XXIX, 1955, p. 49).
34. André Meynieux, 'Pouchkine et Don Juan' (*La Table Ronde*, November 1957, p. 99).
35. D. S. Mirsky, *A History of Russian Literature*, New York, 1960, p. 97.
36. Mirsky, *Pushkin*, p. 164 [my italics].
37. Bayley, *Pushkin*, p. 208.
38. Ibid., p. 199.
39. Anna Akhmatova, *Sochineniya*, ed. G. P. Struve and B. A. Filippova, Washington, II, 1968, p. 259.
40. Heinrich Heine, 'The Romantic School', in *Prose and Poetry*, ed. M. M. Bozman, London, 1934, p. 254.
41. A. D. P. Briggs, 'The Hidden Forces of Unification in *Boris Godunov*' (*New Zealand Slavonic Journal*, 1, 1974, pp. 43—54).
42. Bayley, *Pushkin*, p. 309.
43. Nabokov, op. cit., II, pp. 90, 354, 290; III, p. 471.
44. N. L. Stepanov, 'Pathos of the Novel', in Richards and Cockrell, op. cit., p. 226. (The editors cite this example in their Introduction, p. viii.)
45. Anna H. Semeonoff, ed., *Kapitanskaya dochka*, London, 1962, pp. viii—ix.
46. V. Shklovsky, '*Teoriya prozy* and *Pushkin i Stern*' (*Volya Rossii*, 6, Prague, 1922).
47. Bayley, *Pushkin*, p. 245.
48. Ibid., p. 309.
49. Troyat, op. cit., p. 412.
50. Nabokov, op. cit., III, p. 180.
51. Quoted in Troyat, op. cit., p. 417.
52. Mirsky, *Pushkin*, p. 179.
53. Andrej Kodjak, *Pushkin's I. P. Belkin*, Ohio, 1979, p. 112.
54. John Merserau Jr, 'Yes, Virginia, there was a Russian Romantic Movement' (*Russian Literature Triquarterly*, 3, Spring 1972, p. 142).
55. Some of these ideas have been explained more fully in another article. See A. D. P. Briggs, '*Pikovaya dama* and *Taman*: Questions of Kinship' (*Journal of Russian Studies*, 37, 1979, pp. 13—20).
56. Henry Gifford, *The Novel in Russia*, London, 1964, p. 22.
57. 'Draft article on Prose', in Tatiana Wolff, op. cit., p. 43.
58. Bayley, *Pushkin*, p. 334.
59. From 'Table Talk' (*Sovremennik*, 8, 1837), quoted in T. Wolff, op. cit., pp. 464—5.
60. Bayley, *Pushkin*, p. 164.
61. The main points, as seen by the present author, are set out in greater detail in A. D. P. Briggs, 'The Hidden Qualities of Pushkin's *Mednyi vsadnik*' (*Canadian-American Slavic Studies*, Special Issue, *Pushkin I*, X, 2, Summer 1976, pp. 228—41).
62. D. S. Mirsky, *A History of Russian Literature*, New York, 1960, p. 93 [my italics].

63. Kenneth Clark, *The Romantic Rebellion*, London, 1974, p. 69.
64. Harold C. Schoenberg, *The Lives of the Great Composers*, London, 1971, p. 101.

3 Dmitry Venevitinov and his role in the early development of Russian philosophical romanticism

A. B. McMILLIN

Dmitry Vladimirovich Venevitinov (1805–27) occupies a unique but as yet imprecisely defined place in the history of Russian romanticism. On the one hand he has been recognised by many critics as an almost paradigmatic romantic poet in both theme and language; on the other he has been criticised for excessive adherence to the predominantly elegiac poetic dialect of the 1820s which had been inherited from Zhukovsky, Batyushkov, and, to some degree, Pushkin; adherents of the latter view, amongst whom Lidiya Ginzburg is the most prominent, also attribute his posthumous reputation as a programme poet of philosophical romanticism to the work of his friends in the journal *Moscow Herald*, rather than to any strong intrinsic qualities in Venevitinov's life or work. A survey of the characteristically romantic themes in his original writing and translations casts light on his image as a typically romantic poet, whilst his critical and theoretical prose illustrates, amongst other things, his attitude to Byron, German romantic philosophy, and the romantic Goethe, as well as his role in the controversy over Russian romanticism, particularly in connection with Pushkin and the concept of *narodnost'* (national character). Although the actual achievements of this brilliant but ill-fated youth cannot compare with those of Boratynsky or Tyutchev, none the less he played an important role as both a forerunner and a theoretician, constantly fighting critical oversimplification, and attempting by precept and practice to establish the philosophical basis without which he was convinced true poetry could not develop.

Venevitinov's name has been most frequently related to that of

Friedrich Schelling whose *Naturphilosophie* he and his fellow *lyubo-mudry* (wisdom lovers)[1] had striven to introduce to Russia, but he has also been compared to such disparate figures as Novalis,[2] Keats[3] and Byron.[4] Many critics have described him as a typically romantic poet, the only major voice of dissent being I. Ivanov at the turn of the century who apparently mistook Venevitinov's campaign against critical vagueness and indiscipline of thought for a struggle against romanticism as such.[5] Doubtless the balance and classical harmony of Venevitinov's poetic style influenced Ivanov's belief in his hostility to Byronism,[6] but he was a classicist only by education and training, not by inclination or poetic practice. Opinions have, however, varied as to the precise nature of his romanticism: I. I. Zamotin, for example, in an important early essay suggests that Venevitinov characterised the 'new type' of romantic poet both in his person and in his verse,[7] whilst D. D. Blagoy in his introduction to *Pol. sob.* links Venevitinov with the rebellious strain of romanticism, portraying him as a Decembrist *manqué*, an approach partially supported by Günther Wytrzens who seems surprised that Venevitinov does not even receive a mention in the 1950 anthology *Poeziya Dekabristov.*[8] However, amongst the many other western and Soviet scholars who regard Venevitinov as a typical romantic most would agree with the assessment of the French scholar Jean Bonamour: 's'il a été pour ses contemporains le poète romantique par excellence, ce n'est pas pour s'être rebellé contre la societé, mais pour avoir exprimé dans son oeuvre une certaine conception de l'homme et du monde'.[9]

Venevitinov's life, though not rich in events, was in itself highly romantic, adorned as it was with undisputed charm and brilliance, piquantly melancholy in the poet's unrequited love, and tragic in his virtual exile to St Petersburg and premature death. It finds extensive reflection in his poetry, particularly that of the so-called St Petersburg lyric cycle of 1826—7 where themes that are directly or indirectly autobiographical predominate. Despite the apparently literary nature of some of these lyrics — and subjectivity and autobiography are, of course, part of the common stock of romanticism — they represent a real attempt by Venevitinov to capture and express his innermost thoughts and feelings. As Fyodor Khomyakov, with whom he was rooming at the time, recorded: 'They comprise as it were his diary, expressing, always truthfully, his fleeting feelings of the minute.'[10] Even his earliest and most conventional verse epistles such as the first to his friend N. M. Rozhalin[11] reflect the closeness and warmth of the intellectual circle in which this 'wondrous youth' (*yunosha divnyy*)[12] moved and are not merely expressions of the artificial, 'Lenskian' elegiacism, the feeling of gloom which, according to Kyukhel'beker, writing in 1824, 'has swallowed up all other feelings'.[13] The mignon-esque poems of 1826, *Elegy* (*Elegiya*) and *Italy* (*Italiya*), for all Venevitinov's immense admiration of Goethe,[14] would seem to be at least as much the product of personal sentiment as of any literary inspiration: Zinaida Volkonskaya, the older woman for whom Venevitinov professed an unrequited love, had recently departed to this 'wondrous land of enchantment',[15] and 'home of inspiration',[16] and it was here that the young poet dreamed of finding renewed creative vigour, as Byron, Goethe and many others had done before him. Venevitinov's typically romantic fascination with the exotic may also be seen to derive in part from his work in the Oriental section of the Foreign Ministry archives; it is reflected both in his personal correspondence and in his creative writing: a passing reference in the lyric *Three Roses* (*Tri rozy*) to 'a bright stream . . . beneath the sky of Kashmir'[17] is linked not only with Byron's 'emerald meadows of Kashmeer' (*The Giaour*, line 390), but more intimately with Zinaida Volkonskaya's novella, *L'Enfant de Kaschemyr*;[18] the *Golden Harp* (*Zolotaya arfa*) prose fragment is set in Arabia,[19] and the recently discovered snatches of narrative verse beginning 'In a turban, with a bullet in my back . . .' ('Vchalme, s svintsovkoy za spinoy') also have an exotic background.[20] Hardly less exotic are the two 'Greek' poems *The Death of Byron* (*Smert' Bayrona*) and *The Song of the Greek* (*Pesn' greka*), but any autobiographical connection is decidedly tenuous, as is also the case in his two rather weak 'Ossianic' translations, *The Liberation of the Skald* (*Osvobozhdeniye skal'da*) and *The Song of Kol'ma* (*Pesn' Kol'my*), which, though also typically romantic, are lacking in personal elements; they belong spiritually to the same group of historical poems as the *Yevpraksiya* fragments and, later, *Novgorod*, although it may be noted that the latter is in fact closely bound up with Venevitinov's personal experiences on the way to his northern 'exile'.[21]

Venevitinov's other major verse translations are from Goethe, and also reflect the romantic rather than the classical side of the German's writing, in both selection and treatment. They include some of the best-known passages from the first part of *Faust* (Faust's monologue from the 'Wald und Höhle' scene [v. 3217—50], part of the scene 'Vor dem Tor' [v. 1064—1141], and Gretchen am Spinnrade [v. 3374—413], all emphasising romantic longing, elegiac melancholy and pantheistic communion with enigmatic nature, whilst his versions of *Künstlers Erdewallen* and *Künstlers Apotheose* also underline the romantic aspects of Goethe's ideas on the artist and his role.[22] Like the other *lyubomudry*, Venevitinov saw Goethe somewhat mystically through what Zhirmunsky called, 'the prism of Schelling and romanticism'.[23] To them he represented the ideal embodiment of philosophical romanticism,[24] and nowhere is this image more clearly expressed than in the unfinished fragment of an autobiographical novel, *Vladimir Parensky*, when the eponymous hero, a brilliantly gifted young poet, pays court at Weimar to the 'glorious' Goethe, 'squanderer of heavenly manna'.[25]

In *Vladimir Parensky* Venevitinov, seeking to illustrate the immense significance of Goethe for Russian poets of his generation, was also continuing one of the central — and essentially romantic — themes of his own lyrics, namely that of the poet and his role.[26] From many of Venevitinov's poems of the St Petersburg cycle emerged the image of a rather unearthly poet, proclaiming, as he had done throughout his prose articles and reviews, the inseparability of true poetry from philosophy,[27] and asserting the poet's need to seek freedom from the constraints of the crowd, and union with the natural world,[28] whilst at the same time succumbing to bouts of despair and romantic alienation, with frequent references to his own death. Six lyrics in particular, *Three Fates* (*Tri uchasti*), *The Poet* (*Poet*), *To the Lover of Music* (*K lyubitelyu muzyki*), 'I feel, burning within me . . .' ('Ya chuvstvuyu, vo mne gorit . . .'), *Sacrifice* (*Zhertvoprinosheniye*) and *Poet and Friend* (*Poet i drug*), reflect Venevitinov's rather Germanic self image as the romantic poet for whom 'poetry is inseparable from philosophy'.[29] Here, as elsewhere in his work, it is important to distinguish the romantic *topoi* from the expression of genuinely personal feelings. To take but one example, the 'secret', 'prophetic' voice foretelling doom in several later lyrics such as *Consolation* (*Utesheniye*) and *Testament* (*Zaveshchaniye*), acquires a quite different resonance in the light of his premature death, as indeed do the celebrated last lines of *Poet and Friend*:

> The poet's prophecies came true,
> And at the start of summer
> His friend visited his grave and wept . . .
> How much he had known of life! how little lived![30]

Some critics, most notably Lidiya Ginzburg, have seen Venevitinov as a programme poet of Russian romanticism less on the intrinsic evidence of his own writing than as the, to some extent, artificial posthumous creation of his colleagues in the so-called 'German school' who, she believes, attempted to build up an unrealistic and idealised picture of the dead poet in order to pursue their own literary aims.[31] This, together with the notable variety of critical opinion on the significance of Venevitinov's contribution to philosophical romanticism, forms one of the main points of interpretative divergence between pre-war Soviet attitudes to Venevitinov and the position of more recent scholars like V. L. Komarovich, B. V. Neyman, Ye. A. Maymin, and L. A. Tartakovskaya, who all stress the organic unity of the poet's work, and the importance of the links both between his various poems, and between his creative and theoretical writings. Komarovich first clearly articulated the concept of Venevitinov's St Petersburg poems as a cycle,[32] and Maymin has emphasised the cyclical nature of almost all of his poetry which, with its lofty autobiographical image of the poet, he traces back to early works like *The Liberation of the Skald*, declaring: 'no poet has a more central theme and central hero than Venevitinov'.[33] Ginzburg, on the other hand, has expressed a very different view of the image of an inspired poet in Venevitinov's verse:

> This is less a lyrical hero than a programme poet of romanticism, reflecting the Schellingian concept of poetry as the highest form of cognition and reconciliation of opposites, the concept of the genius as the highest creative power. By the efforts of the friends and people who shared Venevitinov's views the lyrical hero of his poetry arose posthumously. Readers became acquainted with Venevitinov's work through the collection of 1829. In the article attached to the collection Venevitinov's friends created a half-biographical, half-literary image of a fine and inspired youth who died in his 22nd year; at the same time this was the image of a romantic poet. This article seems to become part of the collection, prompting in the reader a certain definite attitude [*vospriyatiye*] to the whole lyric cycle.[34]

Certainly the legendary annual dinners at which Venevitinov's memory was celebrated by his friends have helped to create and preserve a mythical image, although the latter was, predictably, followed by a counter-reaction. Amongst critics rather than colleagues, three, A. P. Pyatkovsky, Ye. A. Bobrov and N. A. Kotlyarevsky, were particularly influential in maintaining the immensely elevated image of Venevitinov, an image which Wytrzens rightly characterises as 'near-mythical although only lightly idealized'.[35]

Whether Venevitinov's image arose naturally from his life and work or represented a posthumous creation, however, its significance in illustrating and advancing the ideas of the Schellingian, German school of romanticism is beyond doubt. As the undisputed leader and inspiration of the *lyubomudry*, he played a major role in laying the philosophical and literary basis for the short-lived but historically important *Moscow Herald*, founded in 1826 after the formal disbandment of the *obshchestvo lyubomudriya* (Society of Wisdom-lovers). Imbued from the start with the spirit of Goethe,[36] the new journal reflected the extensive knowledge of his works enjoyed by Venevitinov and his colleagues, a knowledge and understanding that in fact extended over a wide range of other German writers and philosophers,[37] emerging in a variety of forms as the young enthusiasts sought to popularise German culture through their translations and critical discussions. Ivanov has called the *lyubomudry* poor propagandists for their ideas, being too remote from the general public,[38] and Ginzburg has drawn attention to their lack of technical, that is, poetic, unity (compared with, for instance, the acmeists a century later) as an obstacle to the furtherance of their literary aims, noting also that the end of the 1820s was the end of the age of poetry and the beginning of a period in which 'schools' and fixed literary positions were dissolving in the face of a new emphasis on individual opinions and tastes.[39] Be that as it may, without the *lyubomudry* Russian writers and critics, always spiritually closer to the cultures of France and England than that of Germany, would have remained in even greater ignorance of German traditions and achievements.

Venevitinov's plan for the *Moscow Herald*, *A Few Thoughts on the Plan of a Journal*, was far more than a simple prospectus, as indeed its original title, unacceptable to the censor, implied: *On the State of Enlightenment in Russia*. Rather it constituted a manifesto of the *lyubomudry*'s ideas, and a lucid exposition of some of the endemic weaknesses in contemporary Russian literature, most of which, in Venevitinov's view, derived from the French cultural hegemony which had for too long held Russian literature and thought in thrall. German writing and ideas are prominent both implicitly and explicitly in this essay, as the young critic expounds with conviction the importance of fusing philosophy and literature as the only way of escape from the empty and mechanical imitativeness into which Russian letters, and particularly verse, had degenerated, as what had been the golden age of Russian poetry became, in Belinsky's words, 'a period when versifying turned into utter mania'.[40] As a preliminary to solving the twin problems of literature's crippling dependence on foreign (French) models,[41] and the mechanisation of the language of poetry,[42] Venevitinov proposed the drastic and impractical solution of completely arresting the flow of 'versifying' in order that Russian letters might be made to 'think more and produce less'.[43] Here it should be stressed, however, that he was far from complacent about his own poetic talent and achievement, describing himself in one lyric as 'filled with eternal doubt',[44] and in fact a major point of disagreement between modern critics lies in the assessment of how far the very traditional language, form, and, to some extent, themes of Venevitinov's poetry vitiate his attempts to create a new type of philosophical romanticism.

The overall significance of this new trend in Russian literature is not in doubt: in a recent analysis V. I. Sakharov has contrasted the briefness of the period in which the *lyubomudry*'s poetry flourished with the extent of its importance,[45] whilst earlier P. N. Sakulin described the effect of philosophical romanticism in Russian literature as being the development of a new understanding of *narodnost'* and a great revival in the study of [cultural] history, 'extending its perspectives and deepening its methods'.[46]   Leaving aside for the moment the *lyubomudry*'s critical and theoretical contribution, however, there remains the question of how far Venevitinov's own poetry advanced the new movement. Lidiya Ginzburg perceives a great rift between the poet's creative writing and his theories,[47] a rift which, in her opinion, his verse (like that of Khomyakov and Shevyryov) was too weak to bridge.[48]   In a review of Komarovich's 1940 edition she takes issue with the editor's assertion that Venevitinov was successful in creating a new type of philosophical poetry, and that his philosophical conception gives a new sense to (*pereosmyslyayet*) the elegiac formulas in which he wrote, suggesting, rather, the opposite case, that is, that traditional formulas may in fact drown the philosophical conception.[49]   For her, the inertia of the (dead) poetic dialect of elegiacism prevented Venevitinov from successfully combining his role as a philosophical spokesman with the expression of a truly individual poetic personality: typically, the 'secrets of eternal creation' that he refers to in the lyric 'I feel burning within me . . .' are unveiled in a manner which is 'not in the least philosophical, but entirely elegiac'.[50]   Ginzburg's belief in the severe limitations of the programme and achievements of Venevitinov and the *lyubomudry* has not been shared by more recent commentators who see the group's work in a far more positive light. Tartakovskaya's important monograph is based on a reading of Venevitinov's prose and poetry in the spirit in which they were received by contemporaries, that is as a coherent system of romantic images and ideas, albeit only sketched in outline,[51] as, indeed, is the earlier work of Günther Wytrzens, also written in a spirit of sympathy and understanding.[52] One of the leading Soviet specialists in philosophical poetry, Yevgeniy Maymin, has gone so far as to describe the *lyubomudry*'s work as 'determining the life of Russian verse, both in its evaluation and in its reception'.[53]

It may well be that much of Venevitinov's poetry reflects brilliant promise rather than unequivocal achievement, and that his contribution to the popularisation of Schelling, Goethe and other German writers, though valuable, was perhaps of limited consequence in view of the way Russian literature was to develop in ensuing decades, but his literary criticism on the other hand stands as an unqualified achievement, both in its contribution to the debate about romanticism in the mid-1820s, and more generally in establishing serious standards and criteria for the future development of the art in Russia. Venevitinov's first major critical work, *A Critique of Merzlyakov's Views of the Principles and Nature of Ancient Tragedy* (1825), makes very plain his opposition to the facile juxtaposition of extremes which was characteristic of the period, the definition of romanticism by its differences from an artificially conceived classicism:

Here we are talking only of those works which determine the general direction of ideas in our age. *Extrema coeunt*. The whole world consists of opposites, and our literature is rich in them. But why judge by caricatures? Soulless narrative poems, having neither beginning nor ending, characterless novels and stories, and contentious pieces of criticism written simply to defy the innate laws of logic and conventional rules of decency belong even less to the ranks of romantic works than the poems of Chapelain belong to classical poetry.[54]

In place of such vagueness Venevitinov sought to make criticism more theoretical and more precise. His former teacher Merzlyakov was rebuked for 'lack of theory',[55] whilst literary criticism was presented as a matter of 'new discoveries' and 'proofs derived from them'.[56] No longer could romanticism remain an area of vague emotions and ephemeral feelings, but should rather be perceived as a world-view, approachable only through a unifying, synthesising philosophical theory. Allied to this concept was Venevitinov's clear understanding of literature as a continuous, developing phenomenon rather than as a series of unconnected, disparate periods,[57] and in this connection it may be noted that a recent Soviet scholar has described Venevitinov's critical methods as essentially dialectical.[58] Thus in an unpublished notice of Pushkin's *Boris Godunov* the young champion of romanticism welcomed Pushkin's adoption of the 'popular rules'[59] of Shakespearean drama, and concomitantly his abandonment of the 'arbitrary rules' governing the three unities, since their loss led not to chaos but to a new realistic quality of writing which he termed *'vraisemblance'*.[60]

It was, however, in his commentary on the first chapter of *Yevgeniy Onegin* that Venevitinov made his most important contribution to romantic criticism. Pushkin, with whom he shared a great-great-grandfather,[61] was later to describe him as 'the best of the chosen ones',[62] and welcomed his article as a rare exception to the generally abysmal level of criticism his novel in verse had attracted: 'It is the only article that I have read with love and attention. All the rest is either abuse or over-sweetened nonsense'.[63] *Critique of an Article on 'Yevgeniy Onegin'* takes to task Nikolay Polevoy, editor of the *Moscow Telegraph*, who had published in the fifth issue for 1825 a laudatory but vague review of the novel's first chapter. Venevitinov's response is entirely characteristic: 'Is not the absence of rules also prejudice?' he asks;[64] only the establishing of new positive theories and in particular the acceptance of the inseparability of literature and philosophy will bring the realisation that 'the source of romantic poetry does not consist in *an indeterminate condition of the heart*'.[65] A major part of the article is devoted to defining Pushkin's relationship to Byron, and, at the same time, to defending him from unnecessary and empty comparisons with the

English bard,[66] but no less important are Venevitinov's attempts to bring new understanding to the central romantic concept of *narodnost'*, a term first articulated by Vyazemsky, but generally used in an excessively concrete, material sense which brought it close to mere local colour. In *Critique of an Article on 'Yevgeniy Onegin'* he suggests that *narodnost'* is not to be found in the mentioning of champagne bottles or well-known restaurants,[67] but in a second article, written in response to Polevoy's rejoinder to *Critique . . .*, goes much further, coming close to the view being formulated (though not published) by Pushkin himself at this time,[68] and, indeed later by Belinsky and Gogol':

> I do not suppose *narodnost'* to be found in traditional leather boots, beards, etc. . . . *Narodnost'* is reflected not in pictures belonging to any particular place, but in the very feelings of the poet nourished on the spirit of a particular people, and living, so to say, in the development, successes, and separateness of its character. The concept of *narodnost'* should not be confused with the expression of native customs: such pictures only truly please us when they are justified by the proud sympathy of the poet.[69]

Venevitinov's new interpretation of *narodnost'* represents an important and characteristic instance of his persistent striving to raise the general level of Russian literary criticism of the early romantic period, on the one hand by increasing its terminological and conceptual precision, and on the other by introducing to it a consistent and elevated strain of philosophical reflection.

Poet, translator, philosopher, and critic, Venevitinov did much to develop the theory and practice of philosophical romanticism. His significance as translator, critic, and ideological inspiration for the *lyubomudry* is beyond dispute. As an original poet he does not approach the inspirational depth of, for example, Boratynsky's philosophical lyrics, although on the other hand he certainly anticipated two major features of later Russian romanticism, namely Lermontov's Byronism and Tyutchev's Germanic nature philosophy. His reputation as a poet has moved from early adulation, maintained in romantic memory and revived by idealist critics at the turn of the century, to stern twentieth-century criticism for over-conventional elegiacism; later attempts to emphasise his real or imaginary social concerns and to present him as a potential radical have, most recently, been followed by a more balanced portrayal as a typical early romantic of great promise but only partially fulfilled poetic genius. Once again his role as inspirational leader is important, for just as Venevitinov's poetry as a whole is, by general consent, greater than the sum of its parts, so the collective significance of the *lyubomudry's* philosophical lyrics rises far above the achievement of even their most gifted representative, forming an important and influential trend in Russian romantic literature of the second half of the 1820s.

Notes

* The author is indebted to the British Academy for a grant which facilitated the preparatory research for this article.

1. The terms *lyubomudr* and *lyubomudriye*, formed from the same semantic constituents as *filosof* and *filosofiya*, were intended to distinguish the new school from the French philosophy which had hitherto held sway in Russia.
2. S. H. König (pen-name of N.A. Mel'gunov), *Literarische Bilder aus Russland*, Stuttgart, 1837, p. 176.
3. See Gustav Shpet, *Ocherk razvitiya russkoy filosofii*, Petrograd, 1922, p. 333.
4. Lidiya Tartakovskaya has described him as the prototype for Venevitinov's lyrical hero of the pre-Decembrist period, 'O liricheskom geroye poezii D. Venevitinova podekabr'skoy pory' (*Nauchnyye trudy Tashkentskogo gosudarstvennogo universiteta*, CCCXCVI, Tashkent, 1971, pp. 249—50), and his self-image as the 'smelyy uchenik Bayrona' does indeed emerge from a number of poems of this time: see *K Skaryatinu* (*Pri posylke yemu vodevilya*), in *Polnoye sobraniye sochineniy*, ed. B. V. Smirensky, Moscow-Leningrad, 1934 (hereafter *Pol. sob.*), p. 79. For a fuller description of the relationship between the two poets see A. B. McMillin, 'Byron and Venevitinov' (*Slavonic and East European Review*, CIII, 1975, pp. 188—201).
5. I. Ivanov, *Istoriya russkoy kritiki*, St Petersburg, 1898, I, 2, pp. 421—2.
6. Ibid., p. 424.
7. I. I. Zamotin, 'Obshchestvennyye i literaturnyye epokhi russkoy zhizni XIX v.' (*Russkiy filologicheskiy vestnik*, Warsaw, 1—2, 1906, p. 92). Zamotin's view contrasts sharply with Ginzburg's emphasis on the traditional, conventional elements in Venevitinov's poetry. See, for instance, her 'Opyt filosofskoy liriki (Venevitinov)' (*Poetika*, V, Leningrad, 1929, pp. 72—104).
8. Günther Wytrzens, *Dmitrij Vladimirovic Venevitinov als Dichter der russischen Romantik*, Graz-Cologne, 1962, p. 9.
9. J. Bonamour, 'D. V. Venevitinov, l'homme et l'oeuvre' (supplementary doctoral thesis, University of Paris, 1965, p. 24).
10. Letter to his brother Aleksey, 3 December 1826: *Pol. sob.*, p. 398. Cf. Bonamour, op. cit., p. 25: 'La vie de Venevitinov est déjà une réalité transformée, on dirait presque sublimée, comme sa philosophie et sa poésie'.
11. *Poslaniye k Rozhalinu: Pol. sob.*, p. 69.
12. M. P. Pogodin, 'Vospominaniya o S. P. Shevyryove' (*Zhurnal Ministerstva narodnogo prosveshcheniya*, CXLI, 2, St Petersburg, 1869, p. 406). It is interesting to note that the adjective *divnyy* was one of Venevitinov's own favourites, and indeed plays an important part in one of his most celebrated lyrics, the somewhat Faustian '*Ya chuvstvuyu, vo mne gorit*': 'Teper' gonis' za zhizn' yu divnoy / I kazhdyy mig v ney voskreshay . . .', *Pol. sob.*, p. 107. See also Ian K. Lilly, 'An Adjective-analysis of Venevitinov's Poetry' (M.A. thesis, University of Christchurch, 1968, pp. 33—7, 72), and Kaleriya Yavorskaya, 'Slovar' yazyka D. V. Venevitinova' (Ph.D. thesis, New York University, 1973, p. 84). Of further linguistic interest are Deborah Dunton, 'A Comparison of the Metapoetic Lexicons of A. S. Pushkin and D. V. Venevitinov' (M.A. thesis, University of Toronto, 1979), and Ye. A. Maymin's discussion of the romantic

vocabulary of one of Venevitinov's major lyrics, 'Poet i drug', in *O russkom romantizme*, Moscow, 1975, pp. 168—70.

13. 'We all vie with one another in pining [*vzapuski toskuyem*] about our lost youth, endlessly chewing and re-chewing this pining', V. K. Kyukhel'beker, 'O napravlenii nashey poezii, osobenno liricheskoy, v posledneye desyatiletiye' (*Mnemozina*, 2, Moscow, 1824), quoted from L. Myshkovskaya, *Literaturnyye problemy pushkinskoy pory*, Moscow, 1934, pp. 14—15.

Amongst the many legends to grow up around Venevitinov's name after his death, the idea that he served as a model for Lensky was particularly persistent in the nineteenth century, though plainly without foundation since the second chapter of *Yevgeniy Onegin* was written in Odessa in 1823, whilst Pushkin met his distant cousin only in 1826. Herzen was typical, twice linking the names of Lensky and Venevitinov: A. I. Gertsen, *Polnoye sobraniye sochineniy i pisem v dvadtsati dvukh tomakh*, ed. M. K. Lemke, 1919—22, VI, p. 357; XIII, p. 574.

14. For an analysis of the relationship between the two writers, see A. B. McMillin, 'Venevitinov und Goethe. Zur Geschichte der frühen russischen Romantik', in *Goethe und die Welt der Slawen*, ed. H. B. Harder and H. Rothe, Giessen, 1981 (hereafter 'Venevitinov und Goethe'), pp. 147—57.

15. *Elegiya*, l. 2.

16. *Italiya*, l. 1.

17. Lines 5—6.

18. *Quatre nouvelles par la princesse Zénéide Volkonsky*, Moscow, 1819; these novellas are all extensively alluded to in Venevitinov's effervescent *Fête impromptue* of 1825.

19. See L. Tartakovskaya, 'Novoye o Venevitinove' (*Nauchnyye Trudy Tashkentskogo gosudarstvennogo universiteta*, CCLXXX, Tashkent, 1965, pp. 83—7).

20. D. V. Venevitinov, *Polnoye sobraniye stikhotvoreniy*, ed. B. V. Neyman, Leningrad, 1960, pp. 169—70.

21. *Pesn' Kol'my* is a translation of an excerpt from James Macpherson's *Colna-Dona*, and *Osvobozhdeniye skal'da*, though long thought to be an original work, a free version of Charles Millevoye's *La Rancon d'Égill*. See D. M. Sharypkin, 'Skandinavskaya tema v russkoy romanticheskoy literature', in *Ranniye romanticheskiye veyaniya: Iz istorii mezhdunarodnykh svyazey russkoy literatury*, ed. M. P. Alekseyev, Leningrad, 1972, p. 147. Venevitinov also translated Millevoye's *Plaisir et peine* under the title *Kryl'ya zhizni*, and a lyric by Gresset (*Vetochka*) to which he added four lines of his own.

22. On the *Künstlergedichte* see Wytrzens, op. cit., pp. 45—6, and on Venevitinov's Goethe translations as a whole the present author's 'Venevitinov und Goethe', pp. 151—2. It is interesting to note that in his *Razbor rassuzhdeniya g. Merzlyakova o nachale i dukhe drevney tragedii*, Venevitinov links directly the poetry of Goethe and Byron as 'plod glubokoy mysli', whilst in *Neskol'ko mysley v plan zhurnala* he links the names of Schiller and Goethe: *Pol. sob.*, pp. 210, 216.

23. V. M. Zhirmunsky, *Gete v russkoy literature*, Leningrad, 1937, p. 162.

24. Ibid., p. 172. See also L. Tartakovskaya, *Dmitry Venevitinov* (*Lichnost', mirovozzreniye, tvorchestvo*), Tashkent, 1974, pp. 136—8, and G. V. Venevitinov, *Nekotoryye problemy rannego russkogo romantizma* (*Filosofskiye vzglyady D. V. Venevitinova*), Moscow, 1972, p. 35.

25. D. V. Venevitinov, *Izbrannoye*, Moscow, 1956, p. 143. Venevitinov's tragically premature death prevented his making a pilgrimage to Weimar like that of Parensky, or indeed his fellow *lyubomudr* Shevyryov.

26. Maymin (*O russkom romantizme*, p. 152) stresses the central, 'key' significance of this theme in Venevitinov's verse, whilst Tschiževskij lays particular emphasis on his lofty, essentially Schellingian concept of the poet's role: Dmitrij Tschiževskij, *Russische Literaturgeschichte des 19. Jahrhunderts. I. Die Romantik*, Munich, 1964, p. 83. On the language with which this theme is treated see Dunton, op. cit.

27. 'The true poets of all peoples, of all ages, were deep thinkers, philosophers...', *Neskol'ko mysley v plan zhurnala, Pol. sob.*, p. 218. See also *Anaksagor. Beseda Platona* (ibid., p. 134): 'philosophy is the highest poetry'; and *Razbor stat'i o 'Yevgenii Onegine'* (ibid., p. 225): 'The prime quality in any artist is strength of thought and strength of feeling'.

28. 'Philosophy was born when man lost contact (*razznakomilsya*) with nature'. Letter to A. I. Koshelyov of 1825, *Pol. sob.*, p. 301. This theme, also prominent in the poetry of Tyutchev, is treated philosophically in Venevitinov's prose sketch *Utro, polden', vecher i noch'*, ibid., pp. 130–3.

29. *Razbor stat'i o 'Yevgenii Onegine', Pol. sob.*, p. 224.

30. Sbylis' prorochestva poeta, / I drug v slezakh s nachalom leta / Yego mogilu posetil . . . / Kak znal on zhizn'! kak malo zhil!, *Pol. sob.*, p. 122. Although hints at suicide figure in at least two lyrics, *Kinzhal* and *K moyemu perstnyu*, there appears to be no real justification for Nabokov's assertion that Venevitinov took his own life. See A. S. Pushkin, *Eugene Onegin*, tr. with commentary, Vladimir Nabokov, London, 1964, II, p. 236.

Maymin finds elements of prophecy in Venevitinov's poetry as early as *Osvobozhdeniye skal'da*: see Ye. A. Maymin, 'Poet i filosof: Ocherk tvorcheskogo puti D. V. Venevitinova' (*Uchonyye zapiski Leningradskogo gosudarstvennogo pedagogicheskogo instituta*, CDXXXIV, Leningrad, 1970, p. 43).

31. Ginzburg, 'Opyt filosofskoy liriki', pp. 78–9.

32. In D.V. Venevitinov, *Stikhotvoreniya*, Leningrad, 1940, pp. 146–52.

33. Maymin, 'Poet i filosof', pp. 42–3.

34. L. Ya. Ginzburg, 'Russkaya poeziya 1820–1830–kh godov', in *Poety 1820–1830–kh godov*, ed. Ginzburg and V. E. Vatsuro, Leningrad, 1972, I, p. 40.

35. Wytrzens, op. cit., p. 8.

36. The *pièce de resistance* of the first issue was a letter from the patriarch approving the journal's plan, as well as a number of translations from his works. Thereafter he figured in one way or another in every issue until publication ceased in 1830.

37. Apart from Schelling's nature philosophy and Schillerian aesthetics, the *lyubomudry*, and Venevitinov in particular, showed interest in Klopstock, Friedrich Schlegel, Tieck, Wackenroder, and Novalis. For a somewhat fuller description of the representation of German literature and thought in Venevitinov's writing see A. B. McMillin, 'Venevitinov und Goethe', pp. 148–9.

38. *Istoriya russkoy kritiki*, p. 421.

39. 'Opyt filosofskoy liriki', pp. 92–4.

40. V. G. Belinsky, 'Literaturnyye mechtaniya (1834)', in *Polnoye sobraniye sochineniy v trinadtsati tomakh*, ed. N. F. Bel'chikov, et al., Moscow, 1953–9, I, p. 76. Philosophy as a remedy for imitativeness was also advocated by V. F. Odoyevsky: see Wytrzens, op. cit., p. 75n.

61

41. *Neskol'ko mysley v plan zhurnala*: *Pol. sob.*, p. 217.
42. Ibid., p. 218.
43. Ibid., p. 219.
44. *'Ya chuvstvuyu, vo mne gorit'*, 1. 9.
45. V. I. Sakharov, 'Filosofskiy romantizm lyubomudrov i "poeziya mysli"', in *Istoriya romantizma v russkoy literature, 1825—40*, ed. S. Ye. Shatalov, et al., Moscow, 1979, p. 65.
46. P. N. Sakulin, *Pushkin i Radishchev*, Moscow, 1920, pp. 66—7.
47. Ginzburg, 'Opyt filosofskoy liriki', p. 89.
48. Ibid., p. 104.
49. L. Ya. Ginzburg, 'D. V. Venevitinov, *Stikhotvoreniya*, Leningrad, 1940' (*Zvezda*, 1, 1941, p. 178).
50. Ibid. Her fullest discussion of this subject is to be found in 'Opyt filosofskoy liriki', pp. 80—104, esp. pp. 80—91.
51. L. Tartakovskaya, *Dmitry Venevitinov* (*Lichnost', mirovozzreniye, tvorchestvo*), Tashkent, 1974.
52. Günther Wytrzens, op. cit.
53. Ye. A. Maymin, 'Filosofskaya poeziya Pushkina i lyubomudrov (K razlichiyu khudozhestvennykh metodov)', in *A. S. Pushkin, Issledovaniya i materialy*, VI, Leningrad, 1969, p. 98. See also the same author's *Russkaya filosofskaya poeziya: Poety-lyubomudry, A. S. Pushkin, F. I. Tyutchev*, Moscow, 1976, esp. pp. 23—51.

    Dmitry Blagoy's over-emphasis of Venevitinov's supposed democratic, 'revolutionary' tendencies in the introduction to *Pol. sob.* was typical of the time when it appeared (1934) and has had little support from more realistic recent critics. It was none the less reprinted without amendment almost forty years later: *Ot Kantemira do nashikh dney*, Moscow, 1973, II, pp. 293—331.
54. *Pol. sob.*, p. 210n.
55. Ibid., p. 207.
56. Ibid., p. 209.
57. I. Ye. Usok has described broad historical vision as a quality of the *lyubomudry* as a whole, compared with the narrower view of, for example, the Decembrists. See 'Filosofskaya poeziya lyubomudrov', in *K istorii russkogo romantizma*, ed. Yu. V. Mann, et al., Moscow, 1973, pp. 116—19.
58. Yu. Mann, *Russkaya filosofskaya estetika*, Moscow, 1969, pp. 18, 19.
59. See *Pushkin on Literature*, sel., tr. and ed. Tatiana Wolff, London, 1971, p. 248.
60. *Analyse d'une scène détachée de la tragédie de mr. Pouchkin, Pol. sob.*, pp. 240—1.
61. For details see *Pol. sob.*, p. 353.
62. See Maymin, *O russkom romantizme*, p. 147.
63. A. P. Pyatkovsky, 'O zhizni i sochineniyakh D. V. Venevitinova', in *Sobraniye sochineniy D. V. Venevitinova*, ed. A. P. Pyatkovsky, St Petersburg, 1869, p. 406.
64. *Pol. sob.*, p. 224.
65. Loc. cit.
66. Ibid., pp. 221—2.
67. Ibid., p. 226.

68. An unfinished article, 'O narodnosti v literature', dates from 1825, A. S. Pushkin, *Sobraniye sochineniy v desyati tomakh*, Moscow, 1959—62, VI, pp. 267—78.
69. *Otvet g. Polevomu, Pol. sob.*, p. 237. For a general discussion of the origins and development of the concept of *narodnost'*, see L. G. Leighton, *'Narodnost'* as a Concept of Russian Romanticism', in his *Russian Romanticism: Two Essays*, The Hague-Paris, 1975, pp. 41—108, esp. pp. 79—84.

4 Decembrist romanticism: A. A. Bestuzhev–Marlinsky[1]

NEIL B. LANDSMAN

It is refreshing to see the wealth of attention being lavished recently on romanticism by distinguished Soviet scholars. Particularly heartening is the attempt to extend the bounds of romanticism and allot it its rightful place in the development of Russian literature. N. L. Stepanov, for example, in 1968 rejects the previous commonly-held view of romanticism as something inferior and hostile to realism[2] and in 1973 criticises the general failure to appreciate romanticism by those who consider realism the sole progressive literary force.[3] Marlinsky for the large part remains unaffected by all this reassessment; from the 1820s to the present day he has retained his unshaken position as the most faithful and eclectic adherent to the movement. Indeed his name is synonymous with it; N. K. Piksanov in 1967 equates the man and the movement: 'the basic style of *Vadim* is not romanticism or "Marlinism" . . .'[4] In the 1830s he was a cult figure, the representative of the Romantic school. Turgenev's story, *Knock . . . knock . . . knock!* (*Stuk . . . stuk . . . stuk! . . .*) of 1870 illustrates this beautifully:

> [Marlinsky] in the [18]30s thundered like no one else — even Pushkin, according to the youth of that time, could not be compared to him. He not only enjoyed the fame of being the foremost Russian writer, he even — which is much more difficult and is met with rarely — set his seal to some degree on the generation contemporary to him. Heroes *à la* Marlinsky turned up everywhere, particularly in the provinces and especially amongst soldiers and gunners; they spoke with 'a storm in the heart and fire in the blood'. Women's hearts were 'devoured' by them. The nickname

'fatal' was coined about them. This type, as is generally known, was preserved for a long while until the time of Pechorin.[5]

The criticism of the 1960s and 1970s has come up with a wide variety of labels in an attempt to define romanticism once for all.[6] It is interesting to note that whatever the label, Marlinsky fits it remarkably well. If 'liberalism', then the early stories such as *Roman and Olga* and *Wenden Castle* (*Zamok Venden*) can be viewed as efforts to incorporate progressive Decembrist ideals in literature. If 'individualism' or 'subjectivism', we have an entire panoply of Marlinsky heroes who challenge society and assert their individual rights — Mulla-Nur, Pravin in *The Frigate 'Hope'* (*Fregat 'Nadezhda'*) and Gremin in *The Test* (*Ispytaniye*). If 'the fantastic', there exists a range of Gothic stories from *Eisen Castle* (*Zamok Eyzen*) to *The Cuirassier* (*Latnik*) which show Marlinsky to be a foremost exponent of this trend. If the phrase 'conflict between dream and reality' is used, we can look to a series of heroes who feel disillusioned because their ideals are too bold and lofty for this world — Sitsky in *The Traitor* (*Izmennik*) and Lidin in *Evening on a Bivouac* (*Vecher na bivuake*).

Not only did Marlinsky epitomise the general romantic movement, he was also one of the leading figures (then Bestuzhev) in an important branch of romanticism specific to Russia — Decembrism. Decembrist romanticism flourished in Russia between 1812 and 1825, from the time when the French armies were expelled until the Decembrist revolt. It includes the poetry of Ryleyev and Kyukhel'beker, the stories of Bestuzhev, the political tracts of Orlov, Pestel and Muravyov, the agitational songs of Ryleyev and Bestuzhev. Much of the most recent criticism is devoted to this aspect of romanticism. Ye. M. Pulkhritudova analyses the closeness of the Decembrists to the romantic aesthetic;[7] G. A. Gukovsky maintains that Decembrist poetry was linked with Russian romantic poetry as a whole;[8] B. Meylakh contends that it reflected reality more vividly.[9] V. G. Bazanov has contributed several important works to the subject, in which he allots considerable space to discussion of Bestuzhev.[10] Two of the major anthologies of Decembrist literature, one edited by V. A. Arkhipov, Bazanov and Y. L. Levkovich, the other by Vl. Orlov, reveal the significant role played by Bestuzhev in the development of civic romanticism.[11]

Possibly the only serious bone of contention raised in this spate of criticism is the discussion over whether there is any significant development or change in Marlinsky's work from the early, pre-1825 period to the later, post-Decembrist period. I. V. Kartashova argues that his work undergoes an evolution in the 1830s, when, though not a realist in the strict sense, he is concerned with everyday reality, the life and customs of the Caucasian tribes. While still seeking, as in his early work, the mysterious and extraordinary in the humdrum, and while elevating the imagination, he often shuns the exotic and idealistic and prefers to concentrate on the simple life of the mountaineers. Secondly, whereas earlier he had sharply categorised reality into good and evil, beauty and ugliness, and had divided his heroes into the positive and negative, in the 1830s he attempts to show the capricious complexity of life, its transitions and contradictions. In *The Frigate 'Hope'* he describes not just the external conflicts between man and society so prevalent in the 1820s stories but the inner torments of Pravin and Vera; there is none of the former moralising. Thirdly, the romantic hero changes in essence, as doubt and scepticism encroach after the Decembrist *débâcle* and in the bitterness of exile. Though the 'natural' harmonious man still exists in the person of Iskander-Bek, the contradictory, divided hero, exiled, alone and suffering, makes his appearance with Mulla-Nur. Finally philosophical motifs increase, dealing with the external problems of life and death, the enigmatic human heart, and so on.[12]

F. Z. Kanunova likewise attacks the widely-held opinion that Marlinsky remained true in theme and style to the traditions of Decembrism. She says he moves closer to Kant, Fichte and Schelling, that is, towards German idealistic philosophy, and away from the mechanistic eighteenth-century materialism which had dominated his earlier phase. Thus in his Caucasian tales he glorifies the heroic, active and wilful principle in man and tries to reach some understanding of man's conditioning by history and national culture. In the early stories ethnographic material and folklore had a merely decorative function; in the Caucasian tales they are a psychological factor and demonstrate how man's character is formed in conjunction with history and culture.[13]

But R. F. Yusufov, who has written one of the most authoritative works on romanticism and national cultures, puts forward precisely the opposite theory. He claims that while Pushkin, Lermontov and Gogol overcame romanticism, Marlinsky continued to develop Decembrist romanticism into the 1830s. Admittedly new content was involved since he was dealing with a different society, but his understanding of this society and his method of treatment remained identical. Like Piksanov and others, he employs the term 'Marlinism' to describe what he calls 'the accumulation of internal elements, one-sided judgments and evaluations'.[14]

The benefit of the doubt must be given to Yusufov in this dispute. A careful comparison between the work of the two periods shows the static nature of Marlinsky's talent. The style is still an amalgam of countless sayings, witticisms and turns of phrase. He persists in peppering his stories with metaphors, similes and rhetorical speeches. Dialogue and narrative are still burdened with declamation and clever puns. Gothic tendencies are in evidence along with his typical romantic plots, digressions and incidents. His Byronic method of characterisation remains unaltered: his heroes oppose society, for example Pravin and Vera in *The Frigate 'Hope'*, and Gremin and Olga in *The Test*. They may be endowed with supreme courage and patriotism as is the case with Nikitin and Belozor. They express themselves passionately, as the heroes of *Raids* (*Nayezdy*) do, or display lofty aspirations like the dreamers of *The Cuirassier* and *Raids*. Moreover he continues to write historical, social and military tales as well as poetry, travelogues and literary criticism. There is no doubt that his adaptation of local colour, his feeling for the nature of Russian society, and his lyrical poetry become more impressive, but they are easily recognisable as the work of Marlinsky. They bear the hallmark of 'Marlinism'.

No efforts seem to have been made in the last two decades, however, to resolve the conflict between pre-revolutionary critics, who consider Bestuzhev's tales devoid of political significance, and Soviet critics who take for granted their patent revolutionary ideology. The former emphasise his lack of serious political activity and a consequent absence of political content in his work. S. A. Vengerov, for example, is of the opinion that Bestuzhev's involvement in politics was mere coincidence, the result of his love of danger and the influence of his friends. He contrasts his participation in the Decembrist plot unfavourably with that of other conspirators to whom political activity was second nature. He therefore denies that Bestuzhev's work ever dealt with social and political themes.[15]

I. I. Zamotin too declares that Bestuzhev was only drawn into the Decembrist movement because his own romantic temperament responded impetuously and joyously to the opportunity afforded him to play a leading role in this phenomenon of the romantic revolutionary epoch.[16] Zamotin likewise pays the minimum of attention to social protest in Bestuzhev's work.

A. N. Pypin also adopts this attitude and refuses to admit that Bestuzhev was a sincere and influential member of the Northern Society. Though active in the uprising of 14 December, his conspiratorial role was negligible and his main concerns were always literature, society life and amorous adventures.[17] Pypin goes on to say that there are few traces of political bias in his work, which is thus markedly different from Ryleyev's, where civic themes occupied a prominent place.

Yet another critic of this time, N. A. Kotlyarevsky, insists that Bestuzhev did not consider political thought a necessity of intellect or political action a necessity of temperament. His liberalism was not a matter of deep conviction but a lightly adopted pose. His stories, articles and correspondence do not contain any hints whatsoever of general liberalism, let alone political liberalism.[18]

On the other hand Soviet critics in a body acclaim Bestuzhev as an eminent Decembrist thinker and activist. M. V. Nechkina writes that he was of unquestionable revolutionary zeal and chose to arouse the

Moskovsky regiment on the day of the rebellion as this was the least reliable and would hence require extra effort.[19] A. P. Sharupich numbers him among the most energetic plotters and refers to him as the friend and collaborator of Ryleyev, a member of the supreme Duma of the Northern Society, the organiser and leader of the armed revolt.[20] Nor does N. Maslin have any misgivings about affirming the radical position Bestuzhev occupied in the Northern Society and the active part he played in preparing and carrying out the rebellion.[21] N. L. Stepanov discusses him in the strongest possible political terms and asserts that his publication of the *Polar Star*, his reviews propagandising new political ideas, his agitational songs and his deeds on 14 December all testify to his commitment to revolutionary ideology and his outstanding role in the Decembrist movement.[22] Like the aforementioned, N. Mordovchenko and V. G. Bazanov entirely relate the literary work of Bestuzhev to his participation in the Decembrist secret society and regard the two as inextricably linked and interdependent.[23]

An examination of Bestuzhev's life and literary output before 1825 will go a long way to proving where the truth lies. It is an incontrovertible fact that he sometimes produced an unfavourable impression on his contemporaries. N. I. Grech, while speaking of his intelligence, talent and education, attributes his involvement in the Northern Society to pride, braggadocio and ambition.[24] F. Glinka puts it all down to romantic chivalry and excitable temper.[25] Batenkov asserts that he was a man capable of any extremity[26] and Trubetskoy remarks on his hotheadedness and fiery imagination.[27] Orlov lashes him for his senseless, nonsensical and indecent behaviour in society[28] and Shteyngel' describes Bestuzhev and Kakhovsky as keen terrorists.[29] Bestuzhev himself confessed to the above shortcomings in his character, pointing out that he was boastful, impatient and intemperate, deluded, hasty and over-imaginative.[30]

These comments present a flimsy argument when counterbalanced by the other side of the picture. Indeed there were those among his contemporaries who bore witness to his ardent revolutionary beliefs and his important contribution to the uprising. Kakhovsky states that Bestuzhev's motives were altruistic and disinterested.[31] A. Ye. Rozen wrote that had Ryleyev, the Bestuzhevs, Obolensky and two or three others been arrested, the events of 14 December would never have come about.[32] The statement of the investigatory commission bears eloquent testimony to this fact:

> Junior-captain Alexander Bestuzhev. Plotted regicide and the annihilation of the imperial family; incited others to this; consented also to the deprivation of freedom of the imperial family. Took part in the design of a rebellion through the enticement of comrades and the composition of revolutionary verses and songs; was personally active in the revolt and stirred up lower ranks to take part in it.[33]

It is evident that they clearly comprehended the extent of his implication. This is why they sentenced him to death — later rescinded to twenty years penal servitude.

Statements by Bestuzhev himself over a lengthy period outweigh the faults he had admitted to; like many of his fellow-conspirators he experienced fear and disillusionment when in prison and under the intense pressure of importunate interrogation, and so attributed his crimes to congenital recklessness. His assurances that: 'According to the inclination of the age, I belonged above all to History and Politics',[34] and '. . . in the past I considered literature as a side-line',[35] can be taken as a sign of where his priorities lay. He narrates how he discussed dreams of reform and his willingness to take up arms with Griboyedov,[36] Ryleyev,[37] Batenkov[38] and Obolensky.[39] He directly rebuffs the charges that he was nothing but a scapegrace by saying that he had deliberately contributed to this legend: 'My frivolity was a masquerade for the social carnival . . . Society amused me very rarely, but never captivated me'.[40]

It might well be argued that his whole life had revolved around the revolutionary ferment of the age. His father, Aleksandr Fedoseyevich, was linked with the oppositional groups and radical thought of the previous reign. He belonged to the Radishchevites and together with the most prominent of them, I. P. Pnin, published the short-lived *St Petersburg Journal* in 1798.[41] The young Alexander passed his boyhood in an atmosphere of culture and enlightenment. His father strove to introduce his pedagogical ideas into the education of his own family and after his death the eldest son Nikolay tried to uphold these precepts in the upbringing of his four younger brothers.[42] It follows that they were united by a common bond; they all shared an interest in literature and the pursuit of knowledge, love for their country, and hatred for despotism and serfdom.[43] It is hardly surprising that four of them participated in the Decembrist movement and suffered exile, while the fifth was implicated afterwards.

In his testimony to the Investigatory Commission, Bestuzhev confessed: 'From nineteen years of age I began to read liberal books and this set my head spinning',[44] and 'I adopted a free way of thinking primarily from books, and progressing gradually from one opinion to another, I took to reading the French and English publicists'.[45]

These liberal sympathies, inculcated by education and reading, were manifested in his visit to the Semyonovsky regiment in Kronstadt fortress in the autumn of 1820. The entire regiment had been incarcerated there as a punishment for protesting against the cruelty of Colonel Shvarts, who had restored corporal punishment and had several soldiers flogged.[46] Further evidence as to his growing proclivity towards liberalism can be seen when in 1821 he broke off his literary contributions to *The Loyalist* (*Blagonamerennyy*), the organ of the Society of the

Lovers of Literature, Science and Art, because this organisation was becoming progressively more hostile to romantic tendencies and was headed by the reactionary A. Ye. Izmaylov. He joined at the end of 1820 the Free Society of the Lovers of Russian Literature, made up mostly of Decembrist writers, where he could find a *milieu* conducive to his liberal inclinations.[47]

Now he began to mix with all the leading Decembrist figures, until in 1824 he was accepted into the secret society itself. Such was the esteem in which he was held, he was appointed to the leadership along with Ryleyev and Obolensky in April 1825. That he should have enjoyed the friendship and trust of such an avowed champion of freedom as Ryleyev is an additional pointer to his serious intentions at this juncture.[48] Since 1823 he and Ryleyev had co-operated as the joint editors of *Polar Star*, the highly successful Decembrist anthology of contemporary literature.

On 27 November 1825, together with his brother Nikolay and Ryleyev, he spent the night walking round the town impressing upon the soldiers that they had not been informed about the late Tsar Alexander's will promising an end to serfdom and the reduction of military service from twenty-five to fifteen years. Nikolay claims in his memoirs: 'It is impossible to imagine the eagerness with which the soldiers listened to us; it is impossible to explain the speed with which our words were spread among the troops'.[49]

And on the day of the rebellion itself Bestuzhev was one of the major protagonists in the futile but courageous endeavour to overthrow the autocracy. Early in the morning, accompanied by his brother Mikhail and Shchepin-Rostovsky, he hurried to the barracks of the Moskovsky regiment and roused the soldiers with his fiery oratory.[50] They marched to Senate Square, where Bestuzhev remained until the rebels were routed by the Tsar's cannons. Instead of fleeing in a panic like the majority, he and Nikolay halted several dozen men so as to defend the retreat and repulse a possible cavalry charge.[51] Nor while the grim events of that fateful day unfolded had he been without a definite plan of action: 'If the Izmaylovsky regiment had joined us, I would have taken command and decided on an attempt to attack, the plan of which was already whirling in my head'.[52]

Like all the other Decembrist philosophers and poets, Bestuzhev felt the impact of European developments from 1789. All of them at various stages frankly admitted their allegiance to *avant-garde* European thought from the Enlightenment down to the 1820s. The names of Rousseau, Voltaire, Helvétius, Holbach and Condorcet were constantly on their lips; the works of Byron and Schiller were highly popular; the revolutionary disturbances in Spain, Portugal, Piedmont, Naples and Greece served as reminders and examples to the young Russian nobles;

the latter chose as their real-life heroes men such as Brutus, Riego, Chénier and Byron who laid down their lives for the liberty of their countries. Their literary heroes were also men who rebelled against tyranny, Byron's Corsair and Schiller's Karl Moor. Bitterness was increased by the failure of Tsar Alexander's unofficial committee (Kochubey, Czartoryski, Novosiltsev, Stroganov) and Speransky's reform projects to achieve any positive progress. Moreover the Great Patriotic War of 1812 had brought about no improvement in the lot of the Russian people, who had sacrificed so much in the struggle for the liberation of their country. Affairs of state were hampered by reactionaries: the brutal Count Arakcheyev in the military, the fanatical monk Photius in the church, Prince Golitsyn, aided and abetted by Magnitsky and Runich, in education. A whole series of secret societies sprang up — the Union of Salvation, Union of Welfare, Northern and Southern Societies — to combat the forces of reaction, just as the liberal Carbonari groups in Italy or Hetairea in Greece had done. Bestuzhev, as a central figure in the Decembrist movement, could scarcely have been unaffected by this wave of ideas which swept across Europe and Russia.

Having established Bestuzhev's firm attachment to liberal trends, the way is now open to a study of the political aspects in his early work. This falls into several categories: (1) literary criticism; (2) the travelogue *Journey to Reval* (*Poyezdka v Revel'*); (3) the agitational songs; (4) poetry; (5) the historical tales of old Livonia; and (6) the document, *On the Historical Progress of Free Thought in Russia*.

Bestuzhev's literary criticism, contained in a series of articles he wrote between 1818 and 1825, clearly followed the lines laid down by the civic romanticism of the Decembrists, in particular by their literary society the Republic of Letters. Basically the Decembrists believed that literature had to be harnessed to the politics of the day. It was the Great Patriotic War of 1812 which gave birth to political consciousness. As Bestuzhev explained:

> Napoleon invaded Russia, and then the Russian people for the first time became aware of its strength; then there awoke in all hearts a feeling of independence, at first political, and subsequently national too. This was the beginning of free thought in Russia.[53]

In his article, *A Look at Russian Literature During 1823*, he underlined the link between literature and national crises: '. . . the thunder of distant battles inspires the style of the author and arouses the idle attention of readers; . . . and under a political seal literature revolves in society' (*Soch.*, II, p. 540).

Literature could be used as an educational tool in the battle against prevailing ignorance. If, as Ryleyev asserted, 'The ignorance of peoples is the mother and father of despotism, is the true and chief cause of all the violence and crime which have ever been perpetrated in the world',[54] then it was vital to spread enlightenment. The code of the Union of Welfare assigned it a special category,[55] and Bestuzhev's *Look at Old and New Literature in Russia* blames the retarded development of contemporary Russian literature on the low standards of education in schools and universities, the poor taste of the reading public, the contempt felt for the scholar and writer, and the scorn for the Russian language in society. Literature and Enlightenment thus went hand in hand, and the same code spoke of 'the elegant arts . . . strengthening, ennobling and exalting our moral being'.[56]

The main stress of Decembrist literature was on national spirit, the national independence of Russian literature. The aspiration to create a literature which was not a mere carbon copy of foreign models grew into the prime concern of the Decembrists. They demanded a literature that dealt exclusively with Russian history, folklore and contemporary issues. They called for a renewal of pride in the Russian language itself, which had been so neglected and undergone so much foreign influence. The code of the Union of Welfare urged its members 'to expose the totally absurd attachment to the foreign and its ensuing evil consequences'.[57] Bestuzhev was an indefatigable advocate of the ideal of national spirit and constantly railed against imitativeness of any kind. In his *Look at Russian Literature during 1824 and the Beginning of 1825* he complained bitterly: 'We imbibed with our milk lack of national spirit and admiration for only the foreign' (*Soch.*, II, p. 547).

In 1831 he reiterated this feeling of abhorrence for the foreign in one of his letters: 'I ardently hated German cosmopolitanism, which killed off every noble sentiment of patriotism and nationalism'.[58]

In *A Look at Old and New Literature in Russia* he recommended reliance on national sources and called on writers to study the ancient chronicles such as *The Lay of Igor's Host, The Chronicle of Nestor, Russkaya Pravda* and *The Song of the Battle on the Don*, which offer a faithful reproduction of Russian national characteristics and the roots of the language.[59] Elsewhere he proclaimed: 'I shall not forsake the language of my ancestors, in which they rejoiced and grieved, sang and deliberated'.[60]

In the 1830s he continued to criticise strongly those writers he thought were over-dependent on foreign culture, such as Karamzin[61] and Zhukovsky,[62] just as he had heaped scorn on them in the 1820s:

> There was a time when we sighed irrelevantly in the manner of Sterne, were courteous in the French style, and flew off to the ends of the earth in German fashion. When will we follow our own track? When will we write directly in Russian? God alone knows! (*Soch.*, II, p. 551)

His highest praise is reserved for those writers who were able to capture national spirit — Fonvizin[63] and Krylov.[64] He illustrates the necessity for national spirit in his critical maxim, 'characters and incidents pass, but nations and the elements last forever' (*Soch.*, II, p. 549).

The Decembrist ethic preached that the content of literature must be 'lofty feelings which attract one to good'.[65] Ryleyev's article, *Some Thoughts on Poetry*, contains the words: 'We shall employ all our efforts to realise in our writings the ideals of lofty feelings, thoughts and eternal truths'.[66] Kyukhel'beker led the struggle for lofty themes and genres and hailed 'the sacred mysteries of lofty art'.[67] Bestuzhev was not slow to herald this trend and in his literary criticism systematically eulogised works which were full of 'lofty feelings', such as Ryleyev's *Meditations* (*Dumy*).[68] He sees in Gnedich 'a fiery soul accessible to all that is lofty' (*Soch.*, II, p. 532). He rebukes Pushkin for wasting time and effort on a fashionable dandy like Onegin and assures him: 'I involuntarily give precedence to that which stirs the soul, exalts it, and touches the Russian heart' (*Soch.*, II, p. 627). In the same vein he is extremely critical of literature which is devoid of noble and lofty thoughts and is hard on Karamzin and his followers, treating them with irony.

The travelogue *Journey to Reval*, 1820—1, has been the subject of some controversy. Ostensibly it is an account of a journey to Estonia in the manner of Sterne's *Sentimental Journey* and Karamzin's *Letters of a Russian Traveller*. It has been looked upon by pre-revolutionary critics as belonging to the Karamzinian tradition, along with the travelogues of Sumarokov, Izmaylov, Nevzorov and Shalikov. However, on closer inspection (duly carried out by thorough Soviet critics) it becomes apparent that Bestuzhev's work is of a very different kind. Instead of lyrical enthusiasm for nature, the unfolding of tender feelings, and the relaying of melancholy or pleasant experiences, which the sentimentalists are so fond of indulging in, we get a serious and painstaking attempt to review the position of the Baltic peoples under their foreign oppressors.

He expresses sympathy for the downtrodden Estonians who rebelled against their German overlords in 1343. He castigates the behaviour of the knights, who were coarse and ignorant, besotted and depraved, extravagant and godless. These so-called standard-bearers of religion and culture robbed the Estonians and 'adorned their own wives with pearls and diamonds and themselves with golden chain-mail'.[69] His compassion becomes stronger as his narrative develops and he describes the torments of the vassals, the hunger, pestilence, wars and pillaging they had to endure.[70]

He displays a profound interest in the traditions and customs, the life and history of the Estonian nation. He made a serious study of the region and his references to Estonian sources reveal his knowledge of Livonian works and chronicles.[71] He apparently refutes the theories of the German—Baltic chroniclers who had sung the exploits of the German conquerors, intimating that they combated paganism, brought enlightenment and culture, and were men of honour and justice. Bestuzhev portrays them as taskmasters and represents the struggle of the Estonians for national liberation as a just and righteous one in the true spirit of Decembrist civic romanticism. In fact *Journey to Reval* is in the tradition of Radishchev's *Journey from St Petersburg to Moscow*, Glinka's *Letters of a Russian Officer*, and Von Ferelzt's *Journey of Criticism* — travel books which fearlessly pictured Russian reality, the misfortunes of the people, the horrors of serfdom and the arbitrary rule of landowners.

Yet nowhere did Bestuzhev express the anguish of the people with such vehemence as in the agitational or ritual (*podblyudnyye*) songs. He was the co-author with Ryleyev of 'Ah, I feel wretched . . .' ('Akh, toshno mnye . . .') but was solely responsible for the others.[72] These songs had a great effect on the simple people and spread like wildfire among the troops.[73] Little wonder, since they are written in a straight-forward and forceful style. 'Ah, I feel wretched . . .' surveys the injustices and malpractices suffered by the martyred peasants. It is an outcry against the incredible cruelty of the landowning classes:

> Ah, I feel wretched
> Even in my native land;
> All is in bondage
> . . .
> Will the Russian people
> Long be the junk of masters
> And will they long be traded
> Like cattle?
>
> Who enslaved us,
> Who conferred nobility on them?
> . . .
> And freedom
> Among the people
> Is stifled by the power of the lords.
> . . .
> And now our masters
> Rob us shamelessly
> . . .

> They flay us alive,
> We sow — and they reap.
> They are thieves,
> Fleecers,
> And they suck our blood, like leeches.
>
> (*Soch.*, II, pp. 514—15)

The Decembrists were loud in their denunciation of extortion and bribery in high places, especially the courts. Pestel condemned 'the injustice and venality of the courts and other authorities';[74] Lunin claimed that one of the objects of the secret society was the abolition of procrastination, secretiveness and costs in law-suits;[75] and Bestuzhev himself did not spare the shameful bartering with justice in the judiciary, exclaiming: 'Everywhere honest people suffered, whilst rogues and cheats rejoiced'.[76] 'Ah, I feel wretched . . .' deplores these abuses:

> Peasant, seek no justice
> Anywhere in court
> . . .
> The judges are deaf,
> Though innocent, you are guilty.
> . . .
> There every soul
> Is twisted just for a farthing.
> The assessor,
> The chairman,
> At one with the secretary.
>
> (*Soch.*, II, pp. 515—16)

Even the parish priest joins in the wholesale exploitation of the defenceless peasants. The Tsar has blighted their lives with extortionate taxes and roadwork. The soldiers in the countryside treat them as though they were enemies. They are obliged to pay exorbitant sums even for water. The decrees inspired by Arakcheyev are an added burden. This song is convincing proof that although the Decembrists ignored the people as a concrete factor in the revolutionary struggle against the autocracy, they could reflect their mood and depict their hardships. Ryleyev and Bestuzhev's song is a savage indictment of conditions in Russia and is written with indignation and embitterment.

Military service in Russia was another circumstance the Decembrists found loathsome. They abhorred the system of military colonies established by Arakcheyev, which symbolised the arrant tyranny of the regime and had transformed Russia into a gigantic Prussian barracks. Pestel expressed his horror at 'what he had heard about the military colonies' and at 'the oppression of military service'.[77]

Rayevsky devoted a whole treatise entitled *The Soldier* to this problem; he listed rigid disciplinary procedures, tyrannical, mercenary and unreasonable leadership, disproportionately severe corporal punishment, illegality and inequity, lack of rights of defence or channels of complaint, irksome tasks and duties.[78] A heartfelt protest against the soldier's unenviable fate was voiced by Yakubovich, who singled out the wearisome length of service, the forced abandonment of one's family, the fear dominating one's life, the corruption and ignorance rife amongst officers and their inhumane treatment of subordinates.[79] The management of the military colonies was entrusted to Arakcheyev; the choice could not have been a worse one, for from all accounts he was a bigot and petty bureaucrat, undiplomatic and merciless, the object of universal hatred.[80] Bestuzhev subjected this aspect of life in Russia to harsh criticism:

> The colonies paralysed not only the intellects but all the trades of the places where they were established and struck terror in the remainder. . . . The soldiers grumbled at exhausting drills, fatigues and sentry-duty, the officers at meagre wages and excessive severity.[81]

He had occasion himself to witness the military establishment at first hand as member of a dragoon regiment and later as aide-de-camp in turn to Count Komarovsky, General Bétancourt and Duke Wurtembergsky. Indeed the vanguard of the Decembrist movement consisted of high-ranking officers such as Trubetskoy, Obolensky, Pestel and Orlov.

The song 'Our Tsar is a Russian (Prussian)[82] German . . .' ('Tsar nash, nemets russkiy . . .') satirises Alexander's Prussian-like maniacal obsession with military parades and ostentation:

> Our Tsar is a Russian German
> . . .
> Where does he reign?
> He spends every day at riding-school.
> . . .
> Though the enemy of enlightenment,
> He loves drills.
> . . .
> Only for parades
> Does he dispense rewards.
> . . .
> And for compliments —
> Blue ribbons.
> . . .
> And for mother-truth
> He sends you packing to Kamchatka.

The notorious Arakcheyev comes in for his share of parody both here:
'And Count Arakcheyev / Is the worst of villains . . .' (*Soch.*, II, pp. 512
—13), and in the previously discussed 'Ah, I feel wretched . . .':

> For all these enterprises
> Arakcheyev
> Is the one to blame.
>
> He eggs on the Tsar,
> The Tsar signs a decree.
> To him it's a joke,
> But to us it's terrible.
>
> (*Soch.*, II, pp. 516—17)

Along the River Fontanka (*Vdol' Fontanki-reki*) sketches the misery of
the soldier's lot: 'They are drilled and tortured,/ There is no light, no
dawn' (*Soch.*, II, p. 514). These songs are an open call for reprisals with
the landowners, officials and the Tsar himself. 'Say, Tell Me . . .' ('Ty
skazhi, govori . . .') begins: 'Say, tell me / How in Russia tsars / Are
crushed . . .' (*Soch.*, II, p. 511); while *Along the River Fontanka* asks:

> Have they really no hands
> To save themselves from torments?
>
> Have they really no bayonets
> For snivelling princes?
>
> Have they really no lead
> For the villainous tyrant?
>
> (*Soch.*, II, p. 514)

The peasants in 'Ah, I feel wretched . . .' threaten: 'And what is taken
from us by force / We will restore by force' (*Soch.*, II, p. 515). In the
song 'When the Blacksmith Leaves his Forge . . .' ('Kak idyot kuznets
da iz kuznitsy . . .') we read:

> Here is the first knife — for the evil grandees.
> And the second knife — for the priests, those hypocrites.
> And uttering a prayer — the third knife for the Tsar.
>
> (*Soch.*, II, p. 517)

Another song breathes menace and hostility:

> Now you are weaving ropes for the heads of lords,
> You are sharpening knives for eminent princes:
> And in the place of lamps you will hang tsars!
> Then warmth, intellect and light will reign. Glory be![83]

Much of Bestuzhev's pre-revolutionary poetry contains social comment imbued with Decembrist leanings. In 1819 he wrote *Imitation of Boileau's First Satire* (*Podrazhaniye pervoy satire Bualo*), where he stigmatises the society of St Petersburg for its mercenariness and insincerity. He enumerates the defects which poison it: insidiousness, boastfulness, deceit, slander, flattery, ignorance and arrogance. Judges, clerks and spies are in abundance. Many devote their lives to acquiring wealth which they flaunt instead of knowledge. The servile poor are under the heel of the haughty rich. Fools rise to the highest posts, while the talented are left to starve. The *leitmotif* of the poem is escape:

> I shall flee from you, I shall flee, walls of Petropol,
> I shall hide in the gloom of forests, in remote caverns,
> . . .
> I shall flee! I have found the golden thread of freedom.
> . . .
> Let us leave the corrupt town
> . . .
> I hasten to save myself from corruption.
> Luxurious Babylon! For the last time farewell.
>
> (*Soch.*, II, pp. 465—9)

The whole poem is symptomatic of the typical Decembrist viewpoint and is reminiscent of Chatsky's diatribes in *Woe from Wit* (*Gore ot uma*). It is close in spirit to the first speech in Bestuzhev's extract from *The Optimist* (*Otryvok iz Komedii 'Optimist'*). Here, after delineating the natural phenomena afflicting man, he excoriates the vices introduced into the world by man himself. The main brunt of his attack is borne by the young generation which leads an aimless dissipated life:

> The sources of pleasure are lacklustre from satiety.
> We are old at twenty and dissolute at fifty.
> . . . All men are spiteful, and foolish, and miserable!
>
> (*Soch.*, II, pp. 469—70)

A comparison with Lermontov's similar poem *Meditation* (*Duma*) is all too obvious.

At the heart of the Decembrist ethos were the principles of patriotism and heroic self-sacrifice. The Decembrists were fervid patriots, convinced of the greatness of Russia and its noble people's right to freedom and political justice. They loved their land so passionately that everything concerning its countryside and life in their writing, particularly lyric poetry, is imbued with a highly emotional tone. Glinka, Ryleyev and Rayevsky extolled the beauties of their country and the glory of patriotism.[84] Bestuzhev too filled his work with exclamations like Sitsky's in *The Traitor*:

> Has a Russian suggested to a Russian that he betray his country and become a traitor to his fatherland? (*Soch.*, I, p. 141)

> O my land, my sacred native land! Which heart on earth would not throb on seeing you? Which icy soul would not melt upon breathing your air? (*Soch.*, I, p. 132)

In his poem 'Near the camp stood a handsome youth . . .' ('Bliz stana yunosha prekrasnyy . . .') the young warrior professes that he was always true to his country, which inspired him in battle and implanted the spirit of heroism in his breast.[85]

The precept of self-sacrifice accompanied the patriotic ideal. Ryleyev perpetually exhorted his fellow conspirators to be prepared to die valiantly. Nikolay Bestuzhev relates in his memoirs some truly moving scenes with speeches typical of Ryleyev:

> I am sure we shall die, but the example will remain. We shall sacrifice ourselves for the future freedom of our country . . . . If I fall in the struggle . . . posterity will render me justice and history will write my name together with the names of great men who have died for mankind.[86]

Ryleyev[87] and Odoyevsky[88] acclaimed self-sacrifice as the pinnacle attained by those supreme in bravery. Bestuzhev's *Exploit of Ovechkin and Shcherbina in the Caucasus* (*Podvig Ovechkina i Shcherbiny za Kavkazom*)[89] (written shortly before the Decembrist uprising) is a paean to Russian gallantry in the face of death. In the poem 'Near the Camp . . .' the youth announces his pride at being able to lay down his life: 'Tell her I fell fighting for my country' (*Soch.*, II, p. 475), and in *Mikhail Tverskoy*, a poem which reminds one of Ryleyev's *Meditations*, the scene is set in a sombre prison where a young man bids farewell to his aged father, who remains steadfast at the moment before his execution. In this same poem the motif of revenge on the tyrant is repeated; coming, as it did, only a year before the rebellion it served as a prophetic warning. The young prince observes his father's mutilated corpse, sheds bitter tears and rends his garments. He calls upon the God of vengeance:

> He heeded him, this powerful God,
> Helped Russians to rebel,
> And removed the tyrants from the face of the earth.
> (*Soch.*, II, pp. 477–8)

It is on Bestuzhev's four tales of old Livonia that most debate is centred. To regard them simply as Gothic adventure stories, as pre-revolutionary critics have done, is to miss the point entirely. The Decembrists were of the considered opinion that to set one's narrative in bygone ages was the most effective guise for concealing its true intentions. The historical tale, poem or drama did not incur the censor's wrath. In addition the past was an excellent school for the present; contemporary lessons could be read into heroic accounts of the struggle against the Tartar invasion, or the Ukraine's battle against the Polish gentry, or the republican exploits of ancient Novgorod and Pskov. Objective understanding was not so important; their view of historical events was entirely subjective. Ryleyev's *Meditations* are the best examples of national antiquity employed as material for civic preaching. He confessed that they were intended 'to remind youth of the exploits of their ancestors and to acquaint them with the brightest epochs of national history'.[90] Bestuzhev was captivated by the idea of historical narrative, as he enthusiastically avers in *Andrey, Prince of Pereyaslavl'* (*Andrey, knyaz' pereyaslavskiy*)[91] and *Page from the Diary of a Guards Officer* (*Listok iz dnevnika gvardeyskogo ofitsera*)[92] and always treated it subjectively and imaginatively.[93]

The historical tale of Novgorod *Roman and Olga* is the clearest illustration of how Bestuzhev utilised history for modern purposes. Among the Decembrists Novgorod occupied a symbolic place as the home of freedom and democracy. Ryleyev once advised Pushkin to write about the Novgorod–Pskov region, 'that true land of inspiration' where 'the last sparks of Russian freedom were stifled'.[94] Pestel shared this cult of ancient Novgorod and declared in his testimony: 'The story of great Novgorod also confirmed me in the republican mode of thought'.[95] Bestuzhev at one time was even preparing to undertake a history of Novgorod.[96]

Roman Yasensky is endowed with all the qualities that go to make up the Novgorodian hero; he is above all a good citizen ready to sacrifice himself for a righteous cause. The democratic assembly is a model of the Decembrist ideal of the people's right to self-determination. Roman's speech is replete with the rhythmic style of Decembrist rhetoric and culminates in a powerful battle-cry. The Decembrists attached great importance to political eloquence and among them were men of brilliant oratorical gifts, such as Orlov, Pestel, Muravyov, Bestuzhev-Ryumin, Rayevsky and Lunin. They considered oratory an integral part of revolution. Muravyov-Apostol's *Orthodox Catechism*[97] and Bestuzhev-Ryumin's *Speech at a Meeting of the United Slavs* and *Proclamation to the People*[98] are exemplars of the art. Bestuzhev appreciated the value of eloquence and drew a vivid portrait of Demosthenes in action in his article '*The Orator*'.[99] He himself stirred the soldiers of the Moskovsky regiment with his speech on the morning of 14 December 1825.

Roman speaks warmly of Church and State self-government, the subtleties of international law, the need for a close union between Russia and the West. He tries to destroy the myth of omnipotent Moscow and implores the people not to concede their rights. He appeals to them to choose freedom even at the cost of their lives.

The subsequent trials of Roman, his encounter with the honourable outlaw Berkut, their participation in the battle against Moscow — all propagate the Decembrist ideal of the perfect hero.

It is when the controversial Livonian tales are studied in context, that is, in conjunction with *Roman and Olga* and the foregoing Decembrist philosophy, that their real meaning becomes apparent. Perhaps the worst problem confronting the Decembrists was that of serfdom, an evil which had to be eradicated before any economic or moral progress could be made. Nikolay Turgenev,[100] Pestel[101] and Rayevsky[102] displayed deep concern for the pitiful condition of the peasantry. Bestuzhev's letter to the Tsar[103] and *Journey to Reval* deal with the identical theme — the maltreatment of serfs by their masters. In *Wenden Castle* the brutal and overbearing Von Rorbach has no regard for his vassals, on whose behalf Von Serrat takes up cudgels and proclaims, 'I do not consider it a joke when humanity suffers' (*Soch.*, I, p. 39). Serrat protests passionately against Rorbach's callous flouting of the peasants' rights.[104] Bestuzhev sums up the situation thus:

> The knights who conquered Lithuania and subdued the savages invented everything which the Spaniards later repeated in the New World to torment an unarmed race. Death threatened the stubborn and degrading slavery was the reward for submission . . . the blood of the innocent flowed beneath the swords of warriors and the whips of masters. Arming themselves in the name of sacred truth, the knights acted according to the dictates of grasping self-interest or brutal caprice.
>
> (*Soch.*, I, pp. 38–9)

The individual act of violence perpetrated by Serrat in killing Rorbach is in vain, as Bestuzhev points out: 'The magistrate no longer existed, but his power remained'.[105] Though sympathising with the despair seizing Serrat, Bestuzhev cannot fail to condemn his deed; the leaders of the Northern Society had the utmost trouble in restraining Yakubovich and Kakhovsky from assassinating the Tsar. They believed that such action must be consciously intended for the social good and should not be a matter of momentary rage.

The second Livonian tale, *Neuhausen Castle (Zamok Neygauzen)*[106] affirms Bestuzhev's detestation of feudalism by showing the inner conflicts it produces within a seemingly normal family. The scheming Von Mey, who typifies the unscrupulous feudal lords, is put to death, while again it is the gallant Novgorodians, Vseslav and Andrey, who are portrayed as men of prowess. Furthermore justice is seen as prejudiced and ruthless, administered by a court which operates in secret and favours the mighty and influential.

In the third of the cycle, *The Reval' Tournament* (*Revel'skiy turnir*), the knights and nobles are caustically satirised. The knights are perpetually in a drunken stupor. They are supercilious and have no respect for intellectual qualities. They are devoid of consideration for passing travellers and think nothing of seizing land from each other. Baron Burtneck behaves insultingly to his servants and treats them inhumanely. The nobles likewise are empty-headed and foolish. Pestel,[107] Bestuzhev's brother Nikolay,[108] and Muravyov[109] all spoke with scathing disapproval of the aristocracy, as did Bestuzhev who analysed them thoroughly.[110]

This story also covers a favourite topic of the Decembrists, the rise of the middle class. This class, composed of merchants and petty bourgeoisie, they felt would play an increasingly crucial role in the economic stability of Russia. Like his brother Nikolay,[111] Pestel,[112] and Kakhovsky,[113] Bestuzhev mentioned the handicaps suffered by the middle class: 'The middle class is respected and important in all other countries; in our country this class is miserable, poor, burdened with obligations, deprived of means of a livelihood . . .'; and detailed the causes of the dissatisfaction of the merchants.[114]

In line with these views, Edwin, as representative of the merchant class, holds the centre of the stage. He is morally superior to the knights and nobles. He is brave, sincere and loyal:

> He was able to dream and have feelings, but the Livonian knights could only arouse laughter and rarely amuse. . . . He had grown accustomed to social proprieties, and in education and astuteness surpassed with ease the knights of Livonia . . . (*Soch.*, I, p. 107).

His defeat of Ungern in the tournament leads to open warfare between the merchants and the knights and nobles, a furious battle for supremacy. Bestuzhev refers to the merchants as 'the most active, honourable and useful class' in Livonia (*Soch.*, I, p. 127). They will supersede the knights, who have outlived their age and squandered their wealth, and the nobles, who are now impoverished and lack all progressive inclinations.

The last in this cycle, *Eisen Castle*, has the fearsome Baron Bruno Von Eisen as its centrepiece. He gathers round him hardened criminals for his raids and reckless adventures, but he outdoes them all in ferocity. He maltreats his serfs, kills them and his guests wilfully, and has a vicious, uncontrollable temper. When Reginald redresses wrong by murdering his uncle, we get precisely the same assessment of his act as we had in *Wenden Castle*, that is, approval because it benefited the people and gave rise to rejoicing, but reserve because its motives were selfish:

> Why did he lack the will to refuse resolutely [to plunder] or to rebel against him openly? . . . But no, he did not stand up for the oppressed until he was personally offended; he only rebelled to save his own skin (*Soch.*, I, p. 166).

The final clincher in the argument over the political interests of Bestuzhev must be the letter he wrote to the Tsar when under arrest in the Petropavlovsk fortress, entitled *On the Historical Progress of Free Thought in Russia*.[115] It is outstanding as one of the best Decembrist treatises on the political situation; it discusses the psychological and economic factors which generated social discontent and revolutionary thought. It analyses all the classes in society and draws a picture of Russia after the Napoleonic invasion in a state of devastation and afflicted by harsh measures and innumerable abuses. It includes the projects of reform harboured by the rebels. It is hardly the work of a person indifferent to politics.

There is a second conflict between pre-revolutionary and Soviet critics about Marlinsky's work. With a few notable exceptions the latter utterly ignore the influence of Western European literature on it and their approach is purely nationalistic. The former however pay full tribute to Western European sources. A. Veselovsky,[116] Zamotin,[117] Kotlyarevsky,[118] M. N. Rozanov,[119] et al, carried out exhaustive surveys of the extent and nature of these influences which must be regarded as indisputable. To deny this overwhelming evidence is also to overlook the numerous memoirs of the period which indicate the enormous interest of the public in the works of Rousseau, Byron, Scott, Radcliffe and so on. Even to admit the potent influence of Karamzin, as Soviet critics do, is to pay homage to the Gallic influence in style and theme. And to imply that Marlinsky isolated himself from the European romantic movement is nothing short of ludicrous, when one thinks that Belinsky called him 'our first story-teller . . . the instigator of the Russian tale';[120] that he was the leading literary critic of his day, to whom Pushkin wrote: 'I admit that there is no one I like to argue with more than you and Vyazemsky — only you two can excite me',[121] and whom Pushkin named 'the representative of taste and the true guard and patron of our literature';[122] that he had been appointed censor of bibliography in the Republic of Letters, whose secretary had addressed him in highly respectful terms in 1821, appreciating his 'talents, zeal and labours', praising him as 'one of the society's most honoured and worthy members', entreating further endeavours from his pen.[123]

His articles, reviews and correspondence are brimful of references to all the contemporary English, French and German writers. Here we will concentrate on Byron, Scott and Radcliffe, as well as Rousseau, Balzac and Hugo, the first three of whom represent his early phase and the last three his time in exile.

Bestuzhev wrote to Pushkin on 9 March 1825:

> I thirstily gulp in English literature and my soul is grateful to the English language: it taught me to think, it directed me to nature, it is an inexhaustible spring! I am even prepared to say: *il n'y a point de salut hors la littérature anglaise* (*Soch.*, II, p. 628).

Perhaps his favourite among the English writers was Byron, whose name first appeared in print in Russia as early as 1815 and by 1819 turned up more and more frequently until it was the main talking-point. Zhukovsky, Kozlov, Vyazemsky and Batyushkov were all delighted with him. In the early 1820s his influence was widely acknowledged; the liberal press spoke of him with veneration, the reactionaries with loathing. Bestuzhev's love for Byron was boundless; his letters are sprinkled with comments such as, 'I still read Byron assiduously. What a fiery soul he has!'[124] He never lost an opportunity to discuss him[125] and his articles contain many encomiums to his work:

> [Alfieri and] the matchless Byron proudly cast off the golden chains of fortune, scorned all the allurements of high society — in return the whole world lies at their feet and an eternal day of glory is their inheritance (*Soch.*, II, p. 551).

His enthralment with Byron caused him to misjudge Pushkin and offer him well-meaning advice:

> You grasped St Petersburg society, but did not penetrate it. Read Byron; without knowing our St Petersburg, he described it more exactly where a profound knowledge of people was concerned. . . . I know no one who could sketch characters better or more picturesquely . . . . And how cruel and fresh is his satire!
>
> (*Soch.*, II, p. 627)

His letter of 17 June 1824 to Vyazemsky mourns the loss of Byron as a fellow-poet and a champion of human rights.[126]

The popular romantic contrast between corrupt life in the city and idyllic life in the country or on a desert island or a nomadic existence came to Bestuzhev via Byron. The latter's Don Juan, Corsair, Giaour and Childe Harold escape the chains of society; so do Bestuzhev's Berkut, who lives in the woods unhampered by social prejudice and restrictions, and Vladimir Sitsky, who contrasts stifling court life with the open-air life of freedom and self-indulgence.[127]

Secondly, one of the recurrent themes in Byron which Bestuzhev borrowed was the cowardice, stupidity and cant of English society life. *Night on Board Ship* (*Noch' na korable*) relates how Mary Aston is intoxicated with glamorous society life and is eventually ruined. It is this same society which brings about the downfall of Berkut, who is destroyed by its dissipation and luxury. In *Evening on a Bivouac* the cynical Major Vladov advises Mechin against the folly of choosing a bride from high society, educated to value only clothes, coiffure, fine carriages, visiting cards, dancing, and the social graces.[128]

Thirdly, Byron's attitude to women was not in the usual romantic mould; for him love was not an exalted, divine expression of the soul. His criticism of women was bitter and mocking, and it is that aspect which Bestuzhev takes up. Roman, in his exasperation, berates Olga:

> 'Women, women!' he pronounced with savage mockery, 'and you boast of your love, constancy, sensibility! Your love is mere whim, garrulous, and fleeting like a swallow; but when you have to prove it by deed and not by word, how profuse are your excuses, how generous your advice, old fables and reproaches!' (*Soch.*, I, p. 10)

Major Vladov is just as sharp,[129] Dr Lontzius in *The Reval Tournament* just as biting,[130] and Bestuzhev's own asides just as caustic.[131]

Fourthly, Byron's cult of Hellenism is paralleled by Bestuzhev's admiration for Novgorod, Pskov and Pereyaslavl'. These towns symbolise past glories and exploits and evoke rapture and pride. In the manner of Byron, he stands near the ruins of castles and monuments recollecting former triumphs and events.

Next, Byron's major contribution to European romanticism was his brand of the individual hero. Generally there were two types: the active and the passive. Byron's belonged to the former, the group known as Titans, and were not only outsiders, as was usually the case, but were obsessed by the constant need to prove their value and outshine everyone else. They flouted society and its rules and engaged in astounding exhibitions of energy, emotion and fury or bombastic tirades (Cain, Manfred, Lara). Bestuzhev's heroes are modelled on this prototype. Roman and Edwin, when they feel that their love is unrequited, indulge in outbursts of unbounded despair,[132] but are generous in the extreme when they realise their mistake.[133] All display immense courage: Ronald risks his life and scorns death;[134] Roman faces death stoically;[135] Von Nordeck despises death at the hands of the Teutonic knights;[136] Edwin, quite unpractised in the art of jousting, presumes to challenge the redoubtable Ungern; Ovechkin and Shcherbina cannot contemplate surrender even when the odds are impossibly stacked against them; Von Mey has inflexible will-power.[137] They protest against any social coercion, against the spiritual enslavement of the personality by the conventions and morality of hypocritical society. Schreiterfeld accuses Gideon of ruining his life;[138] Reginald revolts against the ill treatment and evil upbringing he has received at the hands of his uncle;[139] Von Serrat arraigns the rapacity of the feudal order.[140] Nevertheless these Byronic heroes feel no pleasure at such manifestations of delight, courage, feeling or will. They are bored and indifferent. Bestuzhev's knights are afflicted with boredom and the faces of his characters wear a habitually sad expression because 'stern sorrow' involuntarily imparts to their 'pallid' faces 'solemnity and an interesting look'.[141] Their melancholy proceeds from an unsuccessful adventure or personal misfortune (Ronald), or from unrequited love (Edwin), or criminal thoughts (Sitsky), or from an overall pessimistic world-view — the common *mal du siècle* (Sitsky, Lidin).

The sixth way in which Byronic influence is visible is in the use of rapid transitions of action. This did not pass unnoticed by contemporaries. Pushkin advised Bestuzhev in 1825 with particular reference to *The Traitor*: 'Enough of writing rapid tales with romantic transitions — this is all right for a Byronic poem',[142] and it was said of another story: '*Night on Board Ship* can be compared to a poem by Byron'.[143]

If we take *Neuhausen Castle* as an example, we can witness quite conspicuous transitions. At one moment we are faced by the castle itself; then we are transported to a forest glade and its strange occupants; next comes the shore of Livonia and Andrey's band of Russians, the castle tower in which Ewald is held prisoner, the sea where the Russians seize the boat in which Emma is captive, and finally we return to Ewald's cell for the denouement. These switches highlight each scene. They occur without forewarning or intermediate pause. They are meant to emphasise the melodrama inherent in the situation, to heighten the tension and to make all incidents seem more striking.

Lastly we have the device of digression, which Bestuzhev admits to having copied from Byron. The epigraph to Chapter 2 of *The Test* — 'if I have any fault, it is digression'[144] — is taken from Byron. These digressions which allow the author to comment on the action or his characters develop into long and tiresome philosophical paragraphs in the later stories like *Ammalat-Bek* and *Mulla-Nur*.

The influence of Scott is likewise pronounced. Scott was known and loved in all circles and Bestuzhev was likely to have read all the thirteen works published in Russia between 1821 and 1825.[145] Dramatic adaptations from Scott's novels were made by Prince Shakhovskoy.[146] At balls in high society 'they loved to take costumes . . . from the novels of Walter Scott'.[147] Bestuzhev's diary for 1824 mentions *The Abbot, Old Mortality* and other unnamed works.[148] His articles carry numerous references to Scott:

> Walter Scott determined the inclination of the century towards historical details, created the historical novel, which now became required reading . . . (*Soch.*, II, p. 594)

The genius of Walter Scott guessed at the domestic life and everyday tenor of the age of chivalry . . . sprinkled them with the vivifying water of his artistic imagination, breathed into their nostrils, said 'live' — and they came alive, with the flush of life on their cheeks, with the beat of reality in their breasts. (*Soch.*, II, p. 593)

In *The Test* he says that Scott's novels could be found in the homes of country squires[149] and in *The Clock and the Mirror* (*Chasy i zerkalo*) in the boudoirs of society beauties in the capital.[150]

At the beginning of the nineteenth century historical tales derived from chronicles or other sources appeared: Gerakov's *Prince Menshchikov*, 1801, the anonymous *Kseniya, Princess of Galicia*, 1808, the tales of S. Glinka, 1810, and novels based on Ukrainian history by F. Glinka, Somov and Narezhny. But Bestuzhev paid them only desultory attention. His inspiration came directly from Scott, and it was Bestuzhev who laid the foundations for the Russian historical novel. As N. Polevoy said of his tales, 'They were the first attempts at the real historical novel in Russia'.[151] Contemporaries saw plainly the presence of Scott's influence; Pushkin wrote to Bestuzhev at the end of May, 1825: 'Your tournament reminds me of Walter Scott's Tournament'.[152]

Scott's method amounted to the poetisation of national life and national spirit. The first entailed descriptions of the outer trappings of life. Whereas Scott's scenes of town and country were highly impressive, Bestuzhev's were stereotyped and lifeless. Apart from his picture of Reval on the day of the tournament, when he succeeds in capturing the bright revelry, he fails to make his historical scenes seem genuine and satisfying. In spite of taking great pains to refer to ancient armour, clothing, horses, knights, skirmishes, hunting sorties and the like, he appears unable to create the real atmosphere of domestic history. And whilst striving to ratify the historical or ethnographical veracity of his incidents, many of his dates and facts are not authentic. History for him was not archaeological data, but a matter of subjective interpretation, as he explained:

Let others burrow in manuscripts . . . I am sure, I am convinced that it *was* thus . . . in this my Russian heart, my imagination . . . is a guarantee. What purpose has poetry if not to recreate the past and prophesy the future, if not to create always according to the image and likeness of truth![153]

As for national spirit, Scott became the poet of individual nationality. He put Scotland on the map by instilling his characters and landscapes with a true Scottish spirit. Bestuzhev was totally incapable of this. It was Pushkin who fulfilled this task for Russia and so his advice to Bestuzhev is perfectly fitting: 'Abandon these Germans and turn to us Orthodox Russians . . . The novel requires a conversational style;

express everything openly. Your Vladimir speaks the language of German drama, looks at the sun at midnight, etc.'[154]

Indeed Bestuzhev's characters talk and behave like the romantics of Germany, England or France. It is difficult to see them as Russians who have imbibed Russian culture, customs and beliefs. There exists only a superficial treatment — no Russian spirit or soul. The scenery too is not distinctively Russian; his towns, castles and landscapes would serve as well on the pages of any European novel of the period.

After the romantic poem and the historical tale, the most popular genre was the Gothic novel. A host of contemporaries told of their enthusiasm, particularly for Ann Radcliffe. In *Another Page from the Diary of a Guards Officer* (*Yeshcho listok iz dnevnika gvardeyskogo ofitsera*) Bestuzhev remarks jestingly: 'Our journey makes a fine scene for a horror novel', and his companion retorts, 'Yes, and the night is most Radcliffian' (*Pol. sob.*, XII, p. 37).

The Gothic novel of Radcliffe, Lewis and Walpole left its traces on almost all writers, including Shelley, Burns and Keats; Bestuzhev was no exception. The setting, characters and dialogues smack of the Gothic, not to mention the deliberate accumulation of horrific situations. The castles loom dark and menacing, and within Wenden Castle the chilling atmosphere presages brooding evil. Neuhausen Castle is surrounded by lurking shadows and is eerie and forbidding. Eisen Castle is a formidable and awesome edifice. The settings forebode ill and dread, none more so than the following:

> Four torches, thrust into the ground, cast a sort of greenish glow on the menacing faces of those present, and at each flicker of the flame, the shadows of the trees flitted like spectres across the glade. . . . The sky was black, the sepulchral firs whispered in the wind, and when their noise was stilled, at times the splash of waves could be heard on the stones at the river's edge. (*Soch.*, I, pp. 76–7)

In characterisation the men are truculent and passionate, the heroines sweet and innocent maidens. The former cannot control themselves, whether experiencing hatred or love. The text is full of descriptions like:

> Beside himself, rigid, gnashing his teeth in anger . . . feelings of frenzy poured out in oaths and threats. (*Soch.*, I, p. 41)

> His face burned with rage and his bloodshot eyes darted here and there. (*Soch.*, I, p. 70)

> Love sets me aflame but jealousy gnaws my soul still more. (*Soch.*, I, p. 69)

The latter, such as Emma and Minna, swoon at any mishap, are ideal soul-mates, harbour dreams of happiness, and yearn for some indeterminate ideal.

The characters relapse occasionally into dialogue of the Gothic type, a mixture of expletives, insults and threats. They launch into bombastic outbursts so exaggerated that they seem absurd.

Finally the situations usually involve revenge and violence. Incident after incident recounts horror and murder, enough to slake the thirst of any reader: 'Romuald, emaciated, pierced by a sharp log, was hanging head down and flowing with blood; his hands were dying with a convulsive jerk and his lips were uttering indistinct curses, (*Soch.*, I, p. 91). The burial of the heroine alive in *Eisen Castle* is gruesome: 'Poor Louisa came to herself, a shiver ran through her veins . . . Loud, hellish laughter rang out above her. "Death for death, faithless one!" said someone, and her blood ran cold.' (*Soch.*, I, pp. 167–8).

The later work, composed in exile, bore the name Marlinsky. It underwent added influences from western Europe, particularly French. Undoubtedly the most pervasive and enduring influence on Russian sentimentalism and romanticism was Rousseau. Marlinsky embodies in Ammalat-Bek the traits of the 'noble savage', courageous, good-hearted and endowed with rich intellectual potential. His colourful appearance – black curls, red trousers, yellow boots, gold-encrusted gun, dagger, Circassian saddle, stirrups of black steel – symbolise his princely worth and the poetry of free life. Marlinsky follows Rousseau in his extolling of the natural man. In Rousseauist fashion the mountaineers are depicted as independent, freedom-loving, brave, and loyal to their religion and community. The theme of escape by outlaw, criminal or renegade is represented by the bandit Mulla-Nur, who becomes the defender of the poor and oppressed. His protest however is tinged with regret and a sense of alienation. Marlinsky's *Story of an Officer Held Captive by Mountaineers* (*Rasskaz ofitsera byvshego v plenu u gortsev*) shows Marlinsky developing his theories and entering a polemic with Rousseau. Here the Utopian ideal is abandoned in favour of a more realistic and prosaic approach. The poverty and starkness of the mountaineers' lives are underlined, as are their quarrels, reprisals and hard work. The conditions of the natives are primitive and unattractive. Although they are the true children of nature, equal, devoid of vices, passions and ambition, they lack the advantages of civilisation and progress.

Balzac and Hugo are markedly influential in this phase. Marlinsky never tired of re-reading *La Peau de Chagrin* and loved to pit himself against Balzac's talent.[155] He admired Balzac's power of narration, his philosophical gifts, profound emotion, clear, marvellous form, and expressive genius.[156] But as for Hugo, he felt 'humble before him . . . his is not a talent, but a genius in full flower' (*Soch.*, II, p. 650). He called him 'an inimitable, mighty talent . . . a single page of whose work is worth all the Balzacs put together' (*Soch.*, II, p. 660). He had read *Notre Dame de Paris, Marion de Lorme, Le Roi s'amuse, Bug-Jargal, Han d'Islande*, among others. With them, increased depth is attained in the descriptions of society life in stories such as *The Test* and *The Frigate 'Hope'*. Marlinsky satirises the society of the day, empty, vain and frivolous. His heroes reject its values in the name of individual honour and integrity. A more painstaking attempt is made to describe society's conventions, foibles and customs. As the inventor of the military, Caucasian, nautical, social and historical tales, the debt of Russian literature to Marlinksy is enormous. Although much of his style was inflated, it paved the way for Pushkin, Lermontov and Gogol to found the Russian sociological novel. Belinsky's sound comment is a just tribute to his contribution:

> Just as Sumarokov, Kheraskov, Petrov, Bogdanovich and Knyazhnin tried with all their might to withdraw from reality and naturalness in invention and style, so Marlinksy endeavoured to the fullest extent to draw near to both.[157]

Notes

1. Marlinsky was the pseudonym which A. A. Bestuzhev assumed in exile after the Decembrist revolt of 1825. As a member of a dragoon regiment in 1816, he had been stationed in Marli near Peterhof.

2. N. L. Stepanov, 'Chto takoye romantizm?' (*Voprosy Literatury*, XII, 1968, pp. 176—81).

3. N. L. Stepanov, 'Romanticheskiy mir Gogolya', in *K istorii russkogo romantizma*, ed. Yu. V. Mann, et al., Moscow, 1973, pp. 188—218.

4. N. K. Piksanov, *Krest'yanskoye vosstaniye v 'Vadime' Lermontova*, Saratov, 1967, p. 43.

5. I. S. Turgenev, *Polnoye sobraniye sochineniy i pisem'*, Moscow—Leningrad, 1965, X, pp. 266—7.

6. See, for instance, F. Leonidov, 'Romantizm v sovetskom literaturovedenii' (*Voprosy Literatury*, VII, 1971, pp. 199—202); L. Dorofeyeva, 'Silovyye linii romantizma' (*Voprosy Literatury*, IX, 1971, p. 234); I. F. Volkov, 'Osnovnyye problemy izucheniya romantizma', in Mann, op. cit., pp. 5—36; Ye. A. Maymin, *O russkom romantizme*, Moscow, 1975.

7. Ye. M. Pul'khritudova, 'Literaturnaya teoriya dekabristskogo dvizheniya v 30 — ye gody XIX v.', in *Problemy romantizma: Sbornik statey*, Moscow, 1967, pp. 232—91.

8. G. A. Gukovsky, *Pushkin i russkiye romantiki*, Moscow, 1965.

9. B. Meylakh, *Poeziya dekabristov*, Leningrad, 1950, p. 35.

10. V. G. Bazanov, *Ocherki dekabristskoy literatury: Proza*, Moscow, 1953; *Ocherki dekabristskoy literatury: Poeziya*, Moscow—Leningrad, 1961; *Uchonaya respublika*, Moscow—Leningrad, 1964.

11. *Polyarnaya zvezda*, ed. V. A. Arkhipov, et al., Moscow—Leningrad, 1960; *Dekabristy*, ed. Vl. Orlov, Moscow—Leningrad, 1951 (hereafter Orlov).

12. I. V. Kartashova, 'A. A. Bestuzhev-Marlinsky', in *Russkiy romantizm*, ed. N. A. Gulyayev, Moscow, 1974, pp. 86—91.

13. F. Z. Kanunova, *Estetika russkoy romanticheskoy povesti*, Tomsk, 1973.

14. R. F. Yusufov, *Russkiy romantizm nachala XIX veka i natsional'nyye kul'tury*, Moscow, 1970.

15. S. A. Vengerov, *Kritiko-biograficheskiy slovar' russkikh pisateley i uchonykh*, St Petersburg, 1892, III, p. 157.

16. I. I. Zamotin, *Romanticheskiy idealizm v russkom obshchestve i literature 20—30—kh godov XIX stoletiya*, St Petersburg, 1907, p. 170.

17. A. N. Pypin, *Istoriya russkoy literatury*, IV, St Petersburg, 1907, p. 430.

18. N. A. Kotlyarevsky, *Dekabristy Knyaz' A. I. Odoyevskiy i A. A. Bestuzhev-Marlinsky*, St Petersburg, 1907, pp. 122—5.

19. M. V. Nechkina, *Dvizheniye dekabristov*, I, Moscow, 1955, p. 131.

20. A. P. Sharupich, *Dekabrist Aleksandr Bestuzhev*, Minsk, 1962, pp. 15—17.

21. N. Maslin, 'A. A. Bestuzhev-Marlinksy', in A. A. Bestuzhev-Marlinsky, *Sochineniya v dvukh tomakh*, Moscow, 1958, I, p. 3 (hereafter *Soch.*).

22. N. L. Stepanov, 'A. A. Bestuzhev-Marlinsky', in A. Marlinsky, *Izbrannyye povesti*, Leningrad, 1937, p. 6.

23. N. Mordovchenko, 'A. A. Bestuzhev-Marlinsky', in Bestuzhev-Marlinsky, *Sobraniye stikhotvoreniy*, Moscow, 1948; V. G. Bazanov, *Ocherki dekabristskoy literatury*, Moscow, 1953.

24. N. I. Grech, *Zapiski o moyey zhizni*, St Petersburg, 1886, p. 393.
25. F. Glinka, *Pokazaniya*, IRLI (Institut Russkoy Literatury), AN SSSR (Akademiya Nauk SSSR); also see Bazanov, *Uchonaya respublika*, Moscow—Leningrad, 1964, pp. 317—34.
26. M. V. Dovnar-Zapolsky, *Memuary dekabristov*, Kiev, 1906, p. 175.
27. Ibid., pp. 316, 88.
28. Ibid., p. 11.
29. P. Ye. Shchogolev, *Dekabristy*, Moscow—Leningrad, 1926, p. 190.
30. *Vosstaniye dekabristov: Materialy*, ed. M. N. Pokrovsky, Moscow—Leningrad, 1925—58, I, pp. 431—42.
31. Shchogolev, op. cit., p. 193.
32. A. Ye. Rozen, *Zapiski dekabrista*, St Petersburg, 1907, p. 62.
33. *Dekabristy: Otryvki iz istochnikov*, ed. Yu. G. Oksman, Moscow—Leningrad, 1926, pp. 446—7.
34. Pokrovsky, op. cit., I, p. 430.
35. Letter to N. Polevoy, *Russkiy vestnik*, 4, 1861.
36. Shchogolev, op. cit., p. 90.
37. Pokrovsky, op. cit., I, p. 433.
38. Dovnar-Zapolsky, op. cit., pp. 164—6.
39. Pokrovsky, op. cit., p. 435.
40. Letter to N. Polevoy, *Russkiy vestnik*, 3, 1851.
41. M. K. Azadovsky, 'Memuary Bestuzhevykh kak istoricheskiy i literaturnyy pamyatnik', in *Vospominaniya Bestuzhevykh*, ed. M. K. Azadovsky, Moscow —Leningrad, 1951, pp. 597—8.
42. Mikhail Bestuzhev, 'Detstvo i yunost A. A. Bestuzheva-Marlinskogo', in Azadovsky, op. cit., p. 207.
43. Azadovsky, op. cit., p. 600.
44. Pokrovsky, op. cit., p. 433.
45. Ibid., p. 430.
46. Letter to Ye. A. Bestuzheva, *Pamyati dekabristov*, Leningrad, 1926, I, p. 21.
47. Mordovchenko, op. cit., p. 12.
48. Azadovsky, op. cit., pp. 8, 15.
49. Ibid., pp. 30—1.
50. Pokrovsky, op. cit., p. 437.
51. Azadovsky, op. cit., p. 42.
52. Letter to Tsar Nicholas, Orlov, op. cit., p. 513.
53. Orlov, op. cit., p. 510.
54. I. M. Semenko, 'Poeticheskoye naslediye dekabristov', in *Poety-dekabristy*, ed. Semenko, Leningrad, 1960, p. 8.
55. *Izbrannyye sotsial'no — politicheskiye i filosofskiye proizvedeniya dekabristov*, ed. I. Y. Shchipanov, Moscow—Leningrad, 1951, I, p. 266.
56. Ibid., p. 271.
57. Ibid., p. 266.
58. Letter to Polevoy (*Russkiy vestnik*, 3, 1861, p. 296).
59. *Soch.*, II, p. 523.
60. *Syn otechestva*, LXXVII, 20, 1822, pp. 253—69.
61. *Russkiy vestnik*, 6, 1870, p. 507.
62. *Soch.*, II, p. 591.

63. Ibid., p. 526.
64. Ibid., p. 530.
65. Shchipanov, op. cit., p. 270.
66. Orlov, op. cit., p. 559.
67. Ibid., p. 103.
68. *Soch.*, II, p. 554.
69. A. A. Bestuzhev-Marlinsky, *Polnoye sobraniye sochineniy*, St Petersburg, 1838, pp. 70–2 (hereafter *Pol. sob.*).
70. Ibid., pp. 113–14.
71. Ibid., p. 69.
72. Pokrovsky, op. cit., p. 457.
73. Azadovsky, op. cit., pp. 27–8.
74. Orlov, op. cit., p. 503.
75. Ibid., p. 515.
76. Ibid., p. 512.
77. Ibid., p. 503.
78. Ibid., pp. 475–8.
79. A. K. Borozdin, *Iz pisem i pokazaniy dekabristov*, St Petersburg, 1906, p. 78.
80. Orlov, op. cit., p. 3; Azadovsky, op. cit., pp. 11–12.
81. Orlov, op. cit., pp. 511–12.
82. Texts vary.
83. M. P. Alekseyev and B. S. Meylakh, *Dekabristy i ikh vremya*, Moscow–Leningrad, 1951, p. 13.
84. F. Glinka, *Stikhotvoreniya*, Leningrad, 1951, pp. 123–4; Shchipanov, op. cit., p. 519; Orlov, op. cit., p. 475.
85. *Soch.*, II, p. 474.
86. Azadovsky, op. cit., pp. 10, 34.
87. K. F. Ryleyev, *Stikhotvoreniya, stat'i, ocherki, zapiski, pis'ma*, Moscow, 1956, pp. 214–15.
88. A. I. Odoyevsky, *Polnoye sobraniye stikhotvoreniy i pisem*, Moscow–Leningrad, 1934, p. 190.
89. *Soch.*, I, pp. 93–7.
90. Orlov, op. cit., p. 5.
91. Mordovchenko, op. cit., p. 81.
92. Ibid., p. 205.
93. *Syn otechestva*, 4, 1823, pp. 183–4; *Russkiy vestnik*, 3, 1861, p. 328.
94. Shchipanov, op. cit., p. 548.
95. Pokrovsky, op. cit., IV, p. 91.
96. *Russkiy vestnik*, XXXII, 1861, p. 295.
97. Orlov, op. cit., pp. 500–1.
98. Ibid., p. 502.
99. *Sorevnovatel'*, 3, 1824, pp. 302–3.
100. Orlov, op. cit., p. 450.
101. Ibid., p. 503.
102. Ibid., p. 473.
103. Ibid., p. 511.
104. *Soch.*, I, p. 40.
105. Ibid., p. 45.

106. Ibid., pp. 67—92.
107. Shchipanov, op. cit., II, p. 164.
108. Ibid., I, p. 437.
109. Ibid., p. 296.
110. Orlov, op. cit., pp. 511—12.
111. Shchipanov, op. cit., I, p. 435.
112. Ibid., II, p. 164.
113. Borozdin, op. cit., p. 30.
114. Orlov, op. cit., p. 511.
115. Ibid., pp. 510—14.
116. A. Veselovsky, *Zapadnoye vliyaniye v novoy russkoy literature*, Moscow, 1896.
117. I. I. Zamotin, *Ranniye romanticheskiye veyaniya v russkoy literature*, Warsaw, 1900.
118. N. A. Kotlyarevsky, *Literaturnyye napravleniya aleksandrovskoy epokhi*, St Petersburg, 1907; also *Mirovaya skorb' v kontse XVIII i v nachale XIX veka*, St Petersburg, 1910.
119. M. N. Rozanov, *Russo i literaturnoye dvizheniye kontsa XVIII i nachala XIX v.: Ocherki po istorii russoizma na zapade i v Rossii*, I, Moscow, 1910.
120. V. G. Belinsky, *Polnoye sobraniye sochineniy*, Moscow, 1953—6, IV, p. 272.
121. A. S. Pushkin, *Sobraniye sochineniy v desyati tomakh*, Moscow, 1962, IX, p. 67.
122. Ibid., p. 40.
123. IRLI (Institut Russkoy Literatury), AN SSSR (Akademiya Nauk SSSR), *Bumagi Bestuzhevykh*, Arkh., 3 (5572).
124. *Pamyati dekabristov*, p. 69.
125. Ibid., p. 60; see also Azadovsky, op. cit., pp. 524—5.
126. *Soch.*, II, p. 623.
127. Ibid., I, p. 145.
128. Ibid., pp. 49—50.
129. Ibid., p. 65.
130. Ibid., p. 121.
131. Ibid., p. 166.
132. Ibid., pp. 6—7, 116—17.
133. Ibid., pp. 126, 11.
134. *Pol. sob.*, I, p. 178.
135. *Soch.*, I, p. 22.
136. Ibid., p. 78.
137. Ibid., p. 70.
138. *Pol. sob.*, XII, p. 51.
139. *Soch.*, I, pp. 164—5.
140. Ibid., pp. 39—40.
141. *Pol. sob.*, I, p. 171.
142. Pushkin, op. cit., IX, p. 160.
143. *Moskovskiy telegraf*, XLIX, 1833, p. 328.
144. *Soch.*, I, p. 178.
145. *Rospis' rossiyskim knigam dlya chteniya iz biblioteki Aleksandra Smirdina*, St Petersburg, 1828—47.

146. P. Arapov, *Letopis' russkogo teatra*, St Petersburg, 1861.
147. *Zapiski A. O. Smirnovoy*, St Petersburg, 1897, II, p. 49.
148. *Pamyati dekabristov*, I, pp. 60—6.
149. *Soch.*, I, p. 203.
150. *Pol. sob.*, IV, p. 239.
151. N. Polevoy, *Klyatva pri grobe gospodnem*, Moscow, 1832, Part I, Chapters 11 —12.
152. Pushkin, op. cit., IX, p. 160.
153. *Russkiy vestnik*, 3, 1861, p. 328.
154. Pushkin, op. cit., IX, p. 160.
155. *Soch.*, II, p. 643.
156. Ibid., p. 650.
157. Belinsky, op. cit., IV, p. 28.

5 Gogol and romanticism
T. E. LITTLE

I

To assess Gogol in relation to romanticism is an uncertain business because neither the author nor the movement has been properly defined. In 1825[1] Pushkin complains that anything dreamy or Germanic is reckoned to be romantic (*Ruslan and Lyudmila* in 1820 seems to have been considered romantic largely on account of its sheer novelty)[2] and proceeds to give a rather unsatisfactory definition of his own. Prince P. A. Vyazemsky (1792–1878), who had been deeply involved in an unedifying polemic over *The Fountain of Bakhchisaray* (*Bakhchisaray-skiy fontan*) in 1824,[3] observed in deep old age that nobody in the 1820s knew what romanticism was, and that the question was still unresolved in the 1870s.[4] The movement still awaits final definition in the twentieth century. Vyazemsky, who befriended Gogol in the 1830s and wrote perceptively about him,[5] never claimed him as part of the romantic movement, but many others have either professed to see romantic elements in his work, or have reckoned him a fully fledged romantic in his own right.[6]

It is unfortunate that Gogol himself made no substantial pronouncements on the subject of romanticism, and even more unfortunate that his few observations are hostile. By the beginning of his literary career the furious arguments of the 1820s were largely of historical interest, and his only attempt at a definition, as Carl Proffer points out,[7] occurs in a draft version of *Petersburg Notes of 1836*[8] where Gogol writes mainly of the Russian theatre. Romanticism in his view represented a striving to come closer to Russian society. Russians had become distanced from their own society by imitating society and people as portrayed in the authors of antiquity. Gogol sees romanticism as an understandable reaction against imitative literature, but does not approve of those who try to reform the state of affairs. In their eagerness to remove forms and rules which are uncharacteristic of, and do not correspond to, their own (Russian) habits and customs, such people smash a breach through everything. In their attempt to remedy an injustice they cause an equal amount of damage and end up as victims of their own chaos. Tantalisingly Gogol does not state which authors he has in mind. But he does postulate a writer of great talent who creates something new from this chaos and, with the 'inspired tranquillity'of the artist, turns what was romantic into something classic, into a graphic, clear majestic creation. Anybody with a knowledge of Russian literature would expect the name of Pushkin to be mentioned at this point. Instead Gogol singles out Walter Scott! Byron too would have qualified as such a talent, Gogol thinks, had the Englishman had a quieter, more reflective intellect. His dislike of Byron was longstanding. In an article on Kozlov of 1831[9] Gogol had written disapprovingly of Byron's 'gigantically dark' soul which embraced the life of the world, but also mocked it, because Byron was unable to convey life's brightness and greatness. His proud isolated soul wished to live in its own disordered, self-created and fantastic world, having rejected the world of life. (The ironic import of these strictures on Byron is considered later.) Continuing his article of 1836, Gogol condemns romantic dramatists for wishing to relate 'new' events, something hitherto unseen or unheard of, the essential feature of which must be strangeness. Such a desire for strangeness has, in Gogol's opinion, produced preposterous and supernatural plots.

By 1836, therefore, Gogol perceives romantics as destructive innovators, causers of chaos and confusion, swollen with energy and pride and with an aptitude for mockery. Neither the movement nor one of its greatest representatives in Russian eyes, Lord Byron, compares favourably with the clear, calm, majestic and orderly approach of classicism. Elsewhere, as Proffer observes, 'classical' for Gogol means 'of exemplary quality', and the distinctive features of classical works are self-mastery, intellect, natural harmony and prudence. Gogol's identification of romanticism with the Russification of literature would have pleased the movement's supporters.[10] His dislike of its destructive tendencies would have gratified its opponents, but there is little in these theoretical statements on which to build a 'Gogolian approach' to romanticism. An indication that Gogol had nevertheless absorbed romantic attitudes is provided by a number of articles written by him on literary and artistic themes.

Woman, published in 1832,[11] presents an exalted, idealistic view of the female sex. In a dialogue between Plato and Telecles Gogol has Plato speaking of 'eternity in the divine features' of a woman, Alcinoe. We mature and perfect ourselves as we get to know women. Woman, readers are informed, is the 'language of the gods'. In one of those curious transformations foreshadowing the use of Homeric simile in *Dead Souls* (*Myortvyye dushi*), women cease to be discussed as human beings but become imperceptibly identified with the artistic idea. When a picture is still in the mind of the artist it is feminine. When translated into matter and made tangible it is masculine. In striving to express his immortal idea in matter the artist is directed by one high sentiment: to express the divinity within matter itself. The artist makes part of the infinite world within his own soul accessible to other people. An article on Pushkin's *Boris Godunov*,[12] written in 1830, develops the concept of art as a mystical experience. Nowhere is the play itself discussed or analysed. Instead it is presented as an experience beyond empirical analysis the value of which is measured in terms of its effect on the soul. Two critics, Pollior and Elliadiy, agree that there is nothing to compare with the joy which intoxicates the soul when a work of art evokes a response in the heart of others. Pollior suggests that two people should read a work together and, if each finds the other responding to it in the same way as himself, and if one reader finds in the other the matching half of his own beautiful soul, there is no need for the work to be analysed.

In *Arabesques* (1835) Gogol published his much quoted *Sculpture, Painting and Music*.[13] Sculpture is designated a pagan activity from the Greek world of beauty. It is not, in Gogol's view, suited to the expression of Christian ideas. Christianity raised painting and music from insignificance and transformed them into something gigantic. Painting does not merely express a nation. It expresses everything contained within the mysteriously lofty world of Christianity. All beautiful phenomena surrounding men are in its power. In it alone is contained man's link with nature and secret harmony. Within art the sensual and the spiritual are merged. Despite the praise lavished on these art forms, Gogol awards pre-eminence to music. It wrests man from the earth, stuns him with the thunder of powerful notes and plunges him into its own world. At the stroke of a violin bow the perturbed soul of a robber will, for a moment, feel a pang of conscience. The speculator will forget his calculations, and even shamelessness and impudence will shed a tear on encountering a creation of talent.

Gogol's essay, *On the Middle Ages*,[14] the published version of his first lecture at the University of St Petersburg, is written in the by now familiar lofty and hyperbolic style. He speaks with enthusiasm of the growth of papal power, the Inquisition, alchemy and of the military orders. In his relish for the grandiose he describes the inner quality of the Middle Ages as 'gigantic colossalness' of an almost miraculous kind. He praises their bravery and their originality. These qualities he thinks make the Middle Ages unique in the ancient and modern world.

A Few Words about Pushkin[15] is a lyrical expression of praise for Pushkin, whom Gogol considers to be the quintessential Russian poet. In him, Gogol thinks, Russian nature, the Russian soul and the Russian character were reflected in the same purified beauty as a landscape on a convex lens. In the last paragraph, strongly reminiscent of the concluding paragraphs of *Sorochinsky Fair* (*Sorochinskaya yarmarka*), Gogol asserts that the more a poet becomes a poet, the more he depicts feelings known only to poets. The crowd around him diminishes and in the end he can number those who truly appreciate him on the fingers of one hand.

In *Al Mamoun*[16] Gogol extols his ideal monarch and, significantly for his own development, his concept of great poets in the service of a king. Great poets, according to Gogol, combine within themselves the roles of poet, philosopher and historian. They have explored man and nature. They have delved deep into the past and have perceived the future. Their voice (*glagol*) is heard by the whole people and they are great priests (*zhretsy*). Wise rulers honour them with conversation, preserve their valuable lives and do not burden them with the multifarious activities of rulership. Poets are summoned only to the most important state councils because they know the depths of the human heart.

All these views can be traced to the influence of romantic writers and philosophers, chiefly German thinkers such as Wackenroder, Schelling, Novalis and their Russian imitators. Isaiah Berlin points out that Schelling, following Herder, was responsible for the characteristically romantic notion that poets or painters understand the spirit of the age more profoundly than academic historians. Nikolai Stankevich (1813—40) taught that a proper understanding of Kant and Schelling (and later of Hegel) led one to realise that, beneath the apparent disorder, cruelty, ugliness and injustice of daily life, it was possible to discern eternal beauty, peace and harmony. According to Stankevich, men should seek to reform themselves from within. The Kingdom of Heaven — the Hegelian self-transcending spirit — lies within. Salvation comes from individual self-regeneration, and to achieve truth, reality and happiness men must learn from those who truly know: the philosophers, the poets and the sages.[17]

Gogol's views show a close affinity with Berlin's general description of the romantic ethos. Art for him lies beyond empirical analysis, a thing of the soul rather than of the intellect. It expresses divinity, portrays beauty and speaks to the soul of man which the poet has plumbed so deeply. Art and poetry are not of the earth and yet, because of their teaching and counselling roles, they serve a social function like that of the priesthood. The principle of universalisation and the desire to embrace the unembraceable, which V. Zen'kovsky sees as a romantic trait,[18] is evident in the multitude of roles Gogol assigns to the poet or artist. The poet embodies the national spirit, purifies morals, and serves as historian and philosopher to his monarch. Independent of monarch and people (the clear implication is that they depend on him), the poet nevertheless comes under their protection and, because of the uniqueness of his position, he is doomed to isolation.

From the beginning of his career Gogol held a high belief in the vocation of the poet-writer. Derived from romantic notions which were 'in the air' (it is notoriously difficult to identify with certainty specific sources of influence on Gogol),[19] Gogol foresaw a high destiny for the writer and hence for himself. His views on art, history and the function of the artist may now appear to us as idealistic, vague, mystical or simply high-flown gibberish, but they have one supreme virtue: they indicate and inspire enthusiasm for the subject. His historical erudition may have been meagre, but he does make the medieval period sound exciting. The lofty role he assigns to the poet, and the language with which Gogol expounds that role, is lyrical and hyperbolic, but he is merely stating at greater length what Pushkin had already expressed in his lyric verse, particularly *The Prophet* (*Prorok*).[20] Gogol's concern for the influence of art on the soul of man now seems dated in an age when talk of the soul itself, particularly in relation to literature, seems quaintly anachronistic, and yet such an attitude is better than the curious self-destructive assumption that the arts have no influence on man's destiny.[21]

Even Gogol's hyperbole may be seen as a continuation of a wholly laudable vigour and enthusiasm which the romantic movement brought to Russia in the 1820s. Nevertheless it is clear that by 1836 Gogol had broken with one aspect of European romanticism. In his condemnation of supernatural and preposterous plots may be perceived a judgment on himself. Up to and to some extent after 1836 his own works contain frenzied, supernatural and preposterous plots in which critics have professed to find the chief elements of Gogol's romanticism.

II

The very use of the supernatural in Gogol's early stories is in itself a romantic trait, part of the revolt against scientific rationalism prevalent in the eighteenth-century.[22] Gogol's non-rationalistic approach to the arts in general has already been noted, and in his early stories[23] he produces characters and events which defy the scientific order of the 'real' world: witches, wizards, spells and a variety of supernatural beings derived from myth and legend. Another feature of his early tales commonly identified with the romantic movement is the sheer lyricism of his prose, particularly in his rendering of landscape and nature. The often quoted descriptions of a summer day in the Ukraine (*Sorochinsky Fair*), of a Ukrainian night in *A May Night* (*Mayskaya noch'*), or of the Dnieper in *A Terrible Vengeance* (*Strashnaya mest'*), provide striking examples of mellifluous, highly charged and colourful prose in which assonance, alliteration and other poetic devices produce what V. Setchkarev rightly calls a 'fantasy on the theme of nature' rather than a concrete, objective description.[24] Nature, in such descriptions, is no longer an abstract remote entity but is humanised and invested with symbolic significance. The sky 'slumbers and clasps the fair earth'; cherry trees 'timorously push their roots into cold water'; the Dnieper holds all that is reflected in it to its bosom. Lyricism is evident too in the speeches of the characters as when Katerina addresses her husband in Chapter 9 of *A Terrible Vengeance*:

Is it you, lying there, my beloved husband, with closed eyes?
Arise my beloved falcon and stretch out your little hand! Arise!
Look but once at your Katerina, move your lips, utter but one word.
But you are silent, you are silent my noble lord. (*Pol. sob.*, I, pp. 267 —8)

This is the stuff of song, not of speech. Gogol's use of folksongs and folklore as material for his works[25] is entirely in accord with the enthusiasm of Russian romantics for local or ethnic colour — the same enthusiasm which produced Pushkin's *The Gipsies* (*Tsigany*) and *The Fountain of Bakhchisaray*. Another general feature which Gogol shares with romantic writing is his interest in the dark side of human nature. His tales, particularly *Viy* and *A Terrible Vengeance*, treat the sinister themes of necromancy and incest. Eager readers with a taste for psychoanalytical criticism have detected other sexual peculiarities[26] in his works, some of which have been carefully documented by Mario Praz in his study of romantic sexuality.[27]

Apart from noting these general affinities between Gogol's works and romanticism in general, it is possible to see more specific parallels between Gogol's works and German romantic writers, especially Tieck and Hoffmann.[28] *St John's Eve* (*Vecher nakanune Ivana Kupala*) resembles Tieck's *Liebeszauber*. Set at carnival time, the German tale involves the love of a man for a pretty girl, the sacrifice of an innocent child at the instigation of a bloodthirsty witch, the hero's loss of memory and its sudden return at a significant moment.[29] Tieck's *Karl von Barneck* may well have influenced or inspired *A Terrible Vengeance*. In Tieck's tale one brother murders another for his inheritance and the murderer is doomed to remain on earth until two brothers re-enact the drama. This extraordinary condition is fulfilled when a certain Rheinhardt kills his brother Karl and thereafter retires into a monastery. Fratricide among ancestors and a curse descending from one generation to the next are common to both stories, and Tieck's *Pietro von Abano* supplies another motif: the invocation of a soul by a wizard. In Tieck's tale the soul of the dead Crescentia is invoked; in Gogol's tale the wizard summons the soul of his sleeping daughter. The raising of the dead or sleeping souls is a variation on the romantic theme of the double.

The figure of the evil magician in *A Terrible Vengeance* and *The Portrait* (*Portret*) has a long line of colourful antecedents. In Hoffmann's *Ignaz Denner* the title hero wears Spanish-type garments, a gold-edged coat, a distinctive sort of hat and a dagger at his side. Danilo sees his wicked father-in-law wearing Turkish trousers, pistols in his belt and a curious hat. Gogol's wizard murdered his wife, so did Hoffmann's.

Diary of a Madman (*Zapiski sumasshedshego*) treats the common romantic theme of insanity, and the prototype of Poprishchin could well be Geheimsekretär Nettelmann from Hoffmann's *Fragments from the Life of Three Friends*, who believes himself to be a king. Gogol's treatment of Petersburg whereby the city is evoked rather than described might be inspired by Hoffmann's treatment of Berlin. *Nevsky Prospect* deals with the romantic theme of the artist's relationship with his milieu, and the relationship of dream to reality. The concept of the artist as a dreamer living outside the world and divorced from practical life is germane to Hoffmann whose influence is probably at work in *The Portrait*. In *Fragments from the Life of Three Friends* Alexander tells the tale of his dead aunt in whose house he lives, and whose image from her portrait walks round the house at night.

The Nose (*Nos*) seems to mock the romantic mystery tale and the theme of the double. No attempt is made to explain away the anomalies of the tale (the narrator actually gloats over them) or to answer questions raised by the plot. In Adalbert von Chamisso's *Peter Schlemihl's Wonderful Story* a man loses his shadow, while in Hoffmann's *Adventures on New Year's Eve* a man has no reflection in a mirror, a theme taken up in later horror stories such as Bram Stoker's *Dracula*. In *The Nose* Gogol reduces the double theme to comic absurdity by the simple device of removing the dream framework he had originally planned for it, and which would have made all the events 'plausible' as a fiction of the sleeping mind.

Gogol appears to have absorbed themes and episodes from mainly German romantic sources and to have given them a Ukrainian or Russian colouring, a practice entirely in accord with what V. Sipovsky calls romantic individualism, which demanded that a work conveys the atmosphere of the time and place in which it is set.[30] Gogol's dissatisfaction with the preposterous elements of romanticism, and implied criticism of his own earlier works, invites a comparison of the latter with his more 'mature' creations, in particular with *Dead Souls*.

III

A commonplace in studies of Gogol is the assertion that his work evolved from the fantasy of the early period to the realistic mode of his later works. Attention is frequently drawn to the mixture of realism and fantasy allegedly found even in his early works.[31] However, the contrast in the *Dikan'ka* and *Mirgorod* tales is not between realism and fantasy but between the exotically supernatural and the prosaically mundane. Witches, wizards, fairies and demons are juxtaposed to rough peasants and cossacks. The wicked wizard of *A Terrible Vengeance* is proved to be a creature of the devil by his refusal to eat pork and dumplings or to drink vodka and mead! Whether the prosaic details of Ukrainian peasant life are socially and historically true is difficult for modern readers to determine without reliable evidence from social historians. In the absence of such evidence a reader can only suspend judgment on the 'realism' of these tales. There is some reason to believe that Gogol was not always a wholly reliable recorder of his native Ukraine. Contemporary critics pointed out some mistakes,[32] and the very fact that he had to ply his mother for information about Ukrainian life indicates that his own knowledge was sketchy. From what we know of her it may be safely assumed that Maria Gogol was not herself the most perceptive of observers. Fortunately the ethnic accuracy of Gogol's tales is irrelevant to his artistic purpose. For the plots of the Ukrainian tales, and the characters in them, he relies heavily upon the Ukrainian puppet theatre (the boastful Pole, a comic devil, a shrewish wife, a conceited deacon, a crafty gypsy and a brave Cossack),[33] the plays written by his father, and upon folklore. This is a legitimate method of presenting a national ethos. Romanticism as a whole was not concerned with historical or local realism. Many Russians were impressed by what they took to be the Italian atmosphere of some Shakespeare plays, and were thrilled by tales of high adventure in Scott's versions of Scottish and English history. An earlier generation had been beguiled by the bards and warriors of Ossian's (James Macpherson's) Scottish dreamland. Atmosphere for Russian romantics was more important than accuracy,[34] and if Gogol in *Taras Bul'ba* confused three centuries of Cossack history[35] he nevertheless told an exciting tale and projected a vigorous ethnic image. It may be, as V. Gippius

rather sourly observes, that many Russians were deceived into considering the *Dikan'ka* and *Mirgorod* stories as entirely authentic pictures of
Ukrainian life. But perhaps they recognised tales which were Ukrainian
in spirit if not in strict social or historical detail, and the image which a
country projects of itself through its writers is as much part of the
national ethos as are 'scientific' observations.[36]

The supernatural or unrealistic elements of the early tales are their
least successful feature. Pantomime devils, exotically clad wizards,
witches, hags, and all the other stock-in-trade figures of the fairy and
horror story have as little power to frighten as the vampire in the
cinema's endless remakes of *Dracula*. The really frightening entities of
Gogol's stories are the human beings. The *Dikan'ka* and *Mirgorod* tales
leave a confused frieze-like image of swirling Cossacks in a perpetual
dance. Vyazemsky first drew attention to the 'dance of death' of
Gogol's characters[37] and the literalness of his observation is striking.
Sorochinsky Fair ends with the curious dance of the guests at the
wedding feast:

> But an even stranger, unfathomable feeling would have been
> aroused in the depth of the soul at the sight of the old women,
> whose crumbling faces breathed the indifference of the tomb,
> pushing their way through the new, laughing, lively humanity.
> Unconcerned, without even childish joy, with no spark of sym-
> pathy, only intoxication made them do something akin to human
> action; like a mechanic operating a lifeless automaton, they quiet-
> ly shook their drunken heads, danced after the rejoicing crowd,
> paying no attention to the young couple. (*Pol. sob.*, I, pp. 135—6)

There are many strange automaton dances throughout *Mirgorod* and
Dikan'ka. The narrator of *St John's Eve* reminisces about wedding
dances in his youth, and at the end of the tale a tub in which the
church elder's wife is mixing some dough performs a dance with its
arms akimbo, moved by some diabolical force. In *The Lost Letter*
(*Propavshaya gramota*) the narrator describes the dancing of Zaporo-
zhian Cossacks, and the demons seen by Grandad perform a diabolical
khopak. At the end of the tale Grandad's wife performs an involuntary
dance under the influence of Satanic forces. The wicked wizard in *A
Terrible Vengeance* is an excellent dancer, and his daughter is moved by
evil powers to perform an unwilling dance. Pirogov performs a strange
silent dance with Schiller's wife in *Nevsky Prospect* and, having been
beaten up by the Germans, consoles himself with a *mazurka*. Khoma
Brut of *Viy* hires musicians when he is drunk and dances a *tropak*. His
last performance occurs before his final and fatal night of vigil over the
witch's corpse. *Taras Bul'ba* comprises a frenzy of Cossacks who appear
to spend the time they can spare from battle in a routine of energetic
dancing.

Gogol's narrative is also punctuated with strange dumb scenes. In *St John's Eve* the Cossacks stand as though rooted to the spot, with their eyes open and starting out of their heads, not daring to blink. Ivan Shponka sits with Masha for more than quarter of an hour in profound silence, interrupted only by the observation that there are many flies in the summer. The Head and his cronies in *A May Night* are rooted to the spot at the appearance of the Head's sister-in-law.

Even before his strictures on frenzied and supernatural plots in 1836, Gogol was turning away from the more blatantly fantastic elements of *Dikan'ka*. In *Mirgorod* the ostentatiously supernatural devices are reduced. Only *Viy* contains witches and monsters. The intrusion of evil into the narrative of *Old World Landowners* (*Starosvetskiye pomeshchiki*) is a more subtle, sinister process than the activities of wicked wizards. A black cat and a mysterious voice are the only apparent agents of the supernatural and whether they are really such, or merely seen as supernatural by superstitious minds, is left carefully ambiguous. Far more sinister than the cat or the voice are the old landowners themselves. Their sole activity is eating, and beneath the tranquillity of their idyllic relationship lurks, as Richard Peace points out, bitter hostility.[38] The 'evil' of *Taras Bul'ba* is illicit and traitorous love, while in *The Story of How Ivan Ivanovich Quarrelled with Ivan Nikiforovich* (*Povest' o tom kak possorilsya Ivan Ivanovich s Ivanom Nikiforichem*), evil enters the world through a trivial human failing: a man's resentment because his friend called him a 'gander'. The disaster brought about by this mild, if unkind, taunt lacks the theatricality of *A Terrible Vengeance* with its writhing corpses and for that very reason makes a greater impression on the reader. Revising *The Portrait* for a new edition in 1842, Gogol removes the most blatant supernatural occurrences, such as the portrait's self-transportation to the artist's home, and renders the downfall of the painter more 'psychological' in terms of greed for money and fame. But the greed is still demonic, and evil works as devastatingly through human nature as through pantomime devils.

In *Nevsky Prospect* a demon is believed to have shattered the world into pieces which have been senselessly mixed and mingled, and so, as Yu. V. Mann observes,[39] evil in Gogol's view is a lack of logic and order in the world, and behind illogic and chaos lurks demonic force. Nowhere is demonic confusion more effectively shown than in *Dead Souls*. In the early tales evil forces invade the world as monsters or demons, whereas in the later works the very fabric of reality strains under the pressure of situational, logical and linguistic absurdity. After *Mirgorod*, the agents of hell disappear, but the absence of wizards and monsters does not make Gogol's work more realistic, because fantastic events now take place without any obvious supernatural agency.[40]

Kovalyov's nose disappears from his face and turns up later as a high-ranking civil servant. Still later it is nose-size again and can be contained in a policeman's handkerchief. The anomalies in the plot and structure of the tale make it a work of ostentatious fantasy, whereas in *Dead Souls* fantasy is unobtrusive and powerful. No magician casts a spell, and yet strange transmogrifications take place by the subtle workings of innuendo and simile, making the world of NN as fluid in form and identity as Dikan'ka.[41] A melon in Chapter 8 functions as Korobochka's coach. Her clock in Chapter 3 is a nest of hissing snakes. Sobakevich's furniture in Chapter 5 takes on the identity of its owner, because every item of it is as large and as clumsy as he. Nozdryov, who stands among his dogs as a father amidst his family, takes on a canine identity. Chichikov's horses have human thoughts and converse with one another. Gogol's use of the Homeric simile is another powerful instrument of change. The dancers at the ball in Chapter 1 become a squadron of flies. The dogs outside Korobochka's house in Chapter 3 are weirdly transformed into a church choir. In his clash with Nozdryov, Chichikov is turned into a fortress and Nozdryov becomes a lieutenant in the process of besieging it. Throughout the novel a familiar pattern is seen: animate and inanimate objects change identity, human and animal creatures merge into one another, and the distinction between people and things is constantly blurred.[42]

Human logic is also set at naught. A man in *The Government Inspector* (*Revizor*) is reckoned to smell of vodka because he was bumped as a baby. Khlestakov is taken to be the inspector because he does not pay his bill in a local hotel. Two women in *Dead Souls* hear that Chichikov is buying dead serfs and conclude that he must be planning to elope with the governor's daughter. Akakiy Akakiyevich never knows whether he is in the middle of a line of copying or in the middle of the street, and his tailor is held to be good at his job despite his one eye and a pockmarked face. Situational absurdity in Gogol's work owes a great deal to the oddity of his characters' reactions to an event. Kovalyov regards the absence of his nose more as a social outrage than as an event outside the natural order. Akakiy, having elevated his overcoat to the status of a wife, dies of grief when he loses it.[43]

Demonic disorder is accompanied by a continuation of devilish dance and dumb scenes. The dance of the human flies in Chapter 1 of *Dead Souls* has already been mentioned. We observe too Chichikov's obscene little dance of triumph and how the objects on his shelf caper in unison with him.[44] A variation on this theme of frenzied movement is the number of characters who make strange grimaces or have involuntary habits (such as the public prosecutor with his winking eye in *Dead Souls*) and who recall Rudi Panko's friend with the arms which wave like windmills. Chichikov in Chapter 6 of *Dead Souls* goes through all sorts of weird gloating gestures, pursing his lips and blowing into his clenched fist as though it were a trumpet. A similar diabolical little fit of glee is experienced by Akakiy Akakiyevich of *The Overcoat* (*Shinyel'*) when he looks forward to a particularly delicious piece of copying. The famous dumb scene which concludes *The Government Inspector* has overshadowed many others in Gogol's work, particularly in *Dead Souls*. Chichikov and Manilov stare silently at one another for several minutes after Chichikov makes his proposal to purchase dead souls. They stare at one another with tear-filled eyes for a long time before parting and, on meeting again, spend so long in an extended kiss that their teeth ache. A five-minute silence ensues when Chichikov first sits down in Sobakevich's house — Mrs Sobakevich sits without moving eye or eyebrow. There is a two-minute silence during their negotiations for the dead serfs, and another of several minutes' duration occurs when Chichikov first meets Plyushkin. The townsfolk of NN stand rooted to the ground, with eyes bulging like sheep, when they first hear the news of Chichikov's dead souls. Frantic movements and astonished silences are common devices in stage melodrama and yet it is difficult to explain why the cumulative effect here is so eerie. Mann points out that, in folklore, grimaces and facial movements were identified with supernatural forces, a theme which entered romantic literature.[45] There is also perhaps an association between convulsive movements and diabolical possession, or with such phenomena as the legendary Tarantula dance of southern Italy. Static scenes and dumbness are readily associated with fright or paralysis, and one of the consequences of an evil spell in fairy stories is to be struck dumb or rooted to the spot.

Romantic lyricism and treatment of landscape undergo an interesting development in Gogol's later works. Unabashed lyricism of speech is not so evident, but occasionally characters are allowed grotesque flights of rhetoric. Chichikov cleverly adjusts his speech patterns to those of the landowners with whom he is dealing, and his farewell speech to the Manilovs in Chapter 2 is a clever imitation of his host's saccharine style. In his opening speech to Sobakevich he speaks at eloquent length on a number of themes including the vastness and greatness of the Russian Empire. Sobakevich himself grows lyrical on the subject of his dead serfs in Chapter 5, and the public prosecutor's tale of Captain Kopeykin in Chapter 10 is a verbal tour de force. The most exalted lyrical flights are reserved for Gogol himself in the authorial digressions, especially in the *troika* passage of Chapter 11 where he makes his address to Russia,[46] and hints at his own mysterious destiny. *The Overcoat* is a well orchestrated tone poem of assonance, alliteration and euphony where lyricism is weirdly and wonderfully allied to the grotesque subject of Akakiy Akakiyevich and his overcoat.[47]

In *A Terrible Vengeance* Gogol informs us that the forests on the slopes of a hill are not forests but the beard of a wood demon, an appropriate image for a demonic tale. Such extravagant fancies are rarely employed in later works, but landscape and nature still play a symbolic role and adjust themselves to (mainly sinister) themes. The mud-filled desolation and the near-empty church at the conclusion of *The Two Ivans* express the spiritual void of the two title heroes. The deadly boredom of NN and its inhabitants is expressed by the dreary landscape and the tumbledown cottages described during Chichikov's entry into, and his departure from, NN. Whereas some lyrical descriptions in the early tales had been fantasies on the theme of nature, we have now the embellishment of a moral and spiritual theme through which an environment expresses the values of the people who inhabit it. Townscapes too reflect the spiritual values of their dwellers and the demonic confusion of their lives. The Petersburg of Akakiy Akakiyevich, like that of Piskaryov and Poprishchin, is a dream-like town where illusions are stronger than reality, pigs live in houses and dead clerks return in search of their stolen property. It, too, is a geographical desert. As Akakiy returns home from the party:

> Before him stretched deserted streets which are not particularly cheerful in daytime and even less so in the evenings. Now they had become even more God-forsaken and remote: the street lamps began to flicker more seldom — the oil, evidently, had already got low; wooden houses, fences, passed by; not a soul anywhere; only the snow glittered in the streets, and the slumbering shacks with their closed shutters stood out in mournful blackness. He came to a place where the street was intersected by an endless square, with houses scarcely visible on its other side, resembling a terrible desert. In the distance, God knows where, a flame flickered in some watchman's box, apparently standing on the edge of the world. (*Pol. sob.*, III, p. 159)

The living Akakiy is an insignificant mediocrity in this phantom town. Only after his death and bogus resurrection does he assert lively dominion over his surroundings, and the theme of necromancy apparent in Gogol's earlier works assumes a new guise. His post-mortem appearance is the most fantastic or overtly supernatural occurrence of the mature works, and the most frightening. The vengeful ghost, seeking overcoats in a phantasmagoric city, inspires a disquiet which the devils of Dikan'ka fail to do. Pantomime devils, ghosts and spirits, set against the extravagant backcloth of Gogol's Ukraine, are amusing even when designed to be frightening. This spook civil servant is not. Disturbing too are the dead serfs in Chichikov's necromantic drama in Chapter 7 of *Dead Souls*. They have a vigour totally lacking in those who are allegedly alive, as do Sobakevich's dead serfs who come alive in his lyrical flight of Chapter 5. The *real* dead souls of the novel, the landowners and the townsmen, form a pattern of death and decay which reaches a peculiar intensity in Plyushkin. Everything around him shows degeneration and ruin. His peasants' cottages are in disrepair, crops lie rotting on the ground, mould covers his food and dead insects lie in his drink. The garden, a masterpiece of symbolic description, contains living plants and trees being strangled by creepers, and buildings falling into decrepitude. A cold wind blows from his cellar, dust covers the furniture, and the clock, with a spider's web on its pendulum, no longer works.[48]

There is nothing supernatural or ghostly about Plyushkin and his fellow squires and yet they are uncanny and horrible in a manner which surpasses the overtly supernatural and necromantic activities of Gogol's stories.

Illicit sexuality and love which figured discreetly in his early tales can also be read into Gogol's later works by those with eyes to perceive them; but on the whole Gogol is more concerned with moral corruption than with sexual deviation. The hints of incest in *Dikan'ka* are less appalling than peculiarities of love and friendship in later works. The most prominent peculiarity is that love hardly figures at all in Gogol's works, unless it is burlesqued or mocked. The Manilovs have a saccharine relationship in which gooey sentimentality takes the place of love. Chichikov feels the stirrings of a far from disinterested passion for the governor's daughter with a face like a freshly laid egg. Khlestakov's trivial mind sees nothing unusual about making amorous advances to mother and daughter, and such is their mentality that they see nothing strange about a proposal of marriage made to both of them by the same man. Even odder than the absence of love interest is the nonexistence in Gogol's works of genuine, mundane, cordial friendship and affection. Gogol's characters seem to be mainly on terms of hostility, mockery or indifference with one another. There are no 'normal' conversations in his works. People shout, scream, persuade, cajole, coax, bully or threaten. Rarely do they express simple affection or exchange friendly information. Their affections, in any case, are not directed towards people but towards concrete and abstract things. Sobakevich is devoted to food, Plyushkin to money, Korobochka to acquisition and Manilov to his vacuous dreams. Akakiy Akakiyevich, of course, is in love with his coat. Even incest, or castration complexes, have a certain charm in comparison with Gogol's catalogue of strangely directed human affections.

Certain aspects of Gogol's work may be identified with the romantic movement, but in popular and critical parlance to romanticise is to glamorise and make exciting. Attention has been drawn to the alleged idealisation of *Dikan'ka* and *Mirgorod*, as opposed to the squalid realism of later works.[49] This point of view is difficult to accept. Dikan'ka and Mirgorod are glamorised, but not idealised, worlds, because they are hardly ideal places in which to live. Wizards, devils and monsters could be tolerated, but not baggy-trousered, scalp-locked Cossacks with their endless feasting and fun. The Cossack world of *Taras Bul'ba* may be admired for its comradeship, bravery and patriotism,[50] or deplored for its cruelty, savagery and nationalistic bigotry.[51] But even savagery is part of romantic glamour. The glow cast by Scott over the Scottish highlands still makes perfectly sensible people view the history of tribal warfare in that country with keen nostalgia. In similar manner the 'Wild West' is glamorised in film and novel, despite or because of the violence associated with its history. Glamour, however, is not confined only to tales of terror and action, or to stories of the gruesome. There is a putrescent glamour even in tales of boredom and stagnation such as *Old World Landowners* and *The Two Ivans*, or in later works such as *Dead Souls* and *The Overcoat*. Gogol subdues and transmutes the flamboyant elements of romanticism to produce worlds which, in their lyrical grotesqueness, have a baleful splendour. Plyushkin's house and garden, Akakiy's garbage-filled hat, the officials of *The Government Inspector* and the bureaucrats of Petersburg, repel and rivet the attention. They all reflect the glamour of the unbeautiful, and foreshadow the antithesis which in studies of Dostoyevsky would be expressed as the beauty of Sodom in contrast to the beauty of the Madonna. Light and high beauty do not fare well in Gogol's works at the best of times. Chartkov's quest for beauty in *The Portrait* is corrupted by greed. Piskaryov in *Nevsky Prospect* finds that beauty masks sensual and spiritual corruption, and the witch in *Viy* doubles up as a ravishing young beauty and a frightful old hag. Ugliness of body and soul, sourness in human relationships and an absence of spiritual values predominate in Gogol's works, which is remarkable in view of the devotion to goodness, beauty and harmony expressed in his articles. Why should a writer so keen on the good and beautiful[52] be so eager to portray the bad and the ugly in his works? Having considered romantic elements in his works it is now time to consider his personality.

IV

If romanticism represents the triumph of imagination and dream over cold intellect and rationalism, Gogol may be safely reckoned the greatest romantic on the European scene. His works display a fertile imagination and a constant disruption of the logical order. The same powers of imagination may be found in his personal life, and his ability to fantasise (or, bluntly, to lie) has excited the attention of his biographers: his supposedly upside-down stomach, his alleged knowledge of international law, and the lady of wondrous beauty for whose sake he left Russia for a brief period in 1829,[53] to say nothing of the deceptions he practised in literature. His first published work, *Hans Küchelgarten*,[54] was attached to a mendacious preface, and his last, *Selected Passages from a Correspondence with Friends*,[55] contained (apart from some outlandish views) some pretty passages of misinformation.

From early youth Gogol was gripped by a sense of vocation. Fancying himself a poet, historian, philosopher, priest and prophet, he aspired also towards the true and the beautiful, and it is important to understand how compelling and all-embracing his desire for beauty was. As his articles show, he sought beauty in painting, sculpture, music, the divine liturgy,[56] the human soul, and in poetry,[57] but the stronger his ideal, the more terrifying the banal and the vulgar became. While still at school he expresses his distaste for the *sushchestvovateli* of Nezhin, the 'mere existers' devoid of higher ambitions.[58] Like his own Hans Küchelgarten, he was a refugee from the monotony of mundane life which he identified with *poshlost'* but, unlike Hans, Gogol was never reconciled to his former provincial existence.[59] Throughout his life he seemed to be seeking an escape from a world grown dull and trite. While at school he dreamed of a fabulous Petersburg[60] where lofty ambitions of service to State and fellow-countrymen could be fulfilled. A few months in Petersburg left him disillusioned with the civil service. Another vocation, part of his calling as a poet, to teach history, also came to nothing, and creative writing remained the only sphere in which to exercise his mission. Having 'failed' with *The Government Inspector*[61] he set out on a journey abroad to meditate upon his work as an artist, and thus began his years as a wanderer over the face of Europe.

From his ecstatic letters in praise of the city, Gogol seems to have slaked his thirst for beauty in Rome,[62] as indeed did many other romantic writers, but even the glamour of the eternal city failed to satisfy him permanently. He was unfortunate too in his friendships. In his search for communion with beautiful souls he had at least three intense friendships. His letters to Vysotsky from Nezhin express an idealised view of Petersburg and a lofty affection for Vysotsky himself. Their friendship seems to have faded, together with Gogol's ideals of service to the State, after Gogol's arrival in the city. Another friendship, with the poet Nikolay Yazykov, also came to nothing, destroyed, apparently, by the disillusionment of sharing a flat in Rome (Yazykov had a low opinion of Gogol's housekeeping); an example, perhaps, for Gogol of how lofty concepts can be destroyed by mundane details of everyday life. The most intense and poignant of Gogol's friendships was with Iosif Vielgorsky at whose deathbed Gogol kept a long agonising vigil,[63] in a scenario which could well have come from romantic melodrama: an Italian villa, a young handsome nobleman with a beautiful soul dying slowly of consumption, and a distraught writer in attendance. Whether death robbed Gogol of his dearest friend, or merely spared him the disillusionment of seeing that friendship fade in later years, can remain only a subject for speculation. The blow for Gogol can have been no less bitter.

Within the greater quest for fulfilment as a writer, the lesser quests for love and beauty in Gogol's life seem marked for doom. Torn between a vision and the difficulties of its fulfilment, Gogol followed the example of many romantic heroes and took to the road.[64] The wanderer has always had his mystique in literature: Ulysses, pilgrims, crusaders, knights errant and wandering minstrels. In his own wanderings Gogol encapsulates them all. Dismayed by the uproar over *The Government Inspector*, he wrote letters of farewell which recall Childe Harold's departure from Albion. He tells Pogodin he is going abroad to shake off his melancholy and to ponder his duties as a writer.[65] Nearly a year later Gogol again writes in Byronic terms having cast himself in the role of wandering exile: he is homeless, the waves beat and rock him, and he can rely only on the anchor of pride which 'higher powers' have placed in his breast. It is not in his native land, he prophesies wrongly, that he is to die.[66] All this is the stuff of romantic, particularly Byronic, heroism and the suspicion arises that Gogol was not unaware of the similarities. As his wanderings continue, Gogol complains ever more frequently of the 'romantic' maladies of hypochondria and melancholy.[67] Outbreaks of despair alternate with boastfulness until, like a latter-day Melmoth, he almost becomes a demonic figure. And like Melmoth,[68] Gogol wandered with an uneasy conscience for reasons which become apparent as he struggles with the second part of *Dead Souls*.

In 1836, the year of *The Government Inspector* and of his self-imposed exile, Gogol had renounced supernatural and preposterous plots while visualising a great writer of inspired tranquillity who would turn what was romantic into something classic, and come forth with a graphic, clear, majestic creation. Clearly he had cast himself for this role, and the chosen creation would be his new work *Dead Souls*.[69] In renouncing the more flamboyant elements of romanticism Gogol still retained romantic ideas about the function of the poet which were fortified by his religious convictions. It would be a hopeless task to establish in what proportions religion and romantic aesthetics were responsible for his artistic development, but they undoubtedly complemented one another from early years. In 1827 Gogol informs his mother that he is proving his strength for an important noble task to the benefit of the fatherland and of its citizens. His soul appears to see a divine angel pointing to a goal which is constantly being sought.[70] In 1833 he again tells his mother that he would like to assist those who speak of virtue and of God, but few of them possess sufficiently bright and natural minds to see the truth of his words.[71] This less than modest assertion casts an ominous light on Gogol's application to himself of Christ's words, that a prophet is without honour in his own country.[72] His mission to preach and teach was apparent, to himself at least, even as a young man, and so his later bizarre letters to friends in which he claims divine authority for assigning them strange tasks, or giving them spiritual advice, are not the consequence of a new development in his character.[73] They are simply another manifestation of an old trait.

The concept of the prophet-poet is much more ancient than the European romantic movement. In the courts of the Old Testament kings, prophets played an important part and they were often poets in their own right.[74] Their prophecy was not a magical foreseeing of the future but a moral and political commentary on the present. When Gogol in *Al Mamoun* (1835) and in *On the Lyricism of our Poets* (1847) writes of the duties of the poet in relation to the monarch and the nation, he is drawing as much on an ancient Jewish-Christian tradition as on the creed of romanticism.

Another feature of Christianity, especially in eastern Orthodoxy, may be discerned in Gogol's conduct. As he grows more absorbed in the writing of *Dead Souls* he speaks and writes increasingly of the need to withdraw from society and to be free of worldly care. This aspiration reaches its climax when Gogol seriously suggests to three of his friends that they support him financially for three or four years so that he can devote himself to his inspired work.[75] The idea of withdrawing from society in order to be useful to it at a later date is deeply rooted in the Orthodox tradition of the *starets* or elder, who retires to a monastic cell, desert or forest and, on his return to the outside world, gives spiritual counsel.[76] Often the elder has gifts of discernment and prophecy and can read the souls and hearts of men, all virtues which Gogol claimed for the poet in general, and for himself in particular.[77]

The moral purpose of literature had been plain to Gogol from his early years, and was inextricably bound up with aesthetic values. To be moral, in Gogol's view, was to be beautiful. If these ideas were derived from romanticism the religious convictions turned an aesthetic problem into a crisis of the soul. Dualism was second nature to Gogol, and to romantics in general, but an important role in his downfall was played by his dual vision of Russia. In 1836 he writes to Pogodin about 'disgusting mugs' to be found in Russia (by which he means the vulgar types and the 'mere existers'), and makes a distinction between *Rus'*, the poetic, archaic name for Russia, and Russia itself. *Rus'* remains in Gogol's heart, not the nasty Russia but the beautiful Russia of

Zhukovsky, himself, and a few others with beautiful souls and true taste.[78] The authorial digressions in *Dead Souls*, and many statements in various letters, make it plain that the novel is ultimately to portray the spiritual and noble aspects of the Russian nation. The Russian people, Gogol declares in 1849, are more capable than others of taking in the lofty words of the Gospels which lead to the perfection of men.[79] In 1850 he tells Perovsky that he wishes to display what is healthy and strong in his country and to shame those who have neglected the great powers given to Russia.[80] It is clear too that Gogol's quest for a beautiful and holy Russia was closely connected with the task of perfecting his own soul.[81] But even a reader who shares Gogol's general Christian faith must wonder whether this preoccupation with his own spiritual state represents a genuine thirst for perfection or a passion for self-advertisement. When Old Testament prophets describe the moment of their 'calling' and speak as emissaries of Jahweh,[82] there is a humility about them which makes their bold claims bearable. Pushkin, in his poem *Exegi Monumentum*, makes claims for himself which, from most other men, would be intolerable conceit, whereas, coming from him, they sound like a justifiable statement of self-knowledge. None of Gogol's claims inspires confidence. When he informs Zhukovsky in June 1842 that a deep, irresistible faith lives within his (Gogol's) soul, and that heavenly power will help him ascend the ladder which stands before him (although he is standing only on its first and lowest steps), Gogol seems to be boasting of future triumphs rather than outlining a plan of spiritual endeavour. His soul, he claims, must be purer than celestial snow and more radiant than the heavens before he has the power to perform heroic deeds and his great task; only then will the riddle of his existence be solved.[83] In July 1844 he informs Yazykov that the writing of *Dead Souls* is difficult because its subject and matter are linked with his own internal education.[84]

Gogol's predicament was a nasty one. The confusion of aesthetic and moral values has an inexorable logic. If good art is produced only by a morally good artist, it follows that 'bad' art must be the result of moral badness in the artist. In *The Portrait* the old monk in the second half of the tale was deemed a good painter because of his own sanctity and the holiness of the subjects he painted.[85] The idea was hardly new in Russian criticism. In 1793 Karamzin had bluntly stated that a morally bad man could not be a good author[86] and, significantly enough, it is Karamzin whom Gogol cites as a virtuous writer in 1846. He was in Gogol's view endowed with a beautiful harmonious soul, pure aspirations and love of man. With such qualities as Karamzin's one could boldly speak the truth.[87] The pure, Karamzinian, type of author stands in contrast to the disordered, proud and isolated Byronic type of writer whom Gogol had condemned in 1836. Only a brief acquaintance with

Gogol's biography is needed to realise that Gogol's personality had much more in common with the latter than with the former, and it is probable that Gogol was aware of this dismal fact too. He claims to have portrayed his own vices in the figures of *Dead Souls*,[88] and indeed it is easy to find correspondence between the landowners and aspects of Gogol's character,[89] but this is scarcely surprising, for the vices of the landowners are quintessential and can be found in *anybody*, not just in Gogol. Gogol's vaunting of his sinfulness seems as boastful as his prophecies of future purity. Hegelian self-regeneration, if Gogol had even heard of it, became an elaborate and lengthy act of Christian self-purification after which he would, he thought, be in a position to portray a purified Chichikov and a regenerated Russia. The magnitude of the task was daunting, largely because his own, truly inspired talent, was to portray the low and ugly rather than the high and beautiful. Only the demonic 'mere existers' flourished under his pen, among his enemies and, unkindest blow of all, among his supporters. No wonder he professed himself overwhelmed by the darkness of the human soul, and as the gap between his vision and reality became wider, his letters sometimes reflect the dualism in an unconsciously comic manner. Lofty thoughts on the divine alternate with complaints about money and the state of his bowels. A devotion to things of the spirit coexists with a healthy interest in stomach and food. There is a note of despair in his reflections on Easter Sunday as he indicates the discrepancy between the meaning of Christ's resurrection and man's reaction to Easter.[90]

It seems that Gogol ascribed his inability to redeem Chichikov to his own sinfulness, and hence the penitential acts, the pilgrimages and the final bout of fasting. Not only had he to adjust his art to his faith but he had problems about the faith itself. Writing of his own weaknesses and vices in 1848 he claims to acknowledge Christ as the God-Man only because his intellect orders him to do so. He has no faith, but he wants to believe.[91] This uncertainty betrays itself in a number of ways. The suspect optimism expressed in his letters reveals a neurotic hope for future glory rather than a deep-seated conviction of its attainment.[92] In his creative works there are no supernatural powers for good and the Church is powerless against evil forces, whether overtly supernatural as in *Viy* or 'psychological' as in *The Two Ivans*. Another curious feature is the death or punishment of innocent people. In *A Terrible Vengeance* a curse passes down from generation to generation so that many people have to bear a terrible punishment for the sin of an ancestor. Foma Brut is killed by the Viy because he had a chance encounter with a witch. Repentance and forgiveness are absent or ineffective. Stender-Petersen, puzzled by all this, asserts that the idea of an avenging God bringing down wrath upon the innocent is at variance with the Christian doctrine of the Orthodox Church.[93] The point is interesting and requires further scrutiny. Stender-Petersen overlooked the doctrine of the Fall which, in its various theological interpretations, assumes ancestral guilt. The sin of Adam has its effect on all his descendants, weakening man's will and diminishing his ability to respond to divine grace. The Old Testament contains a solemn assurance that the sins of the fathers will be visited upon the children,[94] and only in later Old Testament thought is the doctrine of individual responsibility developed.[95] The Orthodox Church, on the whole, takes a less gloomy view of the Fall than western theology and emphasises the continued existence of man's free will to choose good or evil. The western Church, following Augustine and Anselm, has been sceptical of man's ability to choose for himself, and places more emphasis on the action of divine grace without which man can have no salvation.[96] In some schools of Protestant thought, following Luther and Calvin, this has led to a belief in predestination, both of the damned and the elect. Salvation can be achieved only through God's grace, and so if God chooses to withhold it, a soul is inevitably doomed.

More research is needed into the theological sources of Gogol's thinking. We do know that he had been reared with a fear of death and judgment, and his obliging mother had painted him lurid pictures of tortures meted out to the damned.[97] His long sojourn in Rome may well have exerted some influence on Gogol's theology, and some of his friends certainly entertained the suspicion that he might become a convert to the Roman Church. In 1847, however, he assures Shevyryov that he came to Christ by the Protestant, not the Catholic path.[98] Childhood experience and the general influence of a western or westernised theology[99] might have shaped his ideas on divine vengeance to produce his constant fear of the devil, an awareness tinged with pride of his own sinfulness and apparent doubts about his own salvation. Did he perhaps feel himself in an involuntary league with the Devil, denied God's grace and therefore damned? *Dead Souls* seems to have been his attempt to mock and exorcise the demons who personified his own vices. The characters in it are not glamorous Lucifer types whose evil has a dignified splendour. They are *poshlyaki*, vulgar, trivial little nonentities, forerunners of the shabby little devil who haunts Ivan Karamazov, living lives of subhuman mediocrity.[100] Unfortunately, like Byron's Manfred, Gogol had summoned evil spirits who would not go away but haunted him until his death. His letters and behaviour of his final years indicate an agony of soul which few romantic heroes of literature had had to endure. If, as biographers claim, Gogol did call for a ladder on his deathbed, was he thinking of the ladder he had mentioned to Zhukovsky in 1842, signifying his spiritual aspirations? Or did he have in mind Jacob's ladder, or perhaps the ladder mentioned by Levko in *A May Night* which the angels let down from heaven before Easter Sunday so that God may descend and banish evil spirits from the earth?

There is much in Gogol's works which conforms to the general pattern of European romanticism. The revolt against rationalism is seen in the fertility of his imagination and in the supernatural irrational qualities of his plot and characters. In such works as *Diary of a Madman, Nevsky Prospect* and *The Nose* he explored unconscious regions of the mind, and showed an interest, characteristic of romanticism, in dream and hallucination. Romantics laid great stress on the peculiarities and singularities of groups as well as of individuals which led, according to Schenk, to an interest in minority races, communities and languages.[101] Nostalgia for the past, particularly for the Middle Ages, was a common feature of European romanticism. Gogol in his *Taras Bul'ba* and in his lecture on the Middle Ages follows both these trends. Romantic philosophers of history, particularly Friedrich Schlegel, dealt with the problem of evil, a question ignored by the Enlightenment. Gogol's works are devoted to it.

Despite these similarities, one hesitates to label Gogol's works as definitively romantic. After all, fervent arguments have been made for his position as the founder of Russian realism. He was a slippery person and labels have a tendency to come unstuck. Undeniably he borrowed certain themes and incidents from romantic authors, but we have no proof that without these influences his work would have been all that different. His own temperament, his character, the peculiarities of his upbringing and his religious views have to be taken into account as well. Only a rash critic would state categorically which aspects of Gogol's works derive from the 'age' and which from his own peculiar individual talent and personality.

Ultimately it is Gogol's character rather than his works which has the romantic aura. Schenk draws attention to the preoccupation of romantic philosophers and writers, and their heroes, with themselves.[102] They were often puzzled by the mysteries of the universe and their own place within it. Some sought salvation in religion and, like Leopardi and Lamennais, fell into scepticism. Others accepted the Christian tradition and, like Newman, found refuge in the Roman Church. Introspection, misanthropy, a quest for solitude and the search for the soul mark the heroes of Byron, Chateaubriand and Constant. Some sought escape in nature, in past civilisations, in frantic travelling or in suicide. Romantic love, the perfectly harmonious union between man and woman, a lofty emotion of spiritual love and a feeling of religious fulfilment, was one source of consolation to many of them.[103] Romantic friendship, intense, idealistic and emotional, was another. It is easy to identify Gogol's own life and personality with these general traits: the riddle of his own existence, religious faith and doubt, his love of nature, his fascination with past civilisations, frantic travelling and (depending on one's view of his final fast) even suicide. Romantic love, lacking in practice, was present in theory. The mysterious lady of 1829 and his pronouncements in the article *Woman* indicate a desire to follow the formula of romantic love, even if he could not, or would not, put it into practice himself. Romantic friendships are very much in evidence. Like many romantic heroes Gogol was paradoxical, elusive and, as all his biographers complain, unfathomable. Above all there was about his personality (despite the humorous and grotesque elements in it) something decidedly sinister. Burdened by a prophetic vocation he could not fulfil, tormented by ideals of good and visions of evil, devoted to beauty but attracted to ugliness, a would-be saint but a self-confessed sinner, Gogol was torn asunder. Physical suffering, always present in life, attended his death, the horrors of which are curiously similar to those endured by Byron at the hands of his doctors.[104] A wanderer, a refugee from his own dark mind, striving to be humble yet filled with pride, a comic writer filled with spleen, melancholia and hypochrondria, Gogol has considerable claim to be reckoned a romantic hero.

Notes

1. 'O poezii klassicheskoy i romanticheskoy', A. S. Pushkin, *Polnoye sobraniye sochinyeniy*, 10 vols, AN SSSR (Akademiya Nauk SSSR), Moscow, 1964, VII, pp. 32—6 (hereafter Pushkin, *Pol. sob.*).
2. See V. Zelinsky, *Russkaya kriticheskaya literatura o proizvedeniyakh A. S. Pushkina*, Moscow, 1887, pp. 1—86, where contemporary reviews of Pushkin's poems are reproduced.
3. Ibid., pp. 137—71. Vyazemsky had written a foreword to Pushkin's *Bakhchisarayskiy fontan*, in which he vigorously attacked the classicists. M. Dmitriyev (nephew of I. I. Dmitriyev the fabulist) replied to Vyazemsky in *Vestnik Yevropy*. The argument dragged on for a long time in various periodicals, and might well have been followed by Gogol in Nezhin.
4. P. A. Vyazemsky, *Polnoye sobraniye sochinyeniy*, 12 vols, St Petersburg, 1878, I, p. 75. Vyazemsky wrote this, and other rueful comments on his younger self, in 1876 at the age of 83.
5. He wrote an excellent defence of Gogol's *The Government Inspector* in Pushkin's *Sovremennik*, St Petersburg, 1836, II, pp. 285—309. For a fuller account see T. E. Little, 'P. A. Vyazemsky as a Critic of Gogol' (*New Zealand Slavonic Journal*, 1, 1978, pp. 47—58).
6. Most studies of Gogol deal to some extent with his romanticism. See V. Gippius, *Gogol*, Leningrad, 1924; Vsevolod Setchkarev, *Gogol: His Life and Works*, tr. Robert Kramer, London, 1965; Victor Erlich, *Gogol*, New Haven and Yale, 1969; Prof. V. Zen'kovsky, *N. V. Gogol*, Paris, 1961. Some interesting articles are: Adolph Stender-Petersen, 'Gogol und die deutsche Romantik' (*Euphorion*, XXIV, Leipzig-Vienna, 1922, pp. 628—53); James M. Holquist, 'The Devil in Mufti: The Märchenwelt in Gogol's Short Stories' (*Proceedings of the Modern Languages Association*, LXXXII, 1967), pp. 352—62; Yu. V. Mann, 'Evolyutsiya gogolyevskoy fantastiki' in *K istorii russkogo romantizma*, Moscow, 1973, pp. 219—58, and N. L. Stepanov, 'Romanticheskiy mir Gogolya', ibid., pp. 188—218. See also L. G. Leighton, *Russian Romanticism: Two essays*, The Hague, 1975, and I. V. Kartashova, 'Gogol' i Romantizm' in *Russkiy romantizm*, ed. K. N. Grigoryan, Leningrad, 1978, pp. 58—79.
7. Carl R. Proffer, 'Gogol's definition of Romanticism' (*Studies in Romanticism*, VI, 2, Winter 1967, pp. 120—7).
8. N. V. Gogol, *Polnoye sobraniye sochinyeniy*, 14 vols, AN SSSR, Moscow, 1952, VIII, pp. 550—64 (hereafter *Pol. sob.*).
9. *Pol. sob.*, VIII, pp. 153—5.
10. Vyazemsky to Turgenev, 2 November 1819, complains of the absence of national colour from Russian poetry and coins the word *narodnost'* to express the concept of a national ethos in literature. (*Ostaf'yevskiy arkhiv knyazey Vyazemskikh*, 5 vols, St Petersburg, 1899—1913, I, p. 357). Pushkin too complained in 1824 that Russians have gained all their knowledge and concepts from foreign books (Pushkin, *Pol. sob.*, VII, p. 18). See also the three articles by Orest Somov, 'O romanticheskoy poezii', *Trudy vol'nogo obshchestva lyubitelyey rossiyskoy slovesnosti*, St Petersburg, 1823, 23, pp. 43—59, 151—69, 263—306; 24, pp. 125—47.
11. *Pol. sob.*, VIII, pp. 143—7.

12. Ibid., pp. 148—52.
13. Ibid., pp. 9—13.
14. Ibid., pp. 14—25.
15. Ibid., pp. 50—5.
16. Ibid., pp. 76—81.
17. Isaiah Berlin, *Russian Thinkers*, Harmondsworth, 1978, pp. 137—43.
18. See Zen'kovsky, op. cit., p. 20.
19. Donald Fanger draws attention to this in the first chapter of his book, *The Creation of Nikolai Gogol*, Harvard, 1979.
20. Pushkin, *Pol. sob.*, II, p. 338.
21. Arguments against censorship of the arts in England often seem to be based not so much on a concept of freedom as on an assumption that art has no influence for good or ill anyway. Small wonder that the 'necessity' for art is questioned.
22. Schenk considers that romanticism and the French Revolution began at the same time, and that both marked the eruption of the irrational. It was Rousseau who began the reaction against detached objectivity (H. G. Schenk, *The Mind of the European Romantics*, London, 1966, pp. 3—4).
23. *The Portrait, Nevsky Prospect* and *Diary of a Madman* were published in *Arabesques*, 1835. *Evenings on a Farm near Dikan'ka* was published in two parts, 1831—2, and comprise the following stories: *Sorochinsky Fair, St John's Eve, A May Night or the Drowned Maiden, The Lost Letter; The Night before Christmas, A Terrible Vengeance, Ivan Fyodorovich Shpon'ka and his Aunty, The Bewitched Place. Mirgorod*, published in 1835, comprises *Old World Landowners, Taras Bul'ba, Viy* and *How Ivan Ivanovich Quarrelled with Ivan Nikiforovich* (*Pol. sob.*, I—II). The three stories from *Arabesques* are in *Pol. sob.*, III, together with *The Overcoat* and *The Nose. The Government Inspector, Pol. sob.*, IV, *Dead Souls, Pol. sob.*, VI—VII.
24. Vsevolod Setchkarev, op. cit., p. 96. See also Victor Erlich, op. cit., p. 41.
25. See Gogol's article in *Arabesques: On Ukrainian Songs*. The themes and motifs outlined by him may be found in his works, particularly *Taras Bul'ba*. See also Setchkarev, op. cit., pp. 100—1.
26. Mochul'sky considers *Viy* to be the most erotic of Gogol's works, the beauty of the witch being the 'terrible beauty' of Sodom (K. Mochul'sky, *Dukhovnyy put' Gogolya*, Paris, 1934, pp. 28—9). Castration complexes and anal fixations figure prominently in interpretations of *The Nose*. See Ivan Yermakov, 'The Nose' in *Gogol from the Twentieth Century*, ed. Robert A. Maguire, Princeton, 1974, pp. 156—98. See also Natalia Kolb-Seletski, 'Gastronomy, Gogol and his Fiction' (*Slavic Review*, XXIX, 1, 1970, pp. 35—57), in which it is alleged that food is Gogol's substitute for sex.
27. Mario Praz, *The Romantic Agony*, London, 1933.
28. See Adolph Stender-Petersen, op. cit., passim.
29. Karlinsky points out that the *Dikan'ka* tales owe a great deal to western romantic opera. *St John's Eve* is closer to Weber's opera *Der Freischütz* than to Tieck's tale. (Simon Karlinsky, *The Sexual Labyrinth of Nikolai Gogol*, Harvard, 1976, p. 33).
30. V. Sipovsky, 'Pushkin i Romantizm' in *Pushkin i yego sovremenniki*, Petrograd, 1916, XXIII—XXIV, pp. 231—4.

31. See Zen'kovsky, op. cit., p. 62; Stender-Petersen, op. cit., p. 632; Stepanov, op. cit., p. 192.
32. See Paul Debreczeny, 'Nikolai Gogol and his Contemporary Critics' (*Transactions of the American Philosophical Society*, April 1966, p. 6).
33. See Gippius, op. cit., p. 30.
34. *Narodnost'* was often conceived in terms of 'feeling' or 'soul'. Madame de Staël had written '. . . mais il faut surtout que leurs écrivains (the Russians) puisent la poésie dans ce qu'ils ont de plus intime au fond de l'âme': *Dix années d'exil*, ed. Paul Gautier, Paris, 1904, pp. 314—15. This book exerted considerable influence on Russian romantics. Pushkin praised it (Pushkin, *Pol. sob.*, VII, pp. 22—6), and it helped foster an emotional rather than intellectual response to national ethos.
35. Gippius, op. cit., p. 71. Gogol confused the fifteenth, sixteenth and seventeenth centuries of Cossack history.
36. A similar observation might be made of the Arthurian legends and their treatment in English literature. T. H. White's *The Once and Future King* can scarcely lay claim to historical accuracy, and yet in style and atmosphere it is very British. The first part ('The Sword in the Stone') presents a Britain as the British would like it to have been rather than as it was. Gogol does much the same for his native Ukraine. See Gippius, op. cit., p. 28, for his comments.
37. Vyazemsky, op. cit., II, p. 315.
38. Richard Peace, 'Gogol's Old World Landowners' (*Slavonic and East European Review*, LIII, 133, 1975, pp. 504—20).
39. Yu. Mann, op. cit., p. 230.
40. Yu. Mann (op. cit., passim) speaks of non-fantastic fantasy in Gogol's works. It is interesting to speculate whether a fantastic explanation for a fantastic event is more or less 'realistic' than no explanation at all. If a fairy godmother uses magic to turn a pumpkin into a coach we do, at least, have the workings of cause and effect. If the pumpkin changes without any 'magic' we have a causeless effect which is much more fantastic.
41. Victor Erlich, op. cit., p. 30, points out that in the topsy-turvy world of Gogol's Ukrainian folk tales anything or almost anything can and does happen. Laws of nature are kicked around, fundamental distinctions between the human and subhuman, the whole and the part, the animate and the inanimate are disregarded. It is less often realised that much the same things go on in *Dead Souls* but in a more subtle and much weirder manner.
42. Among modern British writers, Mervyn Peake (1911—68) has a strong affinity with Gogol and uses similar techniques. See T. E. Little, 'Mervyn Peake and Nikolai Gogol' (*Essays in Poetics*, III, 2, September 1978, pp. 87—104).
43. A. Slonimsky, *Tekhnika komicheskogo u Gogolya*, Petrograd, 1923, devotes considerable attention to Gogol's use of illogic.
44. Nabokov points out that this is a parody of the Lacedaemonian girls dancing in Aristophanes' *Lysistrata* (Vladimir Nabokov, *Nikolay Gogol*, London, 1973, p. 71).
45. Yu. Mann, op. cit., p. 254.
46. 'Russia! What do you desire of me? . . . Why do you thus gaze upon me, and why does everything within you turn to me with eyes full of expectation?'

47. 'So to sum up: the story goes this way: mumble, mumble, lyrical wave, mumble, lyrical wave, mumble, lyrical wave, mumble, fantastic climax, mumble, mumble, and back into the chaos from which they all had derived. At this superhigh level of art, literature is of course not concerned with pitying the underdog or cursing the upperdog. It appeals to that secret depth of the human soul where the shadows of other worlds pass like the shadows of nameless and soundless ships' (Vladimir Nabokov, op. cit., p. 149).

48. For the dead, as Proffer observes, there is no time (Carl Proffer, *The Simile and Gogol's 'Dead Souls'*, The Hague, 1967, p. 115).

49. Gippius, op. cit., p. 22.

50. *Dikan'ka* and *Taras Bul'ba* express the romantic ideal of union and unity. Gogol's heroes live according to the unwritten laws of national collectivism, the laws of friendship, mutual support and help (I. V. Kartashova, op. cit., p. 63–4).

51. Karlinsky dwells on the violence and savagery of the Sech in *Taras Bul'ba* (Karlinsky, op. cit., pp. 77–86).

52. Gogol to his mother, 6 April 1827, speaks of satisfying his thirst to see and feel the beautiful (*Pol. sob.*, X, p. 91). To Zhukovsky, 15 June 1848, Gogol describes himself and Zhukovsky as having remained true to the beautiful (Ibid., XIV, p. 74).

53. Gogol's letter to his mother, 24 July 1829 (*Pol. sob.*, X, pp. 145–51), explaining that he left Russia on account of a mysterious female divinity, is famous in Gogolian studies as an example of Gogol's mendacity. Gippius (op. cit., p. 24) thinks Gogol was not lying but merely exaggerating. Gogol's description of his mysterious lady closely resembles the description of women as the artistic idea in his article *Woman*. Perhaps, therefore, Gogol was not lying to his mother but in his own peculiar muddled way was trying to express in terms she might understand the agonies of an artistic crisis. He had just burnt all copies of the disastrous *Hans Küchelgarten*.

54. *Pol. sob.*, I, pp. 61–100. The preface is on p. 60. In it 'the publishers' (Gogol published the work at his own expense) state that they are proud to have the opportunity of acquainting the public with the creation of a new young talent. The poem was published under the *nom de plume* 'V. Alov'.

55. Published 1847 (*Pol. sob.*, VIII, pp. 213–418). In letter no. 10, *On the lyricism of our Poets*, Gogol claims that Pushkin's poem, 'S Gomerom dolgo ty besedoval . . .' (Pushkin, *Pol. sob.*, III, p. 238), was addressed to Nicholas I, and that Pushkin was comparing that monarch to Moses. The poem was in fact addressed to N. I. Gnedich. To assist his deception Gogol omits the last eight lines of the poem.

56. Gogol's commentary on the divine liturgy owes much to a fourteenth-century work by Nicholas Cabasilas, *A Commentary on the Divine Liturgy*, London, 1977; for Gogol's commentary in English, see Rosemary Edmonds (tr.), N. V. Gogol, *The Divine Liturgy*, London, 1960.

57. In his *Textbook of literature for Russian Youth* (*Pol. sob.*, VIII, pp. 468–88), he pronounces beauty to be the wellspring of poetry ('rodnik poezii yest' krasota').

58. See Gogol to G. I. Vysotsky, 26 June 1827. The occupants of the school have crushed the high destiny of man by the crust of their worthless complacency

(*Pol. sob.*, X, p. 98). The *zemnost'* which Gogol attributes to his schoolmates stands in contrast to the vague, lofty and heavenly aspirations he saw in himself. Dualism, whether derived from romanticism or from his own temperament, was evident in Gogol from early years. See Gippius, op. cit., p. 9.

59. Biographers have rightly identified Hans with Gogol himself, but there are strong literary affinities too. Hans setting off on a journey to classical countries recalls many a Byronic hero. The delightful skeleton who fastidiously brushes dust from his bones echoes the graveyard romanticism imported into Russia by Zhukovsky. The disillusionment of the wanderer is reminiscent of Chateaubriand's René. Apart from his brief flight to Germany in 1829 Gogol's wanderings were to start in earnest in 1836.

60. See Gogol to his mother, 26 February 1827 (*Pol. sob.*, X, p. 83), and his letter to Vysotsky, quoted in n. 58.

61. The 'failure' seemed to consist in the public's refusal to be reformed or uplifted by the play's message. To M. S. Shchepkin, 29 April 1836, he complains that all classes are rising against him because of his expression of 'a phantom of truth' (*Pol. sob.*, XI, p. 38). To Zhukovsky, 10 January 1848, he writes that *The Government Inspector* was the first work he wrote with the aim of exerting a good influence on society, and it was unsuccessful (*Pol. sob.*, XIV, p. 34).

62. 'God, God, God! Oh my Rome. My beautiful marvellous Rome!' (Gogol to P. A. Pletnyov, 27 September 1839, *Pol. sob.*, XI, p. 255). See also Gogol to A. S. Danilevsky, 2 February 1838, ibid., p. 121: 'Oh Italy! Whose hand will tear me away from here!' In a letter to M. P. Balabina, April 1838, he expresses the interesting wish to turn into a nose and savour the smells of Rome (ibid., p. 144). Rome was praised by innumerable romantic poets. See Byron's *Childe Harold*, canto IV, stanza 27.

63. The vigil is described in *Nights at a Villa, Pol. sob.*, III, pp. 324–6. Gogol's friendships have been dealt with in some detail by Karlinsky who is convinced that Gogol's relationship with these men was homosexual. Even if the hypothesis is true it does not alter Gogol's idealistic, intense and visionary concept of friendship which matches Schenk's description of romantic friendship (Schenk, op. cit., pp. 152–9).

64. The road restored Gogol's equanimity and was also a source of inspiration. See his letters to S. T. Aksakov, 5 and 13 March 1841, *Pol. sob.*, XI, p. 330 and p. 332.

65. Gogol to M. P. Pogodin, 10 May 1836, *Pol. sob.*, XI, p. 41.

66. Gogol to M. P. Pogodin, 30 March 1837, *Pol. sob.*, XI, p. 92. See n. 77.

67. Gogol to Pogodin, 10 May 1836, wishes to shake off his melancholy (*toska*) by going abroad (*Pol. sob.*, XI, p. 41). See also to Pogodin, 15 May 1836 (ibid., p. 46). To N. Ya. Prokopovich, 19 September 1837 (N.S.), he writes: 'I fear the hypochondria which chases at my heels' (ibid., p. 110). To N. M. Yazykov, 10 February 1842: 'I am tormented by society and assailed by melancholy' (ibid., XII, p. 34). Nabokov points out that French literature of the eighteenth and early nineteenth centuries is full of restless young characters suffering from the spleen (or *ennui*). It was a convenient device to keep the hero on the move. 'Byron endowed it with a new thrill: René, Adolphe,

Oberman and their cosufferers received a transfusion of daemon blood' (Vladimir Nabokov, *Eugene Onegin*, London, 1964, II, p. 152). Pushkin gently mocks the theme in *Eugene Onegin* I, 38. In Gogol's case life seems intent on imitating literature.

68. C. R. Maturin, *Melmoth the Wanderer*, 4 vols, Edinburgh, 1820. The title hero of this work has sold his soul to the devil.

69. Gogol's expectation of a clear, graphic and majestic creation, expressed in 1836, is expressed in similar terms to his hopes for the continuation of *Dead Souls*. See, for example, his letter to S. T. Aksakov, 28 December 1840, in which he claims that 'the continuation (of *Dead Souls*) is being elucidated more clearly and more majestically in my mind, and now I see that, in time, it may be something colossal, if only my weak powers permit' (*Pol. sob.*, XI, p. 322). In 1841 he declares his work to be great and a way to salvation (ibid., p. 332), and in 1842 he tells Pletnyov that the first part of *Dead Souls* is merely the entrance porch to the palace which is being built within himself (ibid., XII, p. 46).

70. Gogol to Mother, 24 March 1827 (*Pol. sob.*, X, p. 90).

71. Gogol to Mother, 2 October 1833 (*Pol. sob.*, X, p. 283).

72. Gogol to Pogodin, 10 May 1836: 'Proroku net slavy v otchizne' (*Pol. sob.*, XI, p. 41). This, of course, was written as Gogol was preparing to leave Russia. See Luke 4:24.

73. To A. S. Danilevsky, 7 August 1841, Gogol writes that his friend should occupy himself with his estate for a year: 'O believe my words! My word from henceforth is invested with a higher power. Everything else may disappoint, deceive, betray you, but my word shall not betray' (*Pol. sob.*, XI, p. 343). Gogol's pronouncement is disturbingly parallel to the words of Christ in Matthew 24:36.

His most quoted piece of divinely inspired advice occurs in a letter addressed collectively to S. T. Aksakov, M. P. Pogodin and S. P. Shevyryov, January 1844, in which he gives them detailed instructions to read *The Imitation of Christ* (*Pol. sob.*, XII, pp. 249–50).

74. Gogol to Pogodin, 28 December 1840, writes: 'Be comforted! Marvellously merciful and great is God' (*Pol. sob.*, XI, p. 325), which in tone and content resembles the opening verse of Isaiah 40 in which Jahweh, through the prophet, gives words of comfort to Israel.

75. Gogol to S. P. Shevyryov, 28 February 1843, *Pol. sob.*, XII, p. 145. The friends in question were Shevyryov himself, Pogodin and S. T. Aksakov, 'Your letters will be even more important and significant for me when I shall remain alone and seek a desert, and isolation from everything, for profound education, for the spiritual education which is being completed within me by the holy, wonderful will of our heavenly father' (ibid., p. 148). To an unknown correspondent, July 1842, Gogol writes: '. . . I have moved far away from society to educate myself in the depth of my soul for others, and my education is far from finished' (ibid., p. 82).

76. '. . . he (the elder) receives no special ordination or appointment to the work of eldership, but is guided to it by the direct inspiration of the Spirit. The elder sees in a concrete and practical way what the will of God is in relation to each person who comes to consult him . . .' (Timothy Ware, *The Orthodox*

Church, Harmondsworth, 1975, pp. 47–8). Father Zossima of Dostoyevsky's *The Brothers Karamazov* is the most famous literary portrait of an elder. Gogol was rather apt to hand out spiritual advice to those who did not ask for it.

77. He writes to Pletnyov, 27 September 1839, that he had a premonition of the death of Pletnyov's wife. His premonitions, Gogol assures his friend, are always accurate. He hints at another premonition which has not yet been fulfilled, but admits that he had had no premonition of Pushkin's death (*Pol. sob.*, XI, pp. 254–5).

78. Gogol to Pogodin, 22/10 September 1836 (*Pol. sob.*, XI, p. 60).

79. Gogol to A. M. V'elgorskaya, 30 March 1849 (*Pol. sob.*, XIV, p. 109).

80. Gogol to A. Perovsky and others, 1–18 July 1850 (*Pol. sob.*, XIV, p. 279).

81. In a letter to the monk Filaret, 19 June 1850, Gogol asks the monk to pray for a writer who dares write about 'the holy and the beautiful' (*Pol. sob.*, XIV, p. 191).

82. See Isaiah 6, part of which Pushkin uses as material for his poem *The Prophet*; and the first chapter of Jeremiah.

83. *Pol. sob.*, XII, p. 69.

84. 'I go ahead, the work progresses too; I come to a halt, so does the work' (*Pol. sob.*, XII, 14 July 1844, p. 332).

85. In several letters Gogol speaks of himself as a monk, a theme closely linked with that of the elder: 'I need solitude, definite solitude . . . with every day and hour I feel there is no higher fate on earth than the vocation of a monk' (*Pol. sob.*, XII, p. 34). In the theology of the Eastern Church, the faith and holiness of the icon painter is of prime importance.

86. N. Karamzin, *Izbrannyye sochinyeniya*, Moscow-Leningrad, 1964, II, p. 122.

87. Gogol to N. M. Yazykov, 5 May 1846, *Pol. sob.*, XIII, p. 62.

88. *Pol. sob.*, VIII, p. 293.

89. Like Sobakevich, Gogol was a glutton and, like Nozdryov, a liar. Gogol's appropriation of his mother's money in 1829, and some of his financial dealings afterwards, are somewhat Chichikovian.

90. 'Easter Sunday', letter 32 of *Selected Passages from a Correspondence with Friends*, *Pol. sob.*, VIII, pp. 409–18.

91. Gogol to M. A. Konstantinovsky (Father Matthew), 12 January 1848 (N.S.), *Pol. sob.*, XIV, p. 41.

92. In the same letter quoted above, Gogol dwells at length, as he was wont to do, on his own ineradicable sinfulness. There are sometimes glimmerings of humour directed at himself. To Zhukovsky, Autumn 1849, he writes 'The beast Chichikov has hardly reached the halfway point of his wanderings . . . the author of *Dead Souls* has to be much better in the soul than beast Chichikov' (*Pol. sob.*, XIV, p. 152).

93. Stender-Petersen, op. cit., p. 636.

94. Exodus 20:5–6; I Kings 21:27–9. Jahweh brings down vengeance upon Ahab's son, not upon Ahab himself. See also Jeremiah 32:18.

95. See Ezekiel 14:12–23.

96. For an exposition of the more optimistic Orthodox view see Vladimir Lossky, *In the Image and Likeness of God*, London and Oxford, 1974, pp. 97–110.

97. Gogol to his mother, 2 October 1833, thanks her for this part of his upbringing and tells her to impart similar doctrine to his sister Olya. His mother must dwell upon the joys awaiting those who get to heaven, and the horrible, cruel torments which await the sinners. He returns to the point later in his letter, and attributes his own sensitivity to his mother's vivid descriptions of eternal torment (*Pol. sob.*, X, pp. 281, 282). This upbringing, as well as German horror stories, does much to explain Gogol's preoccupation with the gruesome.

98. Gogol to S. P. Shevyryov, 11 February 1847 (N.S.), *Pol. sob.*, XIII, p. 214. In the Orthodox view there would be little to choose between Roman Catholic and Protestant attitudes towards the Fall and Redemption. The doctrine of predestination was particularly developed in Calvinism, but there is room for it in Roman Catholicism where it has had its supporters.

99. The Ukraine was influenced by Western theology. The *Orthodox Confession* of Peter of Moghila, Metropolitan of Kiev 1633—47, was the most Latin document ever to be adopted by an official council of the Orthodox Church (see Timothy Ware, op. cit., p. 107), so Gogol's theological orientation could well be traced to influences prevailing generally in his homeland.

100. 'He (the devil) is only a petty official . . . I call the devil directly by his name, I do not give him a magnificent costume à la Byron, for I know he goes around in a frockcoat', Gogol to S. T. Aksakov, 16 May 1844 (*Pol. sob.*, XII, pp. 300, 301). To S. P. Shevyryov, 27 April 1847, Gogol declares it has long been his intention to make people laugh at the devil (ibid., XIII, p. 293).

101. Schenk, op. cit., p. 15.

102. Ibid., Chapter 15, passim.

103. Ibid., p. 154.

104. Leslie A. Marchand, *Byron: A Biography*, London, 1957, III, pp. 1187—1229.

6 Lermontov's *Mtsyri*: themes and structure

ROBERT REID

I

There is general agreement among critics that *Mtsyri* is a particularly pure example of the romantic *poema* or narrative poem. U. R. Fokht calls it 'a most characteristic phenomenon of romantic literature';[1] L. F. Tarasov claims that it represents the genre of the romantic *poema* 'in a typologically pure form'.[2] It does not however enjoy such accolades alone: critics such as Ye. A. Maymin and D. Ye. Maksimov[3] have regarded *Mtsyri* and *The Demon* (*Dyemon*) as equal firsts in the genre, a phenomenon which Yu. V. Mann has called 'the twin-summit-edness of the Russian romantic poem'.[4] However, the 'twin summited' approach is of relatively recent provenance. Maksimov is right to point out that generally speaking *The Demon* and other works of the genre have hogged the critical limelight.[5]

Behind the comparative neglect of *Mtsyri* are preconceptions strong enough to deflect analysis. Maksimov suggests that the superficial simplicity of the poem, a simplicity not only of plot, but of character and motivation, may be to blame.[6] It is as though *Mtsyri* wears its heart on its sleeve. Other reasons for neglect relate specifically to the 'elder brother', *The Demon*: Mtsyri is a mere suckling and a mortal to boot, the Demon is a primeval being and a powerful spirit.

Belinsky may safely be held responsible for initiating this unfavourable comparison, by asserting that 'the idea [of *The Demon*] is deeper and incomparably more mature than the idea of *Mtsyri*'.[7] It is worth bearing in mind however that Belinsky's use of 'mature' in this instance was elicited by his scorn at V. S. Mezhevich's application of the word to *Mtsyri*.[8] Mezhevich's primitive formalism, contrasting the poem's 'sparse content' to its 'inexhaustible depths of thought' can be seen as the earliest ancestor of modern critical approaches to *Mtsyri*.[9]

If 'maturity' is meant to imply artistic maturity then it is hard to regard *Mtsyri* as *The Demon*'s younger brother: both belong to the last period of Lermontov's creativity. If *The Confession* (*Ispoved'*) and *The Boyar Orsha* (*Boyarin Orsha*) be regarded as forerunners or even drafts of the poem, then its gestation period will be seen to have been almost as long as that of *The Demon*. It is however in the disparity between the status of the heroes themselves that *Mtsyri* suffers most: both poems deal with the tragic failure of aspirations and with the weakness and vulnerability of their heroes, but the Demon's failures and weaknesses acquire that grandeur which comes from acting *sub specie aeternitatis*, of existing in a metaphysical stratosphere where significances are initially universal and are only subsequently particularised into inferior interpretations. Mtsyri by contrast is a mortal limited by time and location, and, in the artistic context, to plausible human motivation. In his case interpretations must move cautiously from this narrow framework of particularity towards more universal significances. And what are these significances? *Mtsyri* may indeed seem 'sparse' in this respect. It is notably devoid of two prominent romantic themes, which furthermore are for Lermontov the principal romantic themes of his Caucasian *poemy*: love and crime. *The Demon*, despite its supernatural perspective, does not except itself from these two staples. The love intrigue, the murder of the rival, the motive of revenge (in the early drafts) and the tragic death of the heroine are to be found, either singly or together, in such works as *Aul Bastundzhi*, *Kally* and *Khadzhi Abrek*. In *Mtsyri* the hero peers cautiously from behind a bush at a Georgian girl with a water pot — his closest encounter with a member of the opposite sex. Admittedly some violence is done to a mountain leopard, but not without deadly consequences for the perpetrator of the act, scarcely a crime, and one which it seems others of Lermontov's romantic world carry out as a mere aside to the plot.[10] Mtsyri, then, is as his name implies a true 'novice' in these principal matters of the romantic world. How indeed may the poem aspire to maturity in critical consideration?

The answer to this question lies, paradoxically, in the very absence from the poem of these mature concerns of romanticism. The love intrigue and the vendetta, romantic ends in themselves, do not easily lead out along paths of wider significance; they are rich in *pathos*, perhaps, but not in *ethos*. Their suppression allows the development in *Mtsyri* of subtler themes always present in the background of Lermontov's work. I have called these themes 'Confession and Context', 'The

Ideal' and 'The Encounter with Nature'. They do not necessarily exhaust the thematic content of the work, but they are arguably its principal themes and have been, moreover, traditional preoccupations of European romanticism. But before the last named of these themes, I also discuss *Mtsyri*'s form, that most highly evolved medium of romantic poetry — the 'Lyro-epic'.

II

Confession and Context

It is notable that Lermontov's best works, *A Hero of Our Time* (*Geroy mashego vremeni*), *The Demon* and *Mtsyri* all spring from the transplanting of a cherished theme into a Caucasian context. *The Demon*'s drafts provide the clearest example of this. The early drafts, set supposedly in Spain, have an unsatisfying spectral quality alongside the later drafts which are suffused with the natural colour of the Caucasus. It is not merely that a landscape familiar to the author provided him with an engaging backcloth to the poem. The landscape also participates positively in the plot. The Demon's attitude to the natural surroundings becomes crucial to the unfolding of the story. To this end the Caucasus becomes an Eden with Tamara its Eve. Elsewhere Lermontov has created such a 'virgin of the mountains', but Tamara's encounter with the demonic figure is unique.[11] Able to resist the visual temptations of natural beauty, the Demon succumbs to its chief embodiment: Tamara. Lermontov had, in a sense, been formulating two complimentary themes in isolation: the Demon figure and the Caucasian Eden. The great drama begins with their collision.

Something similar happens with *Mtsyri*: an abstract theme, wandering demon-like in search of substance, encounters a Georgian monastery and the melancholy fate of an exiled Circassian postulant. It is the theme of confession. Lermontov had first used it in his short *poema*, *The Confession* (1830). He later elaborated it into *The Boyar Orsha* (1835) and finally into *Mtsyri* (1839). The heroes of these three poems not only use the same confessional device to express their principal thoughts, but to some extent use the same words to do so. Thus basically the same sentiments are expressed respectively by a victim of the Inquisition, a rebellious thrall of one of Ivan the Terrible's boyars and a novice monk in Georgia who has unsuccessfully tried to escape from his monastery. Early critics were bemused by this reduplication of subject and device. One considered Arseniy from *The Boyar Orsha* as Mtsyri's double.[12] Another, while intrigued by their similarities, noted the crucial contrast between the two *poemy*: *Mtsyri* is characterised by lack of plot, *The Boyar Orsha* by comparative lack of characterisation.[13] Later critics with the benefit of research into Lermontov's creative method have regarded *The Confession* and *The Boyar Orsha* as effectively drafts of *Mtsyri*, a judgment by analogy with *The Demon*.[14] But the gradual refinement of a personality through several drafts is rather different from the preservation, partly verbatim, of a single mode of utterance. For the sake of a climacteric confessional declaration three widely differing sets of *dramatis personae* are tried and three different plots arranged to accommodate them. There is a curious contrast between the durability of the confession and the expendability of its human and geographical context. But this expendability reflects Lermontov's search for a confessional context, which, like the Caucasian setting of *The Demon*, will be an active participant in the plot of the *poema* and not merely a backcloth. This requirement is answered by *Mtsyri*'s Georgian landscape and by the hero's ideal, his Caucasian *rodina*, which motivates the action of the *poema*.[15] Despite this motivation and context, which distinguishes *Mtsyri* from its two forebears, the work must be regarded primarily as the culmination of Lermontov's confessional technique: Lermontov was, as one source puts it, 'a theoretician of confession'.[16]

'Is it possible to relate one's soul?' This line occurs in *The Confession, The Boyar Orsha* and *Mtsyri*.[17] It highlights a persistent problem for the confessee and one which is traceable to Rousseau's *Confessions*: 'Rousseau's *Confession*, a confession made to his peers, opens itself up to charges of self-interest or self-justification', observes a recent critic.[18] Precisely these sentiments are voiced by the narrator in the preface to Pechorin's journal in *A Hero of Our Time*. Rousseau's *Confessions* are important in the history of romanticism not only because they instituted a romantic genre but because they defined, admittedly in a well-known metaphor, that which the romantic sought to do in expressing himself. Indeed V. M. Zhirmunsky speaks of romanticism primarily in terms of confession.[19]

As well as providing a definition of romantic expression, confession also provided, by analogy with contexts already known, a primitive motivation for such utterance; literary confession relied on the concept of real confession to stress the objective value of an essentially subjective utterance. Confession, however, is a multi-connotative term; while it stresses an intention of truthfulness on the part of the utterer, it brings with it two particular preconceptions about the circumstances of the utterance. One suggests legal authority and judgment by society. The other suggests divine authority and reconciliation to God through a confessor. Confession was an attractive concept to the romantic mind, because it pointed inwards to the heart of the individual and outwards towards the religious and secular establishment which were seen as the natural source of individual ills. Viewed aesthetically, confession is a mode of personal expression which implies in itself a pretext or scenario for its utterance. Even if the pretext is disguised or obscured as, for instance, in Dostoyevsky's *Notes from Underground* (*Zapiski iz podpol'ya*), this does not prevent the search for pretext becoming a crucial concern for the confessee himself.

Of the two forms of confession, Lermontov opts, ultimately, for the religious. In his earliest work of the genre, *The Confession*, an errant monk confesses in his cell to the Inquisitor. In *The Boyar Orsha* Lermontov attempts a rather clumsy hybrid — the court in which Arseniy stands accused by both secular (Orsha himself) and religious (the Abbot) interests. In both *The Confession* and *The Boyar Orsha* secular or popular judgment predominates. Both contain the lines:

> Do not say that it is the court of God
> Which decides my fate:
> It is all done by people, people, my father . . .
> (Soch., II, pp. 184, 380)

Though the confessional situation in *The Confession* is superficially similar to that of *Mtsyri* — a private face to face confrontation of confessor and confessee — it is motivated by the unseen power of the Inquisition, which represented for the romantic mind, as for Dostoyevsky, the manipulation of divine authority for secular ends. In *Mtsyri* this sinister organisational background is minimised. One effect of this is to minimise the heroism of the act of utterance. In *The Confession* and *The Boyar Orsha* confession represents the heroic language of truth — the free confession — as opposed to the mere admission demanded by the institution. This helps to stress the ethical quality of the confession. Mtsyri too refuses to use confession for an orthodox reconciliation to the religious life, but the substance of his confession is less ethical than aesthetic: it consists largely of a creative re-telling of a part of his experience. Confession as the occasion for an utterance of an aesthetic character is assumed in the question, 'Is it possible to narrate the soul?' Once institutionalised moral compulsion is transcended, the criteria for judging the confessional utterance do in effect become aesthetic: does it reflect actuality truthfully? *Mtsyri* differs from its predecessors precisely in furnishing the hero with a complex of experiences which he is required to represent meaningfully. From this point of view, Mtsyri's confession may well be regarded as an anatomy of the creative process. It corresponds, for instance, to A. A. Potebnya's conception of the genesis of poetic creativity which he applies particularly to Russian romantic poetry. It begins when:

Something unclear to the author himself (X), presents itself to him as a question. The answer can be found only in the past of his soul, in the content which the soul has already acquired, or deliberately augmented (A) . . . X repels from A everything which is not suitable to it and attracts that which has some affinity.[20]

The result of this selective process is 'a' and the work of art is represented as the equation 'X is a'.[21] The formal implications of this selective process are dealt with in Section IV, but it is appropriate here to note the dynamic function which Potebnya assigns to the question, X, not only as the initiating force of the artistic process, but as an integral part of the finished product 'X is a'. It is noticeable that in the lyrical stanzas of Mtsyri's confession, stanzas 3–8, just such a function is supplied by the question 'Do you want to know what I saw when I was free?' which heads stanzas 3, 6 and 8. Mtsyri is using the confessional situation as the pretext for his creative act, a pretext facilitated by the utter passivity of the confessor, the receptive audience. In this sense the question is rhetorical when addressed to the confessor. Its significant and dynamic force is addressed inwards to the utterer.

The confessional ancestry of *Mtsyri* is only half of its creative pedigree. An objective *fabula* of the poem was sketched out by Lermontov in 1831, between, that is, the writing of *The Confession* and *The Boyar Orsha*. Ostensibly this sketch was intended for a prose work which never materialised: '[Write] the notes of a young monk of 17. He has been in a monastery since childhood. Apart from the lives of the saints he has read no books. His passionate soul languishes. Ideals . . .' (*Soch.*, II, p. 560). This looks very like a schema for the first two stanzas of *Mtsyri*. All that is absent is the catalyst of exile and the consequent motive for escape. P. A. Viskovatov claimed that just such a catalyst was provided when Lermontov, travelling the Georgian military road, received the *Mtsyri fabula* anew from the lips of an old monk, Circassian by origin, who at a tender age had been left by General A. P. Yermolov in the hands of the monks of a Georgian monastery.[22] At the time he met Lermontov the monastery was already deserted and he was the sole survivor of the brotherhood. When he was young he had tried to escape from the monastery several times, but after one attempt had nearly caused his death he relented, settled down and grew attached to the elder of the monastery.

Viskovatov's account, which he had from two of Lermontov's relatives, has traditionally been accepted as an important element in *Mtsyri*'s creative history. However in the 1950s it became the focus of a disagreement between two Lermontov scholars, I. L. Andronikov and A. V. Popov. Andronikov pointed out that since General Yermolov had reached the central Caucasus region no earlier than 1818 (and Lermontov had met the monk in 1837) and assuming the latter was at that time only six years old, the 'old' monk would have been no more than twenty-five when he met Lermontov.[23] Popov points out that Yermolov had in fact been in the Caucasus as early as 1796 as an artillery captain and, had the boy been left with the monks at that time, he would have been nearly fifty when Lermontov met him, 'a respectable age', claims Popov, for 'somebody who has spent upwards of forty years shut in a monastery'.[24]

The true significance of this apparently trifling dissension was revealed in a forthright article by N. Lyubovich. As Lyubovich sees it the writers represent the two principal Soviet critical approaches not only to *Mtsyri* but to Lermontov's works in general.[25] Popov is the traditionalist who believes that *Mtsyri* should be viewed in the context of the 'concrete Russian historical reality' in which Lermontov's 'powerful genius developed'.[26] Andronikov is the principal representative of the 'regional studies' method, of more recent origin, which aims to find many of the sources of Lermontov's Caucasian poetry in local folk legends and traditions. Criticising the 'regional studies' approach for obscuring the literary and philosophical depths of *Mtsyri* and the traditional approach which regards the monastery as an allegory for Nicholas I's prisons, Lyubovich makes a plea for treating the monastery *qua* monastery, and regarding monasteries, or monks, as Lermontov's principal preoccupation in *Mtsyri* and its two predecessors.[27] But this in itself limits his interpretation: despite some interesting remarks on the history of European anti-clericalism and its possible influence on Lermontov, his article refrains from exploring the significance of the monastery much beyond Lermontov's supposed antipathy to the institution, which is presented in the context of ideological trends of the 1830s and 1840s. Where an attempt is made to widen the significance of the 'monastery regime' the result sounds very close to the Popov tradition.[28]

A question which should have been considered more often with reference to the Viskovatov story is the significance of Lermontov's real-life encounter with one of his fictional preoccupations. It must have been gratifying to Lermontov to meet this practical corroboration of the theory he had sketched out in 1831. Even more gratifying, perhaps, if it were to be called coincidence, for it is one of those superficially coincidental phenomena, concealing a ruthless predictability beneath it, which Lermontov would explore fully in *The Fatalist*. For the monastery, in its regulation and restriction of human life, renders the latter curiously predictable. The reason for this is that options in the monastery are disjunctive, or in mathematical terms binary. One either is or is not a monk — there are no half measures. One either is or is not in a state of grace; that is, one has either confessed one's passions and disowned them, or one harbours them. And the harboured passions inevitably lead away from the regime which disowns them to the world outside. And if, as Apollon Grigor'ev puts it, 'passion is brought to a certain degree of energy' escape too is inevitable.[29] In this context, the number two which, as Yu. V. Mann has noted, dominates so many of the images which Mtsyri creates or relays in his confession,[30] may be held to represent in logical terms the excluded middle, that harmonious compromise between opposites which the monastery regime so rigorously opposes. This predictability is not an out and out determinism. Choice exists — some monks choose to conform (most perhaps) — but the choice is between two predictable options. In this way *Mtsyri*'s escape and his act of confession are free but predictable acts. However, as I suggest in Section V, true freedom is not found outside the monastery either: nature imposes her own disjunctions on Mtsyri.

One of the most interesting facets of the history of *Mtsyri* criticism is the varied response to the connotative value of such romantic images as the monastery and *rodina*. Recent critics have accepted the wide connotation of the monastery in particular. A. S. Melikhova and V. N. Turbin place the *Mtsyri* monastery in the category of 'multisignificant phenomena' where 'what is understood . . . is considerably wider than what is said'.[31] The clue to this 'multisignificant' effect is given by another critic: it is enhanced by the fact that 'in depicting the monastery the poet does not resort to concretisation'.[32] The traditional socio-historical criticism has often fallen short of exploring this multisignificance. Among earlier critics, however, Ivanov-Razumnik saw *Mtsyri*, along with much of the rest of Lermontov's work, as inspired by 'anti-meshchanstvo', a term which he used figuratively to mean antipathy towards oppressive and philistine institutionalism.[33] D. N. Ovsyaniko-Kulikovsky also interpreted the monastery's 'seclusion of freedom' in a wide sense: 'it does not matter what kind [of regime] it is: monastery, family, society'.[34] In fact, however, by the early years of this century the process of 'biographising' Lermontov was well under way to the detriment of non-historical interpretations of his work. A. N. Pypin, for instance, criticised those like S. A. Andreyevsky who viewed Lermontov's poetry as something essentially timeless, rather than as a mirror of his age.[35] Andreyevsky himself had a thought-provoking answer to those who saw Lermontov's psychology chiefly in terms of the Nicholas regime 'as though, after the Nicholas epoch, during the era of reforms, Lermontov would have felt perfectly at home'.[36]

Recent Soviet critics have developed an aspect of the monastic regime first noted, I think, by V. Plaksin, who pointed out that Mtsyri had been shown nothing but kindness by the inmates of the monastery.[37] Plaksin thought this a threat to the credible motivation of Mtsyri's flight. Recent commentators such as Yu. V. Mann and D. Ye.

Maksimov take an opposite view: Mann suggests that the 'good monastery' helps to stress the nature of Mtsyri's ideal: 'Evil here exists in goodness itself, in security, in salvation, inasmuch as these things threaten to fetter the will and to thwart desire of its realisation';[38] Maksimov says that: 'the monks have created for Mtsyri a prison unknown, it would seem, in the history of romanticism — a friendly, kind prison, and hence a particularly terrible one . . .'[39] In fact, however, as Victor Brombert points out, 'Examples of the happy prison abound in Romantic literature'.[40] Prison traditionally has a benign monastic aspect of refuge and tranquillity as well as a Gothic dimension of oppression and terror. 'The romantic fascination with the sequestered poet' in particular derives from the fact that there is a metaphoric correspondence between the free soul made prisoner and the creative act in which inspiration is held captive by verbal or formal constraint.[41]

It is this correspondence in particular which illuminates the relationship between the monastery and the confession in *Mtsyri*. The monastery, itself a source of constraint for the individual inside it, provides in confession a particular idiom of utterance wherein the individual can align his aspirations as nearly as possible with those of the institution. Is such confession merely a metaphor of artistic creativity, or is it in itself a creative act? Certainly the content of Mtsyri's confession suggests a creative, poetical act, just as his question, 'Is it possible to narrate the soul?', is addressed towards the aesthetic rather than the sacramental validity of his confession. Nevertheless *Mtsyri* may be regarded as an exploration not only of the aesthetic implications of the romantic confessional genre, but also of that genre's relationship to its religious origins.

III

The Ideal

The literary historian A. M. Skabichevsky viewed the emergence of romanticism in terms readily applicable to *Mtsyri*. Exploring the affinity between romanticism and the medieval world, in itself a traditional romantic preoccupation, Skabichevsky concluded that both were dominated by a profound dualism wherein the ideal, in Platonic terms, was opposed to the world of false realities. Here, however, the affinity ends, for the medieval ideal — the *via negativa* — seeks above all to subjugate the passions, whereas the romantic ideal is centred upon the passions themselves and abhors the passionless social conformity of the common herd. Thus two outlooks, the medieval and the romantic, are conceived by Skabichevsky to be at the same time formally similar but substantially opposed.[42]

It is interesting to question whether Lermontov's 1831 description of the youth in the monastery ('His passionate soul languishes. Ideals . . .') is 'medieval' or 'romantic' according to Skabichevsky's prescription. The answer remains uncertain because Lermontov's sketch fails to spell out the precise relationship in the context between ideals and passion, between that which the individual aspires to, and that which is outlawed by his 'medieval' monastic community. But the relationship can be inferred, not only from the subsequent development of the sketch in *Mtsyri* but also from a principle widespread in Lermontov's work, namely that 'passions, for all their significance, are merely a preparatory stage towards the development of ideas, thoughts, knowledge and self-awareness'.[43] For Lermontov, then, passion is not an end in itself, but an integral part of the epistemological process. Whatever the end of this process, it will inevitably reflect the 'passionate' component. Mtsyri's *rodina* adequately demonstrates the resultant harmony of passion and idea: at source an unintellectualised human instinct to belong, it develops into a symbolic representation of the romantic ideal.

The potency of *rodina* in *Mtsyri* is that it combines in it two well-recognised, but not easily reconcilable, versions of the romantic ideal. The first is the Odyssey or epic journey: 'Romance is a journey towards home, the hero's home, but not the reader's and more of an ideal than a real home, where the hero might bear to abide.'[44] This is the spatio-temporal expression of the ideal. There is secondly a static conception of the ideal, Platonic in character, whereby the real world is situated 'above' the false world of illusion and change. A case may be made for seeing much of Lermontov's poetry as constructed upon such a vertical axis: above is heaven, below is earth, and between soar such creations as the Demon.[45] The Caucasus has in Lermontov's poetry the unique quality of closeness to heaven:

> But may the prayer of the rested heart
> Be borne away on your cliffs
> Into the land beyond the stars, which you possess,
> As far as the eternal throne of Allah.
>
> (*Soch.*, I, p. 36)

It is such distant peaks seen by Mtsyri from his monk's cell which form the focus for his ideal. Estrangement from the ideal, as a tragic stasis, and therefore an allegory of the human condition, is, of its nature, a lyrical rather than an epic preoccupation with Lermontov, and is typified by the eternal separations of *The Rock* (*Utyos*, 1841) and 'In the wild North there stands a pine . . .' ('Na severe dikom . . .', 1841). Nevertheless the true return home, 'a circular, rather than a linear journey',[46] although it is a major philosophical concern of Lermontov, is hinted at, but never fully achieved in his work. Both the Demon and Mtsyri fail in their pursuits of a former state. In *The Angel* (*Angel*, 1831), the home and the starting out are depicted, but not the return. In *Izmayl Bey* the return is depicted but in terms of what M. H. Abrams calls 'the romantic spiral': the hero returns to the same place but on a different level.[47] That different level is determined by changes in the exiled hero and changes in *rodina* and the chief worker of these changes is time. Time is the dimension which converts the circularity of true return into the tragic spiral.

Of course some critics have treated Mtsyri's *rodina* principally as a straightforward patriotic concept in need of no further clarification.[48] In a lexical context this has resulted in the placing of *rodina* and its synonym *otchizna* in the category of socio-political and publicistic lexis, alongside *freedom, captive* and *prison*.[49] The definition of *rodina within* the poem however is more elusive. Belinsky was right in calling Mtsyri's idea of *rodina* 'a ghost'.[50] It has developed from childhood memories 'strengthened in proportion to his conflict' with the monastic establishment.[51] Stanza 7 shows that Mtsyri's pictorial evocation of *rodina* is still entirely that of a child, with its stress on the peace of the family and its mention of his cradle. Relationships in the 'real' *rodina*, were Mtsyri to return, might not be so ideal. But how is one to check this? Commentators with leanings towards 'regional studies' have been inclined to interpret some of Mtsyri's actions, notably his fight with the mountain leopard, in terms of ethnological and folkloric data, but these in general illuminate *Mtsyri*'s Georgian setting as much as its hero's cultural origins.[52] If anywhere, however, the true character of *rodina* is to be found in Lermontov's works, particularly in the Caucasian *poemy*. It is less a depiction of objective reality, 'less an analysis, than an inner experience of the world',[53] inseparable from the poet's individuality: a poetical world of the Caucasus. This world, however much an emanation of Lermontov's subjectivity, is, relative to Mtsyri's private dream of it, an objectivity. A 'fictionalised', regional studies technique, directed towards the canon of Lermontov's Caucasian poems, illuminates the meaning of *rodina* and places Mtsyri himself in the context of other Caucasian heroes.

Though Lermontov's Caucasian geography shows glimpses of an Eden, it is in terms of human behaviour strikingly post-lapsarian. Mtsyri may dream of idyllic human relationships but the reality of such works as *Kally, The Fugitive* (*Beglets*), *Aul Bastundzhi* and *Izmayl Bey* is deeply tragic. In the case of *Izmayl Bey* the tragedy is not unconnected with concrete historical fact, and the poem may be read as supporting the plight of the Caucasian tribes and as an indictment of war in general.[54] However, as in the other Caucasian *poemy*, it is timeless psychological conflicts which preponderate and Lermontov shows some ingenuity in bolstering these against the national question: the initial encounter between Izmayl and the Russian officer who has sworn to kill him is doubly removed from the field of conflict, not only in the solitude of their confrontation but also in the fact that the officer fails to recognise Izmayl and takes him for a friendly tribesman. The confrontation on the battlefield is merely private enmity expressed in a historic context.

The historic context of *Izmayl Bey* ought, one would think, to provide some definition of Circassian patriotism and one indeed emerges:

> Silence is dear to the Circassian,
> His native land is dear to him,
> But freedom! freedom! To the hero
> This is dearer than homeland and repose.
>
> (*Soch.*, II, p. 249)

Freedom, it seems, is capable of supplanting *rodina* as the highest ideal. So too is love. In *Aul Bastundzhi* Akbulat, totally absorbed in his new wife and unaware of his brother's murderous covetousness towards her, declares: 'Zara! She is my homeland / And all my riches and all my family!' (*Soch.*, II, p. 333). Leila in *Khadzhi Abrek*, perfectly happy with the man who has abducted her, says of her exile:

> 'I am better and happier
> In the upland mists.
> God's world is everywhere lovely.
> The heart has no homeland!'   (*Soch.*, II, p. 358)

She too is unaware that she is speaking to her father's avenger who will shortly murder her. In such cases *rodina* is taken as the norm of highest loyalty which exceptional persons may surpass with some greater passion. It is synonymous with passionate longing and only passionless entities, like the subject of *Clouds* (*Tuchi*, 1840), 'Know neither homeland nor exile' (*Soch.*, I, p. 91). In the same way *rodina* may imply some sustaining spiritual possession, clearly without geographical basis, as when Lermontov says of himself in *Aul Bastundzhi*:

> . . . Its [my soul's] gloom is deep
> And like the secret darkness of eternity,
> No man's living eye may penetrate it.
> And in that gloom, inaccessible to the mind,
> Live memories of a distant
> Holy land . . . and neither the world nor its noise
> Will kill them . . .   (*Soch.*, II, p. 328)

138

The affinity between Mtsyri's idea of *rodina* and this 'holy land' are obvious. But it is a far cry from such a secret Utopia to the true nature of life and relationships in the *rodina* depicted in the Caucasian *poemy*. There the emphasis is almost without exception on extraordinary characters, violent passions and the disruption of relationships. Bastundzhi is burnt to the ground not by invaders but, in a sense, by the primeval passion of Selim, who, failing to seduce his brother's wife, kills her and is then ostracised. To a considerable extent however the community itself is shown as sanctioning violent behaviour: revenge, and therefore violence, is institutionalised. Leila, though happy to have been abducted, is slain in vengeance for her abduction. Kally, who carries out to the letter a mullah's command to avenge his family, carries vengeance to its logical conclusion in also murdering the mullah, whose harsh commands have made him a multiple murderer. Vengeance, therefore, operates at every level, 'for oneself, or for one's relatives, or for one's people'[55] and whether socially or religiously justified or not it invariably rebounds on the perpetrator and leads to his social ostracism.

The way in which Lermontov presents such ostracism is in itself noteworthy: Leila's father, alone and thirsting for revenge, wanders the hills 'like a snake, crushed by a horse's hoof' (*Soch.*, II, p. 353). Selim, anathematised for the murder of his brother's wife, is sentenced to die like an animal:

> . . . not in battle — but from the arrow
> Of an unknown night robber;
> And may he lie three days and nights without shelter
> Half dead on a mountain peak . . .
>
> (*Soch.*, II, p. 348)

Kally, the arch-avenger, becomes a dangerous wanderer: 'Like a wild beast he shunned people; / Unable to seek women's love!' (*Soch.*, II, p. 218). Finally the hero of *The Fugitive*, Garun, who has fled from the field of battle and is therefore a legitimate target for everybody's hatred, even his mother's: 'Runs swifter than a deer, / Swifter than hare from eagle' (*Soch.*, II, p. 46); and: 'Hides alone in the wilderness, / Like a beast, pursued and hunted' (*Soch.*, II, p. 47).

There is a marked similarity between the fate of these social outcasts from tribal society and that of Mtsyri. Mtsyri 'crawled and hid like a snake'; he too spent three days and nights without shelter on a mountain peak; he 'was foreign to people, like a beast' and, as stanzas 12—15 show, he, like Kally, was unable to seek love. But the closest psychological parallel to Mtsyri is provided by Garun, the Fugitive. G. V. Filatova observes with some understatement that the subjects of *Mtsyri* and *The Fugitive* are 'not typical phenomena in mountain life'.[56] Garun's sin is the most heinous conceivable in the context of *rodina*: he flees the battlefield 'during a national war of liberation, a "holy" war by Caucasian lights'.[57] By refusing to stay and avenge his kinsmen he offends too against the vengeance ethic and, in this flight from violence, he becomes utterly estranged from his people. Probably the most important excision from *Mtsyri*'s final draft illustrates precisely this estrangement: after the dream of the fish in stanza 24 Mtsyri imagines he sees a Circassian war party, with his father at the rear, galloping past him:

> With a wild whistle, like a storm,
> They rushed by close to me.
> And each one, leaning over from his mount,
> Threw a scornful glance
> At my monkish garb . . .   (*Soch*., II, p. 563)

Durylin's explanation for Lermontov's omission of this remarkable passage in the purely formal terms of its immediate context is hardly satisfying.[58] If it is out of place at all, then it must be because its ruthlessly realistic view of *rodina* runs entirely counter to the benevolent and childlike projection of it which has sustained Mtsyri in his captivity and which continues to do so.

But in excising this passage Lermontov did not exclude all evidence of a *rodina* independent of Mtsyri's lovingly formulated private ideal. Like the Fugitive, Mtsyri in the very act of flight acquires almost involuntarily a similarity to a hunted animal. But whereas the Fugitive receives this animal characterisation objectively, as it were, from Lermontov, Mtsyri is an active, not to say willing, participant in the animalising process. Some of the earliest critics of *Mtsyri* were aware of this singular preponderance in its hero's characterisation without, necessarily, exploring its full significance or the complexity of the poem's zoology.[59] Mtsyri's self-definition in animal terms is dictated by his alienation from the only community he has mature knowledge of — the monastic community. The animal, as the works of writers such as Kafka and Hesse show, can provide a potent allegory of social alienation and existential isolation. Herein lies the essential contradiction and ultimately the tragedy of Mtsyri's adoption of the role of 'little beast'.[60] For alienation from one community is only half of Mtsyri's goal; the other half is complete acceptance by another, and, as he thinks, more perfect community. But the beast identity is one of universal social isolation and, as we see, the pariah of the hill community has characteristics remarkably similar to those of Mtsyri. In this there is a majestic irony: Mtsyri, armed with the idealised memories of a six-year-old, puts all his energies into a definition of himself which would render him as alien to the community he aspires to as to that from which he seeks to separate himself. In this way *Mtsyri* hints prematurely at the likely fate of its monasticised hero were he ever to reach the object of his desires. He suffers in advance of his goal the fate of the dissenter from tribal rule, though, in his ignorance, he eagerly seeks this bestial role. The *Fugitive* and *Kally* stand as the terrible and extreme options which would face a hero who has 'done no evil to people' were he to realise his dream of the romantic return.

Two romantic homelands therefore are clearly at work in *Mtsyri*: one is Mtsyri's private idyll; the other the tragic reality of the Caucasian *poemy*. Despite this dominant role, neither of the variants of *rodina* is fully present in the poem: as in the case of the monastery, it is precisely the lack of concretisation which invests the image with symbolic power. Of the two homelands, it is natural perhaps that Mtsyri's private idyll should have traditionally dominated the critical mind to the extent of becoming the major theme of the work: '*Rodina* in the poem is the embodiment of man's dream of high standards of life, of brotherly relationships, of concern and kindness in human behaviour'.[61] But one finds too what is in effect an unthought-out hybrid:

> What is Mtsyri's ideal, his *Rodina*, towards which he is striving? It is above all a kingdom of freedom where people are 'free as eagles', it is a kingdom of honour in which all things appear in their true light: *the enemy frankly calls himself an enemy*, love and friendship really are love and friendship. Appearance is stripped away from things — it is a world diametrically opposed to the 'masquerade'. Consequently, relations between people may be relations of love and *enmity* but never of lies.[62] [My italics]

Such extrapolations go somewhat beyond the continents of Mtsyri's own formulation of *rodina*: it contains no enemies at all because it is based on the reminiscences of a child and is formulated by somebody 'unacquainted with the noisy world' who 'wished to take monk's vows' and who has 'done no evil to people'. For enemies 'frankly called' or otherwise we must look to the 'real' *rodina* of The Fugitive and *Kally* whose appalling estrangement Mtsyri blindly re-enacted when in the depths of the forest he 'lost the mountains [of his home] from view and at once began to lose his way' (*Soch.*, II, p. 63).

Critics of *Mtsyri* generally point out that like Pushkin's The Gypsies (*Tsygany*) the poem addresses itself to Rousseauism.[63] *The Gypsies* effectively refuted the myth of the noble savage and Lermontov's presentation of the life of Caucasian tribes may be regarded as taking its cue from the famous lines from the epilogue of Pushkin's poem:

> Beneath your tattered tents
> Dwell torturing dreams,
> And your wild nomadic shelters
> Have not escaped troubles,
> And everywhere are fateful passions,
> And from the Fates there is no defence.[64]

In sympathy with these sentiments Lermontov creates a Caucasian Eden but one in which, symbolically speaking, 'the snake receives too much attention in comparison with other details of the landscape'.[65] Yet he still manages to create a hero who cherishes the dream of human innocence, by preventing that hero from testing his dream against fallen reality. It is perhaps by now a truism in the comparative study of Aleko and Mtsyri to state that the latter, unlike the former, is, in seeking his ideal, also seeking to return home. This is Lermontov's particular intensification of a romantic theme. In failing in his greatest desire to achieve the great circle of home-coming (or spiral, as was suggested above) Mtsyri achieves, against his desire, another and more terrible circle from exile to exile, from the monastery to the monastery. Paradoxically, however, it is this second circle, this false returning, which ensures that Mtsyri's *rodina* will remain untested and intact.

Attempting to characterise Mtsyri's attempted return, Durylin says that 'he has left one bank and not reached the other', envisaging, presumably, the monastery and *rodina* respectively.[66] In terms of this second circle, Mtsyri may be said to have left the bank and reluctantly returned to it again. The significance of this, in romantic terms problematic, returning, lies not in the goal of the journey, but in the journey itself and Mtsyri's encounter thereon with the natural world. The impact of this encounter is complicated by the hero's mode of narrating it, as well as by the presence in the poem of non-narrational elements which alter the reader's perspective. What follows in Section IV therefore is in part a necessary preamble to the last section, in part too an anatomy of a uniquely romantic structure.

IV

The Lyro-epic[67]

It is a noticeable fact that the plot summaries of *Mtsyri* provided by critics often show wide variation. This is, perhaps, a measure of the poem's considerable formal complexity which derives from the interrelationship of its epic and lyric elements and from the presence in the work of more than one creative point of view. The precise nature of this interrelationship has been an abiding interest of students of *Mtsyri* and is of more than purely formal interest, since, ultimately, the differentiation of epic and lyric in the poem coincides with a differentiation of philosophical viewpoint.

Some of the earliest responses to Lermontov's poetry opine on the lyro-epic question in general terms and though written in a 'positive' age, 'doomed to live and die without poetry', manage to anticipate much of the later critical discussion.[68] A. Nikitenko and S. Shevyryov both think that the usual development for a poet is from the lyric towards the epic. Shevyryov sees the process as 'an undefined ether' emerging into the 'varied, living world of the epos'.[69] Nikitenko compares the lyric to a 'patriarchal age' during which the poet is in harmony with nature; this gives way at length to the 'rising and falling of buildings' — the epic's work of 'moral world construction'.[70] Shevyryov considers Lermontov as competent in both the creative spheres defined; Nikitenko views him as essentially 'patriarchal'. In their brief comments on the subject these two critics manage not only to relate formal and psychological aspects of poetic creativity but to illuminate both by a historical perspective: on one level the lyric reflects a primal age of innocence in the poet's creative history while the epic reflects his coming to terms with the real world. On another level the temporal metaphor offers a definition of the genres themselves: the lyric's temporal precedence is here symbolic of its timelessness, a notion inseparable from its 'undefinedness' and 'patriarchality'. Time, change and specificity begin with the epos which in Nikitenko's more connotative image runs its eventful course between two stases: that from which the epos has emerged and that towards which it is moving — 'the patriarchal age' and 'moral world construction' respectively.

Such a characterisation of epos in terms of causal change or eventfulness is still in general currency among contemporary critics but 'lyric' in the context of Russian romanticism and of Lermontov in particular has for the purpose of definition become inseparable from the authorial 'I'. Thus for K. N. Grigoryan the presence of the author throughout *Mtsyri* makes it Lermontov's highest lyrical achievement.[71]   O. I. Fedotov calls it Lermontov's 'most subjective and lyrical of poems'.[72] But what is the nature of the author's presence in *Mtsyri*? Lermontov differentiates himself from Mtsyri not as lyrical commentator from epic hero, not as creator from creation, but, in effect, as one narrating subject from another. That is why the story of Mtsyri's escape is told twice, once by the author and once by the hero. Admittedly the author's account is somewhat briefer:

He disappeared suddenly
One autumn night. The dark wood
Covered the hills about.
For three days all search for him
Was vain, but then,
They found him senseless on the steppe
And brought him home again to shelter.

(*Soch.*, II, p. 53)

It is in fact the fabula to the hero's plot and as such as inherently objective and unaesthetic as the plot is subjective and creatively transformative. But the plot is Mtsyri's preserve and the author's terse pretelling of it stresses his formal disinvolvement from it and underlines the autonomy of Mtsyri himself as character-narrator. The presence of the authorial 'I' throughout *Mtsyri* is therefore something of only marginal artistic significance. Fedotov unwittingly underlines this when he quotes in support of his lyrical view of *Mtsyri* the following remarks by Kotlyarevsky: 'Who would not recognise the author himself in this Mtsyri? With the exception of the monastery . . .all else is taken straight from personal recollections: the lonely childhood, the thirst for great deeds, the longing for love and freedom'.[73]

The psychological validity of the above is not in question but there is no reason to suppose that such wholly biographical raw material would be more likely to produce a lyrical work than an epic or drama. If Potebnya is right in claiming that 'all poetry, not just lyrical, is subjective' then this must mean that subjectivity itself is not sufficient definition of the lyric.[74] Indeed, as A. N. Sokolov points out, many of Lermontov's lyrics (e.g. *The Sail* (*Parus*, 1832), *The Leaf* (*Listok*, 1841), *The Rock* are innocent of the lyric 'I' and his further observation that, however 'objective' they may be, 'the subject is always present in some form or other' merely confirms Potebnya's truism about poetry in general.[75]

A rather more satisfying approach to lyrical definition is to regard the monologue, 'the recounting of one's own experiences' as essentially lyrical.[76] Thus for critics like S. I. Leusheva and G. K. Bocharov, the prevalence of monologue in *Mtsyri* ensures the preponderantly lyrical character of the poem; however, they do admit the presence in it of 'some narrative elements'.[77] It will generally be found that narrative in this context is to be understood in terms of action or events. The defenders of the lyrical view who admit the presence of events are careful to underline that their organisation is largely weak and unsystematic. Possibly this impression derives from the chronic passivity of the hero even in the presumably dynamic context of escape, for though Mtsyri sometimes 'acts in the literal sense of the word' he is often merely 'dependent on circumstances', on the unfolding of contingent events.[78] But for an epic it perhaps matters less whether the author is the passive or active subject of events than that these events should exhibit what V. G. Yolkin calls 'logical and chronological consecutiveness', a feature which he believes is present in *Mtsyri*.[79] Interesting in this connection is L. Ye. Slashcheva's work on time in Lermontov's poetry. She divides the latter into two broad categories: one in which time unfolds logically in a single tense or in logical sequence of tenses; the second in which there is an 'arbitrary mixing of all three time plans'.[80] In the first category the poet refrains from arbitrariness of tense usage in order faithfully to reproduce 'the objective temporal consecutiveness of phenomena';[81] in the second, time becomes a descriptive ancillary to the author's theme and the work unfolds according to some other logical principle than the strictly temporal.

Slashcheva deals exclusively with Lermontov's shorter poems, but in essence the distinction she makes between *The Angel* and *The Rock* on the one hand and 'I look at the future with fear . . .' ('Glyazhu na budushchnost' . . .', 1838) on the other is between story and description and therefore between epic and lyric. In this way it can be used to clarify the views of Nikitenko and Shevyryov already mentioned. To the definition of epic little need be added, but the lyric, far from appearing an 'undefined ether', may be profitably seen in terms of the appropriation of time by the poet for descriptive purposes. To this extent time is mastered in the lyric whereas in the epic it rules, sometimes tyrannically.

Mtsyri is best thought of as a regular oscillation between the lyrical and epic genres: the author's lyric in stanza 1 is a prologue to the author's epic in stanza 2; the hero's lyric (3—8) is a prologue to the hero's epic (8—24) and the poem concludes with the hero's lyrical epilogue. Superficially there is similarity between the author's section of the poem (lyric preceding story) and the hero's section (lyric preceding same story). In each case the lyric prologue represents a state of mind later in time than the events described in the story. In each case there is the 'arbitrary mixing of three time plans': the present tense of utterance and observation, a distant past of hallowed memory — the kings of Georgia and the childhood of Mtsyri — and the more recent past of the monastery in use, or, in Mtsyri's case, of his impressions of freedom.

But there are limits to this similarity. That objective viewpoint which, as observed above, so radically separates the author's description of Mtsyri's flight from the hero's own, applies equally to the two lyrical prologues. While Mtsyri's prologue anticipates his escape and attempts to synthesise it with the hero's memories and aspirations, there is nothing in stanza 1 of the poem to anticipate the biographical contents of stanza 2. This is because, whether in lyric or epic, the author's perspective is essentially that of the monastery and its fate. Thus while he is deafeningly silent about Mtsyri's experiences during his escape, he does offer us the only image in the poem of the monks searching for Mtsyri for three days. Mtsyri's view of the matter is of course different: 'I listened hard: there was no pursuit' (*Soch.*, II, p. 58). Not, of course, to suggest that Lermontov is in any sense the monastery's spokesman. The monastery before his gaze is a ruin. In the long history of its decline, what are three days? Stanza 1 expands this Aurelian perspective on human affairs: beside the history of a nation, what is the fate of a single monastery? And finally, what is this catalogue of human vicissitudes, when compared to the immutability of nature, represented by the eternal sisterhood of the Aragva and Kura?

Yet despite the withering objectivity of stanzas 1 and 2, the author's section and the hero's section of the poem are not merely the immemorial irreconcilables of philosophical detachment and passionate solipsism. Though the author has anticipated Mtsyri's biography and flight, he has not anticipated the latter's act of story-telling. Mtsyri's creative re-telling of his experience is therefore a fact in its own right, a meaningful consecutive step in a story which has hitherto been told by somebody else. Thus the subjective account of Mtsyri is logically locked into the objective chain of events initiated by the author and it is an indispensable link in that chain. A price however is exacted for this incorporation into objectivity.

It will be noticed that the structure of Mtsyri's utterance is lyric prologue — epic — lyric epilogue. By contrast the author has merely lyric prologue — epic. Having handed the baton to Mtsyri he does not see fit to return at the end with his own epilogic comment. Formally, Mtsyri has the last word, but it is a somewhat indecisive one: we do not know whether Mtsyri, who has been close to death before, really will die and consequently the status of his auto-elegy in stanza 26 remains ambiguous. Baron Rozen thought such an ending to the poem unsatisfactory: Lermontov should have said something over Mtsyri's corpse to contrast it 'with the life of a few moments before'.[82] But, in a way, he does just that. Stanza 1 answers all but the positional requirements of an epilogue: it is temporally, but not formally, posterior to all the events in the poem. Significantly it does not point us to Mtsyri's grave. It is, as we have seen, concerned with the fate of the monastery itself. Herein is the price exacted for objectivity: Mtsyri's confession is not a self-sufficient unmotivated utterance such as that in *The Confession*; unlike too the confession of Arseniy in *The Boyar Orsha*, it derives much of its unique colour from the circumstances and particularities of the hero's captivity and escape. It is, as we shall see, in an essential way a monk's account, albeit a monk of unique origin and situation. Mtsyri's fate is an inseparable element in the wider fate of the monastery.

Stanza 1 as combined prologue/epilogue relates to fate in a way characteristic of Lermontov. For the return from ruined monastery to ruined monastery implied by the dual role of the stanza naturally parallels Mtsyri's own cyclical journey from the monastery and back again. Particularly notable is the fact that the gradual reassertion of lyric begins from Mtsyri's realisation, in stanza 20, that his journey is in fact over. This realisation, anticipated in the last line of stanza 19, associates the return with fate. The first line of stanza 21 also implies the same thing. Awareness of fate in the poem is essentially a lyrical concern, and the body of Mtsyri's epic is free from its mention, except in the closing lines of stanza 16 where it occurs as a lyrical aside. In stanza 4 we have an overt association of fate with the idea of the monastery in the line, 'In my soul a child, by my fate a monk' (*Soch.*, II, p. 54). Fate is a lyrical concern because it is a supratemporal concept according to which events do not merely come to be at a given point, but in their fated inevitability pre-exist their manifestation. This is the Aristotelian view of fate by which the immutability of future events is deduced by analogy with the immutability of past events and by the susceptibility of all propositions, even those pertaining to the future, to the verdict of true or false.[83] This analogic view of fate is well illustrated by the discrepancy between the temporal and formal status of stanza 1. Temporally it is the last thing of all, but for the plot it is the first thing. By the time Mtsyri begins his confession, it is, in terms of plot, a past event and yet, in terms of real time, it is the future which lies ahead of Mtsyri. For Mtsyri, as for everyman, the future remains dark. For the reader it is clear because it has happened already, not in a temporal sense but by an artificial transposition of the future into the past, an arbitrary rearrangement of time by the artist. Thus from Mtsyri's point of view at any given stage in his story, it may be said that, although the future is yet to be, it is already written.

The anticipatory role of Mtsyri's lyric prologue is to be viewed differently from the author's. Both prologues aim at imposing a free a-temporal wholeness on material which will shortly be converted into a causally entrapped epic. In both lyric overviews, some vital particularity is lost: in the grandeur of stanza 1's historical sweep Mtsyri is missing. In Mtsyri's prologue what is ignored is the shameful failure of his escape which will shortly be unfolded in detail by the epic. For in this integral overview, where the ideal of *rodina* commands and rearranges Mtsyri's experiences, there is no room for the forests or dark nights which bedevil the epic quest for the real *rodina*.

The relation between Mtsyri's prologue and his subsequent narrative and epilogue illustrates some characteristic features of romantic epistemology. It reflects in particular 'a notion crucial to romanticism' — the three-stage unfolding of consciousness which originates in Kant's analytic and has affinities with Hegel's dialectic of self-consciousness.[84] According to Richard Jackson's exposition of this process, the first stage is one of 'intuitive awe' essentially unanalytical, in which the imagination 'prepossesses' the entire object of thought in a single vision; in temporal terms this is also a 'leaping-ahead' to the achievement of a given desire or aim.[85] Next comes the more dogged process of breaking that which has been grasped intuitively into parts for separate contemplation. In temporal terms this is a 'holding back' from the achievement of the proposed vision in order to test it against experience. The third phase is in effect a synthesis of the two foregoing phases. In the sense of restoring the integral vision this phase is a return to or repetition of the first phase, but, 'because repetition is a "transforming process", it is not a simple return to the beginning, but a return with a difference'.[86]

Viewed in these epistemological terms, stanzas 3—8 of Mtsyri's confession, the lyric prologue, may be held to represent Mtsyri's prepossession of his experience as yet untested by analysis. Stanzas 8—20, the epic proper, is the second phase in which temporality is asserted and the minutiae of the escape explored; only through this process is the tragedy of the episode revealed, reaching its greatest intensity as the epic declines again into lyric (21—4). During this third stage an integral view of both his life and escape is again acquired by Mtsyri but it is irrevocably altered by his failure to achieve his goal. Even in the epilogue proper (25 and 26) where the *rodina* ideal is restated in terms similar to the prologue, it is coloured by the imminence of Mtsyri's death and the impossibility of its realisation.

In this way, while Mtsyri's return to the monastery may be conceived as a circle in physical or geographical terms, it is in psychological terms helical, and the events which take place during the epic may be regarded as determining the vertical discrepancy between the point of departure and the point of arrival. Such is not the case with the author's prologue/epilogue, stanza 1. It is offered to us not as a transitional state of consciousness to be superseded but as ineluctable objective fact. There is no need for the author to alter his prologue in the light of the hero's confession, for the confession itself cannot alter the future. The reader himself, though, returning to stanza 1, finds that he is now able to discern in it specifically epilogic elements, logically undetectable at its prologue stage. Where, for instance, is Mtsyri's grave? Or were his last wishes not carried out? Or is it perhaps the case, as Ivanova suggests, that there never was a flowery garden beside the monastery and that this was the last and highest of Mtsyri's flights of fancy?[87] Or is he the wretched figure sweeping the flagstones? These are the dormant questions called to life in stanza 1 by its epilogic application.

V

The Encounter with Nature

N. Ye. Mednis, characterising what he calls 'the second part' of Mtsyri's monologue, stanzas 9–26, calls it a subjective narrative, but one in which 'the subjective does not obscure the objective'.[88] In support of the view that *Mtsyri* is a consistent story in terms of plot development, he quotes Maksimov:

> In *Mtsyri* in contrast to the tradition of Byronic *poemy*, events develop quite coherently, in an uninterrupted chain, without chronological upheavals, with complete adherence to temporal and spacial contiguity, with no breaks or missing links and with a measured emphasis on the key moments, the narrative peaks.[89]

Maksimov is saying in effect that Mtsyri faithfully reproduces the consecutiveness of the events he has experienced and so to this extent his story corresponds with fact. V. I. Korovin goes as far as to call this correspondence 'synchroneity of word and action', which is more a characterisation of the effect Mtsyri's narrative has on the reader than a proper reflection of the relationship of real event to narrated event.[90] For whereas, at any point in the unfolding of Mtsyri's narration, the reader is encountering Mtsyri's actions for the first time, Mtsyri as narrator is re-living them. For Mtsyri as narrator, the episode of his escape is already a closed system with a clearly defined beginning in stanza 9 and ending in stanza 24. Each recounted event, by the very fact that it is now perceived as part of that system as a link in an 'uninterrupted chain', differs in value from the original experiential phenomenon. The act of revaluing that experience in terms of the new causal perspective is a creative act. Like the retrospective first person narratives *Taman'* and *The Fatalist, Mtsyri* is not only a re-telling of events but also an interpretation of their causal relations. In *Mtsyri* the difference between event and gloss frequently corresponds to what Marshall Brown calls 'propulsive narration and lyrical pause'.[91]

By lyrical pause in this context is meant explanatory interpolation into the narrative. Such, for instance, is all of stanza 8 after the words 'I ran away'. In this case the raw material of Mtsyri's escape, unglossed by motive, would suggest that the catatonic prostration of the monks and the headlong flight of the novice are merely differing manifestations of a common terror of the storm. This impression is overridden by the lines: 'O, I like a brother / Would have gladly embraced the storm!' (*Soch.*, **II, p. 58**). Flight *from* now becomes flight *into* and Mtsyri has thus utterly dissociated himself from the reactions of his brethren. Wherever in the plot Mtsyri himself becomes the agent for physical change, a change, that is, in setting rather than in the hero's mental state, some lyrical clarification of motive inverts or modifies the literal implications of the objective event. The descent into the gorge in stanza 12 becomes a heroic act because we are told that: 'Youthfulness is free and strong, / And death did not seem terrible!' (*Soch.*, II, p. 60) lest indeed we should simply compare the cassocked awkwardness of the escaped novice, notwithstanding his highland stock, with the easy grace of the autochthon with the waterpot in stanza 13. This comparison can still be made by the reader, not only retrospectively, after having first encountered the phenomenon of descent as a fusion of objective fact and interpretation. Again, Mtsyri's failure to go up to the Georgian girl's hut — 'I wanted . . . but / I didn't dare go up there . . .' (*Soch.*, II, p. 63) seems quite in keeping with the diffidence he has displayed towards her in stanza 13. Mtsyri manages instead to represent this failure as a noble abstinence:

> I had a single aim in my soul —
> To reach my native land —
> And overcame the suffering of hunger as best I could.
>
> (*Soch.*, II, p. 63)

Similar too is the treatment of Mtsyri's frenzied rage in stanza 15 when the hero

> . . . sobbed,
> And gnawed at the damp breast of the earth,
> And tears, tears flowed
> Into it like scorching dew.   (*Soch.*, II, p. 63)

Mtsyri is at pains to assure the elder that he did not want human help, that the gnawing of the ground is not to be taken as a symptom of human despair, but a sign of his defiant anti-humanity. Also, somewhat ingeniously, the sobbing is interpreted not as a loss of restraint, but rather as its exercise, so that:

> If even a momentary cry
> Had betrayed me — I swear, old man,
> I would have torn out my weak tongue.
>
> (*Soch.*, II, p. 63)

Finally Mtsyri's representation of his fight with the leopard as an actively sought proof of his warriorhood overshadows the fact that it is the leopard which attacks, not Mtsyri, who is immobile and on the defensive: 'Seizing a forked branch / I awaited the moment of battle' (*Soch.*, II, p. 64); and again, in stanza 17: 'I waited. And in the shadows of night / He sensed his enemy' (*Soch.*, II, p. 64). By such exegesis, Mtsyri attempts to establish plausible justification for his own deeds within the context of the ideals he has spoken of in the lyrical prologue.

There is however another sense in which lyrical pause may be understood within Mtsyri's escape narrative. There are stanzas such as 10, 11, 14 and 22 in which physical activity on the part of the hero is suspended. His psychic activity is proportionally heightened. Nevertheless psychic activity is still conveyed epically rather than lyrically in these stanzas, because Mtsyri's thoughts are recorded in the order in which they took place and because 'time envelops both the subjective and objective worlds in the same way and unlike space makes no distinction between them'.[92] Clearly however Mtsyri's epic is nothing if not a quest for a spacially located ideal and with respect to this ideal there is a great distinction between the physical activity meant to bring it closer and the psychic events which merely delay its realisation. Thus the possibility of an epic realisation of the ideal — that is, of a physical return to homeland — supersedes the former lyric mode of realisation, whereby the reality of the ideal was in direct proportion to the imaginative effort required to sustain it. Psychic events, consecutive or otherwise, are, relative to the aims of the epic, asides from the proper action.

Usually, of course, an authentic act by the hero of an epic quest has both subjective and objective validity. It is the objective realisation of a conscious aim. In *Mtsyri*, however, subjective and objective events occupy their separate monadic compartments. Mtsyri's movements are blunderings from his goal and his psychically enriched pauses can take him no nearer to it. How is this to be explained?

Undoubtedly the laws of nature have much to do with blowing Mtsyri off course. The elevated situation of the monastery which affords Mtsyri visual access to the hills of *rodina* also ensures that his flight will require a steep descent, during which, while getting no closer to his goal, he also loses sight of it. Nature, while obstructing Mtsyri in the linear attainment of his ideal, also cheats him of linear time, essential to the epic quest. Instead he is at the mercy of the circadian alternation of day and night in which change is perceived not quantatively but qualitatively. Day offers a superfluity of sensual stimuli to psychic activity and a disincentive to objective action. Night provides the possibility of action without the vital guidance of the senses. In this circadian context, Mtsyri's absence, represented by the succession night-day-night-day, is to be understood as the completion of a cycle rather than the achievement of linear progression: night 2 reasserts night 1, day 2 reasserts day 1. Mtsyri is at large long enough to demonstrate the cycle.

The repetitions which flow from the cycle are obvious enough: both nights are the occasion for Mtsyri's disoriented flight through darkness. Both have strong overtones of the hunt: Mtsyri is the hunted on night 1, the hunter on night 2. Both days, by contrast, are characterised by an immobility after the night's exertions and by a specificity of setting ('God's garden' in the first instance, 'God's world' in the second) which becomes the subject of Mtsyri's observation. In both cases the intensifying heat of noon causes thirst, slaked physically on the first day and mirageously on the second. Clearly however the repetitions are not exact: hunted to hunter is a considerable modification. 'God's garden' and 'God's world' are far from identical religious concepts. The mirage is at once formally similar to water and substantially dissimilar. Thus the periodicity of natural time enforces only the partial recurrence of phenomena. Linear time, in which change is absolute and non-alternating, persists through the four stages of the circadian cycle (night-day-night-day) as a continuous process. This linear time is, of course, Mtsyri's own. This is the time which registers the hero's cumulative fatigue, hunger and thirst, the accretion of experience and alteration of attitude. In the perspective of this experiential time, the change from 'God's garden' at one noon to 'God's world' at another is to be explained by the unbroken chain of cause and effect linking one day to the other through the intervening night. The change like the chain itself is subjective and pertains only to Mtsyri's psychic history. Nature is immune to such progression.

Experiential time provides some clue towards explaining *Mtsyri*'s striking anachronism, so striking that, as Fedotov puts it: 'Neither the author himself, nor Belinsky, nor Kotlyarevsky, nor the overwhelming majority of other researchers have noted the verbal discrepancy between the "three blissful days" and Mtsyri's factual two-day absence from the monastery'.[93] Implicit in this criticism are two possible understandings of 'day': it may be the natural day reckoned from dawn to dusk or it may be the astronomical day reckoned as twenty-four hours and applied as day measurement from Mtsyri's time of departure. According to either of these scales Mtsyri is indeed absent for two days at most and in all likelihood for less than this period of time. There is, of course, a third understanding of 'day' which yields somewhat different results: the so-called 'civil day', be it of the week or of the month, whereby the twenty-four hour cycle is treated 'without reference to its length as a point or unit of time on which anything happens . . . .'[94] According to this third mode of reckoning it would indeed have been possible for Mtsyri to have been absent for three days, for, assuming he fled the monastery before midnight, his absence would have affected three days of the week. This problematic mensuration invites comparison with the three days of Christ's resurrection. Here too three days are covered with the same economy: Christ is hastily entombed on Friday evening and before dawn on Sunday he is already risen, having nevertheless fulfilled the three days prophecy.

Underlying both *Mtsyri* and the Gospel account is the notion that experience is more important than duration in evaluating time.[95] Mtsyri emphasises this in his remarks to the elder who has lived long enough to find 'the beautiful world hateful' and to have 'lost the habit of wanting' (*Soch.*, II, p. 55). Without his three days of freedom, Mtsyri's own life would have been 'sadder and darker' than the elder's 'impotent old age' (*Soch.*, II, p. 57). Abstract chronological measurement of a period of time says nothing of the quality of the experiences involved in it. The nature of Mtsyri's experiences at large depends very considerably on his point of entry into the elastic three-day period. He uses only the late night of the first day, all the obligatory middle daylight and night and most of the daylight of the third day. Temporal *quality* is vital to the plot of *Mtsyri*. It is important to the concept of the work that it should begin during the late hours of night, that the hero should exhaust himself in random flight during the initial stages of his journey and thus be all the readier to remain inactive by day and to forget his goal.[96] This temporal quality lies neither wholly in the alternation of nature's circadian time nor wholly in the hero's experiential time but in the interaction of the two, in the historic intervention of the hero's time at a point in the natural cycle.

The *triduum* is but one of a number of important religious elements in *Mtsyri* which colour the hero's perception of nature. It should not be surprising that Mtsyri, brought up by monks and himself intending to become one, should use religious imagery in his narrative. On one level, Mtsyri may be regarded merely as larding his text with images which would readily occur to a monk: the mountain peaks smoking like altars in stanza 6, the Devil's fall from heaven in stanza 10, 'God's garden' and the flight of the angel in stanza 11, 'God's world' in stanzas 20 and 22, the crown of thorns in stanza 22. On the other hand, as can readily be seen, the order in which these images occur is far from random: the Fall of Satan precedes 'God's garden' (Eden), which, after the Fall of Man becomes 'God's world', which is redeemed by Christ's passion, represented by the crown of thorns. These images furthermore, together with others not explicitly religious but coloured by juxtaposition, cluster for the most part around the two meridians of Mtsyri's days at large.

There is a certain impetus to the daylight stanzas 9—13. The observations of stanza 9 culminate with a five-line treatment of the serpent and Mtsyri's fellowship with it. Stanza 10 culminates with the legend of the Devil thrown down from heaven into the gorge. Stanza 11 shows us God's garden but ends with the hero's thirst forcing his tortuous climb down into the gorge in stanza 12. Stanza 13 begins with the Georgian girl's graceful descent by a narrow path. An Eden scenario is created but the affinities and motivations are strangely altered. It is not Eve who is tempted but Adam, for it is Mtsyri who, in some detail, describes his fellowship with the serpent. Furthermore it is this very fellowship which, far from leading this Adam to tempt his Eve, causes him to be 'foreign to people like a beast' and to 'crawl and hide like a snake'. For this default and after much procrastination, Mtsyri flings himself out of Eden uttering the hollow barrage of excuses which conclude stanza 14. This treatment of the Fall, while it retains the *dramatis personae* of Genesis, has strong affinities with the Koranic tradition which Lermontov may have imbibed from Byron's *Turkish Tales* or perhaps from more direct sources. Apart from the Koranic predilection for detailing the beauties of Eden as a garden, the *houris* or 'maids of Paradise' represent in the Moslem tradition that possibility of redemption through love which Mtsyri refuses by his self-assimilation to the serpent.[97]

Expulsion from 'God's garden' leads to 'God's world' and to fallen man's estrangement from nature. In stanza 22 nature sleeps and the grass which, in stanza 9, had proved a comfortable resting place for Mtsyri now becomes a crown of thorns. The only animal not immobilised by the heat is the serpent, which now receives even more detailed treatment than in stanza 9, without, however, the hero's confession of fellowship with it:

> . . . Only the snake
> Rustled through the dry weeds
> Its yellow back glinting
> Like a blade with a gilt inscription;
> Furrowing the scattered sand
> It slid along with care. Then
> Playing and basking in it,
> It wound into a triple coil
> And, as if suddenly scorched,
> Rushed and jumped
> And hid itself in some distant bushes.
>
> (*Soch.*, II, p. 68–9)

There is perhaps a hint here of the crucifixional placard, but the 'inscribed blade' and the serpent-weapon have clear parallels elsewhere in

Lermontov's work. In the Caucasian *poemy* the serpent is sometimes compared to a piece of discarded weaponry as though taking upon itself the representation of human discord within nature (for example, *Soch.*, II, pp. 257, 329). The gilt inscribed blade of a redundant dagger hung up for decoration is used in *The Poet* (*Poet*, 1838) to represent the poet's treatment by the crowd. In two other poems of the same year (*The Dagger* (*Kinzhal*) and 'Like the heavens, your gaze . . .' ('Kak nebesa, tvoy vzor . . .'), the dagger is shown as faithful executor of its owner's deeds whether of valour or perfidy and the essential ambiguity of the weapon symbol is hinted at in the oxymoron at the end of stanza 1 of *Mtsyri*:

> . . . She has flourished
> Since then in the shade of her gardens,
> Fearing no enemies,
> Behind a marge of friendly bayonets.
>
> (*Soch.*, II, p. 52)

Significantly too, the crown of thorns is used elsewhere by Lermontov to represent the poet as 'a sufferer, a prophet, misunderstood and harassed by the crowd'.[98] Lermontov thus uses it to ally the creative status of Mtsyri with that of the 'romantic poet' who 'takes on himself the role of Christ'.[99]

The road out of Eden does not lead directly to Calvary. The intervening night and the fight with the leopard contain that which converts the fellowship with the serpent into the glaring menace of the dagger. Lost in the wood in stanza 15 Mtsyri reiterates the closing lines of stanza 9 in which he voiced fellowship with the snake:

> I was alien
> To them forever,
> Like a beast of the steppe.   (*Soch.*, II, p. 63)

However, a physical encounter with a wild beast on its own terms leads not to fellowship but to a struggle to the death. This struggle offers Mtsyri a fleeting sensation of friendship, anticipated in stanza 17 by the leopard 'groaning like a man' but reaching its climax in the desperate struggle during which

> We fell at once,
> Woven together like a pair of snakes,
> Embracing more firmly than two friends.
>
> (*Soch.*, II, p. 65)

In a moment the animal is dead. The experiment in fellowship has proved illusory and over this failure presides the image of the embracing serpents with its rich irony.

In effect, it is a failure to mythologise adequately. Mtsyri personifies a singular attempt to solve the romantic problem of man's estrangement from nature by a single-minded zoanthropy which shuns humanity. In so doing he succumbs to an urge as old as the madness of Nebuchadnezzar and as new as behaviourism and thereby merely aggravates the corollary problem of man's alienation from self. *Mtsyri* exemplifies a peculiarly romantic ecology whereby 'nature is not the source of value but the occasion for projecting it'.[100] The denizens of Mtsyri's natural world relate to him symbolically. Some live purely in the metaphorical habitat created for them by the hero, others, such as the jackal in stanza 9, the snake and the leopard, have an objective existence which is however metaphorised by Mtsyri himself.

The natural symbols which Mtsyri uses in stanzas 3—5 refer less to the escape proper than to Mtsyri's spiritual growth prior to it. They are significant in their own right but also in the order in which they occur: the worm, the eagle (stanza 3), the leaf (stanza 4) and the pigeon (stanza 5). The worm represents Mtsyri's gnawing ideal, the eagle represents the qualities of his race, the storm-tossed leaf his emotional state, and the pigeon is a homing exile like himself, temporarily stranded. Thus nature provides Mtsyri with explicit images of his condition. But there is also an implicit symbolism in the ecological interrelation of these images. The worm is inimical to the leaf, the eagle to the pigeon and the pigeon to the worm; and the storm is inimical at least to the leaf and the pigeon, if not to all. On one level the inevitable antagonism which supports the natural order may be held to reflect the basic inconsistencies of Mtsyri's philosophy: Mtsyri the homing pigeon and gentle dove might well be slain by his eagle compatriots. On a psychological level it hints at the futility of Mtsyri's zoanthropic quest for identity. For no such identification can be found which is immune from the tyranny of the natural order. The epic section of the poem from stanza 9 onwards demonstrates this clearly.

There is, for instance, a patent inconsistency between the attitude Mtsyri claims to have taken to the storm while it was going on ('I . . . would have gladly embraced the storm!') and his lyric self-characterisation as a 'storm-wrenched leaf' or his implied similarity to the pigeon sheltering from the storm. The truth is that however Mtsyri acted in the storm, whether ecstatically or in panic, he, like the prostrate monks, was acting in a uniquely human way, for which nothing in nature can furnish an exact analogy.[101] Although Mtsyri feels misanthropic fellowship with the snake in stanza 9, by stanza 22 there is nothing in common between the defeated parched and delirious

Mtsyri and the quick-moving reptile which **alone of creatures** braves the sun at midday. Of the inadequacy of fellowship with the leopard something has been said already. It is notable in context however that, although Mtsyri may wish a beast-to-beast contest, he prevails over the leopard because he is human, for his forked stick is symbolic of a peculiarly human ascendancy over the animal world.

Mtsyri's slaying of the leopard and his realisation that he has returned full circle to the monastery effect a marked change in his zoanthropy. Realising its mythological inadequacy, he produces a new image which better accords with his latest condition — the riderless horse:

> The powerful horse on an unfamiliar steppe,
> Throwing its clumsy rider,
> Would find the straight and short way
> To its homeland from afar . . . .
> What am I next to him?   (*Soch.*, II, p. 67)

The wisdom of hindsight teaches Mtsyri that his condition is closer to that of a captive animal returning instinctively to its home than to that of a wild one in its habitat. In this connection it becomes clear that the pigeon of stanza 5 is perhaps the latest and most highly developed of Mtsyri's zoanthropic images. The image comes verbatim from *The Confession* and *The Boyar Orsha*, but its context in these works leaves the image's full connotative power unexploited. The pigeon represents man's subtlest control over the animal since, though its physical freedom is unrestricted, its homing instinct is exploited, and it will return eagerly to captivity. Lermontov's use of the pigeon thus represents an advance on the 'orthodox' ambiguity of the romantic bird image, whereby 'the bird flies freely, but in its flight it also recalls the cage from which it flew away . . .',[102] and also on the bird in stanza 10 of *The Prisoner of Chillon* which is its probable inspiration. For Byron the bird's visitation is essentially unmotivated and open to miraculous interpretation. It comes as a consolatory apparition of visual and aural beauty. The pigeon's function is more didactic than aesthetic. Its appearance is motivated purely by its need for shelter from the elements which the monastery can provide. The monastery thus temporarily furthers the pigeon's goal of a complete return, of a restitution of what was before. Mtsyri falls short of this desideratum and thereby underlines his humanity; for, being human, Mtsyri, unlike a pigeon, cannot derive adequate shelter from the structural shell of the monastery, but having once entered its inner living structure, he has become an organic part of it.[103]

Only by delirious distortion is Mtsyri able to force the natural world into yielding him exacter paradigms of human desires. The fish, a dumb creature, offers him a deathlike peace and fellowship beneath the waves. This is the final bankruptcy of zoanthropy in the poem. It should however be noted that the narrator himself, in accordance with the objective functions of the author's prologue, offers an impartial assessment of Mtsyri in terms of the animal kingdom: he is 'like a mountain gazelle, fearful and wild' (*Soch.*, II, p. 52). The value of this simile is that, not originating with the hero, it is neither a role to which Mtsyri aspires (like the serpent or leopard) nor one from which (like the horse or pigeon) he has fallen short. However it does place Mtsyri firmly among the fearful victims of the natural world rather than among the predators.

Donald Davidson claims that 'the most obvious semantic difference between simile and metaphor is that all similes are true and most metaphors are false'.[104] The proof of this is that we tend to use similes when the corresponding metaphor would be false: 'We say Mr S is like a pig because we know he isn't one'.[105] Thus although in terms of identity the simile's claim is more modest than the metaphor's, its claims to plausibility are the greater. *Mtsyri*'s general use of simile rather than metaphor to compare animals with the hero must be explicable in part by Lermontov's purely artistic predilection for this familiar mainstay of narrative poetry. Still, it may well be argued that the preponderance of adverbial similes in *Mtsyri* suggests that the hero's purpose in applying them is as much aetiological as rhetorical. Of course, the failure of all Mtsyri's attempts at self-assimilation to nature lies in the essential non-congruence between Mtsyri as subject and nature as modifier.[106] All metaphorisation is, to some extent, a defamiliarisation of subject by modifier and so, in proportion to his fulfilment of a bestial role, Mtsyri becomes estranged from his human self. The prominence of the serpent in this false quest for identity suggests that the quest itself should be understood as a fall from authentic human existence;[107] the self is defined in terms contingent to it rather than, in Kierkegaard's words, 'as a relation which relates itself to its own self' and not to anything else.[108]

Equally, however, the metaphorical relation between man and nature can be inverted: the jackal in stanza 9 'shouts and weeps like a child' (*Soch.*, II, p. 58). The leopard, it will be recalled, 'groaned like a man' (*Soch.*, II, p. 65). Herein lies the positive aspect of Mtsyri's encounter with nature. If defining the human self in terms of nature depletes and estranges it, defining nature in terms of the self augments the self.[109] Man imaginatively tames and modifies nature by perceiving it either anthropomorphically or in terms which assimilate it to human needs and experience. In this way, nature is capable of being 'the accomplice' of man as well as 'the persecutor'.[110]

Stanza 6 is the principal repository of such a familiarisation of nature: the ivy-clad hills seem like a ring of dancing brothers; the rocks think thoughts which Mtsyri is able to divine and

> Long have their stony embraces
> Reached out into the air,
> Every moment thirsting to touch;
> But days and years pass fleeting by
> And never will their union be.　　　(*Soch.*, II, p. 56)

The mountain peaks become the smoking altars familiar to a monk. Such animations and humanisations are a typical feature of Lermontov's lyric poetry. In *The Gifts of the Terek* (*Dary Tereka*, 1839), the river Terek attempts to bribe the Caspian Sea with dead bodies in order to be allowed to flow into it; in *The Leaf* a wind-blown oak-leaf begs shelter in the foliage of a plane tree; in *The Rock* a cliff grieves for a rain-cloud which has spent the night with it and moved on. 'In the wild North there stands a pine . . .' describes a pine tree helplessly dreaming of a distant palm. Lermontov appears to single out for such attention either inanimate or immovable features of landscape, generally to exemplify a tragedy stemming from this very lifelessness or motionlessness. Separation, helplessness and yearning for fellowship are therefore often the themes of such poems or images.

In the lyrics concerned animated nature, in the broad tradition of romantic lyrics, is unmotivated. Likewise such animations as occur regularly in the Caucasian *poemy* appear either as the poet's lyrical asides or as a pathetic fallacy connected with a character's mood. Thus in *Aul Bastundzhi* Akbulat gazes passively at clouds which resemble a hunt in full cry; the image, however, is the poet's, not his, and is setting the scene for impending fraternal dissension. In *Izmayl Bey*, in a curiously transcendental aside, the poet teeters between anthropomorphising the rocks and petrifying the Chechen sitting next to him:

> Like a grey rock, the grizzled old man
> Lolled his head, sunk in thought . . .
> His silence and the silence of the rocks;
> I could scarcely distinguish them at that moment!
> 　　　　　　　　　　　(*Soch.*, II, p. 247)

The case stands differently, however, when such images issue from the mouths of the characters themselves and hence acquire a psychological motivation for their utterance. Take, for instance, the following extended simile from the speech of Leila's father in *Khadzhi Abrek*:

Three gentle daughters and three sons
God gave me for my old age;
But evil storms came lashing,
And the tree's boughs came crashing,
And now I stand alone,
Like a bare stump in the valley(s).

(Soch., II, p. 352)

There can be less scope here for interpreting the image either as romantic stylistic convention or as an example of romantic nature philosophy of the Blakean 'Sick Rose' or 'Clod and Pebble' type, however legitimate this may be elsewhere in Lermontov's poetry. The principal justification of the image rests in its applicability to the old man's emotional state.

If the nature imagery in Mtsyri's confession is similarly psychologically motivated, then it is less a romantic nature philosophy of enduring significance than an ephemeral manifestation of one particular psyche — Mtsyri's. Heightened motivation, indeed, is not necessarily a symptom of heightened realism — 'romantic works . . . have their own mode of motivation, albeit idiosyncratic'[111] — and the effect of psychological motivation is the substitution of one romantic mode for another: romantic solipsism in place of a metaphysics of nature. And yet V. F. Savodnik writes of Lermontov's view of nature:

> . . . he uses an *association of ideas* taken from *nature*; thus he does not interpret nature from the data of direct inner experience in order to humanise it and bring it closer to our understanding, but on the contrary, he finds in nature herself forms and colours, analogies and parables . . .[112]

Is Mtsyri then some strange dissenter from his creator's philosophy, since he does precisely those things excluded above? Mtsyri indeed, but not *Mtsyri*. For the authorial prologue of the poem provides an apparatus whereby the subjective propositions of the hero may be tested objectively. The hero's principal conceptual modes — the zoanthropic and the anthropomorphic — are represented in the prologue. The comparison of Mtsyri to a frightened gazelle in stanza 2 is therefore not only one more animal comparison to add to the list; Lermontov's use of the zoomorphic image represents its legitimate aesthetic application, whereas Mtsyri's attempt to squeeze something more out of it results in the protean contradictions of zoanthropy. If the gazelle image represents Lermontov's critical dissociation from Mtsyri's zoanthropy, the description of the two rivers in the opening lines of the poem represents an endorsement of Mtsyri's anthropomorphic images in stanza 6. Without objective corroboration, these too might have seemed products of Mtsyri's imagination. Here, however, Lermontov offers us just such an image because it is most appropriate to the exact depiction of something which really exists in time and place:

> A few years ago,
> Where the rivers Aragva and Kura
> Noisily flow into one another,
> Embracing like two sisters . . . .

(Soch., II, p. 51)

The image may be verified against the reality. Mtsyri's anthropomorphism is vindicated.

This use of 'exact topological location', in Howard Mumford Jones' phrase, does exemplify a certain interfusion of realism and romanticism.[113] But in general, specificity of location in Lermontov, particularly of Caucasian location, serves to refine and purify the romantic effect, rather than to dilute it. In this connection it is interesting to note that the traditional Soviet view of Lermontov's creative career as romanticism ultimately 'surmounted' by realism has yielded in more recent years to the view that Lermontov did indeed remain a romantic to the end, though during his mature period romantic works may be said to 'coexist' with examples of realism.[114]

In conclusion, it is perhaps worth remembering that 'exact topological location' brings with it inevitable extra-textual implications. The first line of *Mtsyri* implies that the decline of the monastery has been fairly quick. Human conceits fade away, but Nature endures and Mtsyri's artistic vision is and will be vindicated by her. How fares this process now? 'The monastery described in the poem remains', wrote T. Ivanova in 1969; 'it is now called *Mtsyri* and tourist excursions go to it'. She continues:

> The scenery is just the same [as described in *Mtsyri*]. The small town of Mkhet, ancient capital of Georgia, spreads out at the foot of the mountain in just the same way; the church dome is etched just as clearly against the blue sky and, as one gets closer, one can make out the 'pillars of the ruined gates and towers'. But the Kura and Aragva, though they 'flow into one another' no longer do so 'noisily' but flow smoothly since the installation here of a hydro-electric station.[115]

A strange sequel, the implications of which lie, alas, beyond the bounds of critical application.

Notes

1. U. R. Fokht, *Lermontov: Logika tvorchestva*, Moscow, 1975, p. 95.
2. L. F. Tarasov, 'Poema M. Yu. Lermontova *Mtsyri*: Stilisticheskiy kommentariy' (*Russkiy yazyk v shkole*, 5, 1976, p. 58).
3. Ye. A. Maymin, *O russkom romantizme*, Moscow, 1975, pp. 141ff; D. Ye. Maksimov, *Poeziya Lermontova*, Moscow, 1964, pp. 178ff.
4. Yu. V. Mann, *Poetika russkogo romantizma*, Moscow, 1976, p. 197.
5. D. Ye. Maksimov, op. cit., p. 178. For a survey of major trends in *Demon* criticism see Robert Reid, 'Lermontov's *Demon*: A Question of Identity' (*Slavonic and East European Review*, LX, 2, 1982, pp. 189—210).
6. Loc. cit.
7. V. G. Belinsky, *Polnoye sobraniye sochineniy*, ed. N. F. Bel'chikov, et al., Moscow, 1954, IV, p. 544.
8. V. S. Mezhevich (pseud. L. L.), 'Stikhotvoreniya Lermontova' (*Severnaya pchela*, 1840), in *Russkaya kriticheskaya literatura o proizvedeniyakh M. Yu. Lermontova: Khronologicheskiy sbornik kritiko-bibliograficheskikh statey*, ed. N. Zelinsky, Moscow, 1913, I, pp. 120—5 (hereafter *Russk. krit. lit.*).
9. Ibid., p. 130. Compare, for instance D. A. Gireyev's observations on *Mtsyri*: M. Yu. Lermontov, *Mtsyri*, ed. D. A. Gireyev, Pyatigorsk, 1948, p. 18.
10. In *Aul Bastundzhi* (Part II, stanza 8), Selim boasts of polishing off two of the beasts single-handed in order to get possession of their cave.
11. For instance, in *Izmayl Bey*, Part I, stanza 24.
12. A. Galakhov, 'Lermontov' (*Ruskiy vestnik*, XVI, 1, p. 76, and more particularly, II, p. 259). Later A. L. Bem developed the idea of self-imitation as a principle of Lermontov's creativity: 'Samopovtoreniya v tvorchestve Lermontova', in *Istoriko-literaturnyy sbornik*, Leningrad, 1924, pp. 268—90.
13. V. Plaksin, 'O sochineniyakh Lermontova' (*Severnoye obozreniye*, III, 3), in *Russk. krit. lit.*, p. 130.
14. S. I. Durylin puts forward this view in *Kak rabotal Lermontov*, Moscow, 1934, p. 79.
15. *Rodina*: homeland, motherland, fatherland — no exact English equivalent.
16. L. S. Melikhova and V. N. Turbin, *Poemy Lermontova: Opyt analiza zhanrovogo svoyeobraziya khudozhestvennogo proizvedeniya*, Moscow, 1969, p. 35.
17. M. Yu. Lermontov, *Sobraniye sochineniy v chetyrokh tomakh*, ed. I. L. Andronikov, Moscow, 1964—5, II: *Poemy i povesti v stikhakh*, pp. 53, 185, 376 respectively. All subsequent quotations in the text are from this edition (hereafter *Soch.*).
18. Robin F. Miller, 'Rousseau and Dostoyevsky: the Morality of Confession Reconsidered', in *Western Philosophical Systems in Russian Literature: A Collection of Critical Studies*, Series in Slavic Humanities, 3, ed. Anthony M. Mlikotin, Los Angeles, 1980, p. 99.
19. V. M. Zhirmunsky, *Izbranniye trudy: Teoriya literatury, poetika, stilistika*, ed. Yu. D. Levin and D. S. Likhachev, Leningrad, 1977, pp. 134—5.
20. A. K. Potebnya, *Estetika i poetika*, Moscow, 1976, p. 311.
21. Loc. cit.

22. P. A. Viskovatyy, 'Ispoved' (*Russkaya starina*, 10, 1887, pp. 124—5).

23. I. L. Andronikov, *Lermontov*, Moscow, 1951, pp. 151—2.

24. A. V. Popov, 'Sokrovennoye sozdaniye tvorcheskogo geniya Lermontova', in *Sbornik trudov Stavropol'skogo gos. ped. instituta*, vyp. 13, Stavropol', 1958, p. 362.

25. N. Lyubovich, '*Mtsyri* v ideynoy bor'be 30—40-kh godov', in *Tvorchestvo M. Yu. Lermontova*, ed. U. R. Fokht, Moscow, 1964, p. 107.

26. A. V. Popov, op. cit., p. 364.

27. N. Lyubovich, op. cit., p. 108.

28. Ibid., p. 126: second paragraph, for instance. A more recent commentator, Anatoly Liberman, also implies that Lermontov wrote *Mtsyri* as an anti-clerical work. However, he interprets the poem as 'a defence of freedom in its most abstract (romantic) form'. *Mikhail Lermontov: Major Poetical Works*, tr. Anatoly Liberman, London, 1983, p. 579.

29. Apollon Grigor'ev (*Russkoye slovo*, 3, 1850) in *Russk. krit. lit.*, p. 56.

30. Yu. V. Mann, op. cit., p. 202.

31. L. S. Melikhova and V. N. Turbin, op. cit., p. 35.

32. V. S. Yashina, 'Konflikt peredovoy lichnosti s obshchestvom v romanticheskoy poeme Lermontova *Mtsyri*', in *K Problemam teorii i istorii literatury*, Stavropol', 1966, p. 117.

33. R. V. Ivanov Razumnik, *Istoriya russkoy obshchestvennoy mysli*, 2nd edn, St Petersburg, 1908, pp. 155, 162.

34. D. N. Ovsyaniko-Kulikovsky, *M. Yu. Lermontov: K stoletiyu so dnya rozhdeniya velikogo poeta*, St Petersburg, 1914, p. 64.

35. A. N. Pypin, *Istoriya russkoy literatury*, St Petersburg, 1907, IV, p. 53.

36. S. A. Andreyevsky, *Literaturnyye ocherki*, St Petersburg, 1902, p. 203.

37. V. Plaksin, op. cit., p. 133.

38. Yu. V. Mann, op. cit., p. 207.

39. D. Ye. Maksimov, op. cit., p. 233.

40. Victor Brombert, 'The Happy Prison: A recurring Romantic Metaphor', in *Romanticism: Vistas, Instances, Continuities*, ed. David Thorburn and Geoffrey Hartman, Ithaca and London, 1973, p. 63.

41. Ibid., p. 67.

42. A. M. Skabichevsky, *Sochineniya v dvukh tomakh*, St Petersburg, 1895, I, pp. 217—18.

43. V. Asmus, 'Krug idey Lermontova', in *Literaturnoye nasledstvo*, XLIII—XLIV, Moscow, 1941, p. 86.

44. Harold Bloom, 'The First and Last Romantics' (*Studies in Romanticism*, IX, 1970, p. 225).

45. In this respect Lermontov seems an exception to Northrop Frye's rule that 'after Newton ups and downs become hopelessly confused' resulting in 'a profound change . . . in the spatial projection of reality'. Northrop Frye, 'The Drunken Boat: The Revolutionary Element in Romanticism', in *Romanticism Reconsidered*, ed. Northrop Frye, New York, 1963, p. 5.

46. M. H. Abrams, *Natural Supernaturalism: Tradition and Revolution in Romantic Literature*, London, 1971, p. 165.

47. Ibid., p. 183.

48. For instance D. A. Gireyev in his introduction to an edition of the poem: 'Poema o velikoy lyubvi k rodine', in M. Yu. Lermontov, *Mtsyri*, Pyatigorsk, 1948, pp. 5—31; also B. V. Neyman, 'Mtsyri', in *Istoriya russkoy literatury XIX veka*, ed. F. M. Golovenchenko and S. M. Petrova, 2nd edn, 1963, I, pp. 410—13.

49. See Ye. A. Polukarova, 'Iz nablyudeniy nad upotrebleniyem otvlechonnoy leksiki v poeme M. Yu. Lermontova *Mtsyri*', in *Yazyk i stil' proizvedeniy M. Yu. Lermontova (Uchonyye zapiski Ryazanskogo ped. instituta*, LXXVIII, Penza, 1969, p. 33).

50. V. I. Belinsky, op. cit., IV, p. 537.

51. A. L. Rubanovich, *Problemy masterstva Lermontova*, ed. V. P. Trushkin, Irkutsk, 1963, p. 161.

52. T. Ivanova draws some interesting inferences from the incident: Mtsyri probably originates from one of three Caucasian tribes typified by such hand-to-hand combat and his forked stick probably represents a characteristic tribal weapon. In these tribes it is not unusual for children under thirteen years to indulge in warfare, and capture by an enemy is considered by them the greatest disgrace. Mtsyri, then, has not only suffered the latter but, in exile, is still only a novice while his native peers are already fully-fledged members of the tribal community. T. Ivanova, in her introduction to *M. Yu. Lermontov, Poemy*, Moscow, 1969: 'Poeticheskiy mir Lermontova', pp. 28—30. I. L. Andronikov, by contrast, considers that the inspiration for the fight was a medieval Georgian song about a youth fighting a tiger. He believes that Georgian folkloric influence on the poem is strong, to the extent that: 'each day of Mtsyri's freedom involuntarily evokes in the memory the knights and giants of Georgian folk poetry'. I. L. Andronikov, *Lermontov v Gruzii v 1837-om godu*, Moscow, 1955, pp. 39ff.

53. L. F. Tarasov, 'Poema M. Yu. Lermontova *Mtsyri*: Stilisticheskiy komment-ariy' (*Russkiy yazyk v shkole*, 5, 1976, p. 58).

54. As K. N. Grigoryan suggests in *Lermontov i romantizm*, Moscow-Leningrad, p. 108. For differing views on Lermontov's attitude to the national question in the Caucasus, see A. N. Sokolov, *Ocherki po istorii russkoy poemy XVIII i pervoy poloviny XIX veka*, Moscow, 1955, pp. 592—7, and Vl. A. Arkhipov's critique of the latter in Vl. Arkhipov, *M. Yu. Lermontov: Poeziya poznaniya i deystviya*, Moscow, 1965, pp. 426ff.

55. S. V. Shuvalov, *M. Yu. Lermontov: Zhizn' i tvorchestvo*, Moscow-Leningrad, 1925, p. 96.

56. G. V. Filatova, 'Problema polozhitel'nogo geroya v poemakh Lermontova *Beglets* i *Mtsyri*' (*Uchonyye zapiski Mosk. obl. ped. instituta im. Krupskoy*, 186, vyp. 11, p. 114).

57. Loc. cit. For more detailed discussion of Lermontov's other Caucasian *poemy* see Robert Reid, 'Hero, Plot and Myth: Some Aspects of Lermontov's Caucasian *Poemy*' (*Essays in Poetics*, VII, 2, 1982, pp. 39—64).

58. Durylin holds that its retention would have detracted from the impact of the fish vision by 'bringing a new motif into the integrated psyche of a person dying of thirst'. S. I. Durylin, op. cit., p. 73.

59. Apollon Grigor'ev, op. cit., p. 156: Mtsyri is here called a 'little beast' (*zveryonok*). See also Herzen's brief observations on the poem: A. I.

Herzen, *Sobraniye sochineniy*, ed. V. P. Volgin, et al., Moscow, 1965, XXX, 2, p. 751.

60. See n. 59.

61. V. A. Yevzerikhina, 'Poema Lermontova *Mtsyri*: k voprosu o tvorcheskoy evolyutsii', in *Novosibirskaya vysshaya partiynaya shkola, 13-ya nauchnaya konferentsiya*, Novosibirsk, 1972, p. 109.

62. Yu. Lotman, 'Istochnik "tolstovskogo napravleniya" v russkoy literature 1830–kh godov' (*Trudy po russkoy i slavyanskoy filologii*, 5: *Uchonyye zapiski Tartuskogo universiteta*, vyp. 119, 1962, p. 43).

63. For instance: S. I. Durylin, op. cit., p. 77; V. I. Korovin, *Tvorcheskiy put' Lermontova*, Moscow, 1973, p. 182; Yu. Lotman, op. cit., pp. 37, 43; D. Ye. Maksimov, op. cit., pp. 182, 190: Maksimov stresses Lermontov's modification of the Rousseau tradition.

64. A. S. Pushkin, *Sobraniye sochineniy*, ed. D. D. Blagoy, et al., Moscow, 1960, p. 180. In this connection L. N. Nazarova notes that 'Mtsyri's flight from the monastery into nature is not an attempt to become part of a new cultural world (as was Aleko's journey) but rather a break with a philosophy and mode of life which are constitutionally alien to him. Its goal is a return to the self, to the source and first principles of his own being – to that from which he has been forcibly removed'. *Lermontovskaya Entsiklopediya*, ed. V. A. Manuylov, et al., Moscow, 1981, p. 325.

65. V. M. Fisher, 'Poetika Lermontova', in *Vyenok M. Yu. Lermontovu: Yubileynyy sbornik*, Moscow-Petrograd, 1914, p. 205.

66. S. I. Durylin, op. cit., p. 77.

67. L. Todorov characterises the lyro-epic genre as follows: 'In depicting reality [it] combines features present in both epic and lyric . . . in an organic, qualitatively new compound. The lyro-epic genre was at its height during the age of romanticism when the lyric principle pervaded many genres, a tendency most fully and diversely displayed in the *poemy* of Byron, Shelley, Vigny, Mickiewicz, the young Pushkin and Lermontov'. L. Todorov in *Slovar' literaturovedcheskikh terminov*, Moscow, 1974, p. 178.

68. A. Nikitenko, 'Stikhotvoreniya Lermontova' (*Syn otechestva*, I, 1, 1841), in *Russk. krit. lit.*, I, p. 174.

69. S. Shevyryov, 'Geroy nashego vremeni' (*Moskvityanin*, 1841), in *Russk. krit. lit.*, I, p. 152.

70. A. Nikitenko, op. cit., p. 184.

71. K. N. Grigoryan, op. cit., p. 110.

72. O. I. Fedotov, 'Lirizm vysokogo napryazheniya: O zhanrovom svoyeobrazii poemy Lermontova *Mtsyri*', in *Voprosy literatury: K 160-letiyu so dnya rozhdeniya M. Yu. Lermontova*, vyp. 10, Vladimir, 1975, p. 77.

73. N. A. Kotlyarevsky, *M. Yu. Lermontov: Lichnost' poeta i ego proizvedeniya*, Petrograd, 1915, p. 112. Quoted in O. I. Fedotov, op. cit., p. 78.

74. A. K. Potebnya, op. cit., p. 314.

75. A. N. Sokolov, 'Khudozhestvennyy obraz v lirike Lermontova', in *Tvorchestvo M. Yu. Lermontova: 150 let so dnya rozhdeniya*, Moscow, 1964, p. 188.

76. S. I. Leusheva, 'Poemy Lermontova *Dyemon* i *Mtsyri*' (*Literatura v shkole*, 1, 1940, p. 37).

77. G. K. Bocharov, *Za sorok let: Zapiski slovesnika*, Moscow, 1972, p. 174.
78. Ye. A. Vedenyapina, 'O tipologicheskoy strukture obraza geroya russkoy romanticheskoy poemy 20—30-kh godov XIX v.' (*Vestnik Moskovskogo universiteta*, 1, 1972, p. 30).
79. V. G. Yolkin, '*Mtsyri* Lermontova kak liro-epicheskaya poema', in *Voprosy esteticheskogo vospitaniya uchashchikhsya na urokakh literatury*, Vladimir, 1973, p. 86.
80. L. Ye. Slashcheva, 'Kategoriya vremeni v khudozhestvennom soderzhanii: na materiale liriki M. Yu. Lermontova', *Filologicheskiy sbornik*, vyp. 6—7, Alma Ata, 1963, p. 330.
81. Ibid., p. 329.
82. Baron Rozen, 'O stikhotvoreniyakh Lermontova' (*Syn otechestva*, III, 1843), in *Russk. krit. lit.*, II, p. 91. John Garrard also thinks that the brief role played by the 'nameless narrator' is a 'narrative shortcoming' in the poem. Another is the lack of dialogue between Mtsyri and the old monk. These weaknesses were inherited from Byron. However Garrard does not show why such narrative features should inevitably be flaws in a work of literature. John Garrard, *Mikhail Lermontov*, Boston, 1982, pp. 94—5.
83. See Steven M. Cahn, *Fate, Logic and Time*, Yale, 1967, p. 9, and for an exposition of the Aristotelian view, p. 27. Cahn however also argues that Aristotle was unwilling to accept the full rigours of logical fatalism; see p. 24.
84. Richard Jackson, 'The Romantic Metaphysics of Time' (*Studies in Romanticism*, XIX, 1980, p. 24).
85. Ibid., pp. 23, 24.
86. Ibid., p. 25.
87. T. Ivanova, op. cit., p. 27. Ivanova considers that a neighbouring hill, Zeda-Zeni, to that on which the prototype for *Mtsyri* is situated, is more likely to have inspired the natural setting of the poem.
88. N. Ye. Mednis, 'Stikh i kompozitsiya poemy M. Yu. Lermontova *Mtsyri*', in *Russkaya literatura XIX v.: Voprosy syuzheta i kompozitsii* (*Uchonyye zapiski Gor'kovskogo universiteta*, vyp. 32, p. 122).
89. D. Ye. Maksimov, op. cit., p. 225. Quoted in N. Ye. Mednis, loc. cit.
90. V. I. Korovin, *Tvorcheskiy put' Lermontova*, Moscow, 1973, p. 171.
91. Marshall Brown, *The Shape of German Romanticism*, Ithaca and London, 1979, p. 212.
92. Jakob Johann von Uexkull, *Theoretical Biology*, tr. D. L. Mackinnon, London, 1926. Quoted in John Bleibtreu, *The Parable of the Beast*, St Albans, 1970, p. 27.
93. O. I. Fedotov, op. cit., p. 92.
94. *The Compact Edition of The Oxford English Dictionary*, Oxford, 1971, I, p. 650 (reduced O.E.D., p. 49), Section 7.
95. See for instance the parable of the labourers in the vineyard, Matthew 20.
96. The religious symbolism of this idea underlies John 9:9—10.
97. See B. Blackstone, 'Byron and Islam: the Triple Eros' (*Journal of European Studies*, IV, 1974, pp. 358—9).
98. Leonid Semeonov, M. Yu. Lermontov, *Stat'i i zametki*, Moscow, I, 1915, p. 249. Other examples are in *Death of a Poet* (1837): '. . . and taking off

his former crown — a crown of thorns, / with laurels plaited in, they placed upon him: / but the secret needles sorely / hurt his glorious brow' (*Soch.*, I, p. 22); *Pamyati A. I. Odoyevskogo* (1839): 'What are these to you: the crowns of its [the world's] attentiveness / and the thorns of its vain calumnies?' (ibid., p. 64); *A. G. Khomutovoy* (1838): 'But may a blessing descend / on your life for / momentarily / having lifted the crown of thorns / from his [Lermontov's] bowed head' (ibid., p. 45).

99. Morse Peckham, 'Toward a Theory of Romanticism: II, Reconsiderations' (*Studies in Romanticism*, I, 1, 1961, p. 6).

100. Ibid., p. 5.

101. S. Lominadze usefully contrasts Mtsyri's attitude to the storm with that expressed by the lyric voice in *Parus* (1832). He notes that Mtsyri, unlike the lyricist, is ignorant of the inherent contradiction of seeking peace in a storm. S. Lominadze, 'Kuda bezhit Mtsyri' (*Voprosy literatury*, X, 1984, p. 158).

102. Victor Brombert, op. cit., p. 74.

103. The monastery in context thus exemplifies an ambiguity which helped to make buildings, and particularly houses, a Gothic and romantic staple, an ambiguity which D. Punter ascribes partly to the Greek *oikos* signifying both house as structure and house as family. D. Punter, *The History of Terror*, London, 1980, p. 199.

104. Donald Davidson, 'What Metaphors mean', in *On Metaphor*, ed. Sheldon Sacks, Chicago, 1979, p. 39.

105. Loc. cit.

106. I here follow the terminology used by David S. Miall, in 'Metaphor and Literal Meaning' (*British Journal of Aesthetics*, 1977, 17, pp. 49—59, esp. p. 55).

107. As André Lacocque puts it: 'The serpent in Genesis, the representative par excellence of the animals of the fields, introduces itself into the dialogue between God and man and pulls man down towards the ground, where it is henceforth condemned to crawl and grovel.' André Lacocque, *Le Livre de Daniel*, Paris, 1976, p. 74.

108. S. Kierkegaard, *Fear and Trembling and The Sickness unto Death*, tr. and ed. Walter Lowrie, Princeton, 1973, p. 146.

109. Animality seems to have been a preoccupation of the more heterodox and arcane strands of the Judaeo-Christian tradition, represented by such works as the Book of Daniel where 'beasts play a considerable role, always to the detriment of man's integrity' (André Lacocque, loc. cit.), and the Apocryphal Gospel of Thomas where we find this nice example of the potential reversibility of the metaphorical relation between man and animal: 'Jesus said: Blessed is the lion which the man shall eat, and the lion become man; and cursed is the man whom the lion shall eat and the lion become man', *The New Testament Apocrypha*, ed. E. Hennecke, London, 1963, I, p. 511, verse 7; see also loc. cit., verse 3: 'If they say unto you it [the Kingdom] is in the sea, then the fish will be there before you.' In marked contrast an apothegm in the Oxyrhynchus papyri declares: 'Who are they that draw us and when shall come the Kingdom that is in heaven? The fowls of the air and of [sic] the beasts whatever is beneath the earth or upon the earth, and

the fishes of the sea, these they are that draw you.' F. C. Happold, *Mysticism: A Study and an Anthology*, Harmondsworth, 1963, p. 195. Canonical N. T. animal imagery is comparatively less ambitious and extreme; it is intriguing that something akin to heterodox or schismatic animal symbolism should assert itself precisely in the context of a young monk's disaffection with the monastic *status quo*.

110.   A. D. Zhizhina, 'Ideyno-obraznaya sistema poemy Lermontova *Mtsyri*' (*Literatura v shkole*, 5, 1976, p. 18).

111.   N. A. Lisenkova, 'Motivirovka i yeyo rol′ v khudozhestvennom proizvedenii', in *A. N. Radishchev, V. G. Belinsky, M. Yu. Lermontov (Zhanr i stil′ khudozhestvennogo proizvedeniya)*, ed. A. K. Bocharova, et al., Ryazan′, 1974, p. 78.

112.   V. F. Savodnik, *Chuvstvo prirody v poezii Pushkina, Lermontova i Tyutcheva*, Moscow, 1911, p. 119.

113.   Howard Mumford Jones, *Romanticism and Revolution*, Cambridge, Mass., 1974, p. 3.

114.   See I. Ye. Usok's observations in 'K sporam o khudozhestvennom metode M. Yu. Lermontova', in *K istorii russkogo romantizma*, Moscow, 1973, pp. 283ff.

115.   T. Ivanova, op. cit., p. 25.

7 Perspectives on the romanticism of V. F. Odoyevsky

NEIL CORNWELL

I

Western histories of Russian literature have generally relegated V. F. Odoyevsky to the sidelines as a minor figure of romantic prose, with a brief mention of *Russian Nights* (*Russkiye nochi*) and little else. He has been accorded the occasional chapter in more specialised studies dealing with a particular theme, such as the impact on Russian literature of the German romantics, Goethe and Hoffmann.[1] John Mersereau, in his article 'The Chorus and Spear Carriers of Russian Romantic Fiction', said that 'Prince V. F. Odoyevsky was good enough at least part of the time to take a leading role, especially when compared with Gogol in poor form (e.g. *The Portrait*)'; Terras called him 'Russia's leading romantic storyteller'; while Fanger referred to Odoyevsky as 'one of the visitors to Russian literature of the twenties, described by Marlinsky in 1825 as a "steppe, occasionally enlivened by the swift passage of journalistic Bedouins or ponderously moving caravans of translations"' and as a 'prospector in search of the philosopher's stone'.[2] An eloquent plea for Odoyevsky to be treated as a major figure was made by Simon Karlinsky in an article of 1966.[3] This kind of prominence for Odoyevsky has never really been acknowledged, however, in Russian and Soviet criticism of the past 150 years.

One of a number of curious circumstances arising from the creative biography of V. F. Odoyevsky is the fact that, apart from his voluminous efforts in the fields of philosophy, musicology and popular education, he had three virtually self-contained and separate literary careers.[4]

The first began in the early 1820s, reached its height with the publication of the almanac *Mnemozina* in 1824—5 and fizzled out in the aftermath of the Decembrist revolt. The tail end of this period merged indeterminately with the beginnings of the second period which really started from about 1830 and again faded after the publication in 1844 of a three-volume 'Collected Works'.[5] The third period can be said to start in the mid 1850s and to continue until Odoyevsky's death in 1869. The first period made perhaps the greatest immediate impact on the advanced reading public of the day and is remembered not only as Odoyevsky's formative period, but as the only stage (the heyday of the *lyubomudry* or wisdom-lovers) when his ideas could be said to have been at the forefront of the development of Russian thought. The middle period was his most productive and successful from an artistic point of view and has naturally provided the staple diet for the bulk of Odoyevsky criticism. The third period resulted in very little completed or published work and has been accorded much less attention.

Odoyevsky's work of the first part of the 1820s attracted considerable attention almost from the start. *Mnemozina* quickly aroused, as had been its intention, critical controversy and a number of leading figures have recorded its impact.[6] Odoyevsky began to publish in the 1830s his mature romantic and society tales, both singly and in cycles, and these attracted mixed critical comment. Pushkin and Gogol, for example, are both on record as admiring at least some of Odoyevsky's work.[7] However, it was with the publication of *Russian Nights* as part of the three-volume collection of 1844 and Belinsky's review article of that year that Odoyevsky criticism proper can be said to have commenced.

Critical discussion of Odoyevsky's work has been largely dominated, from Belinsky to the present day, by the attitude adopted towards the romantic elements, whether identified as such or not.

Before 1844 Belinsky had published only brief comments on Odoyevsky's work, but in a generally enthusiastic tone. Following his early didactic phase, Belinsky wrote in 1835, Odoyevsky had taken a different direction, focusing in his mature work on the artist ('that marvellous riddle'), whose loftiest moments were expressed 'with amazing truthfulness . . . in profound, poetic symbols', in allegoric form: *Beethoven's Last Quartet* (*Posledniy kvartet Betkhovena*) and *Sebastian Bach* were obviously in Belinsky's mind. 'Prince Odoyevsky is a poet of the ideal world and not the real world', says Belinsky with apparent approval. There is, however, another side, in Belinsky's view, to Odoyevsky's work: that represented in stories such as *The Story of a Cockerel, a Cat and a Frog* (*Istoriya o petukhe, koshke i lyagushke*) and *Princess Mimi* (*Knyazhna Mimi*): 'two true pictures of our heterogeneous society'.[8]

Belinsky's references to Odoyevsky during the period of his 'reconciliation with reality' were at least equally favourable. He found *Princess Zizi* (*Knyazhna Zizi*), in 1839, an enjoyable story to read and the incomplete Utopian novel *The Year 4338* (*4338-y god*) 'an excerpt rich in original thoughts'.[9] The publication of the 1844 works, however, elicited Belinsky's only extensive essay on Odoyevsky's fiction.[10] Included were a number of previously published stories with various additions — most notably the trappings of the philosophical 'frame-tale' — now entitled *Russian Nights*. The other volumes consisted of stories and miscellaneous writings, mainly of the 1830s and early 1840s.

Had Odoyevsky's collection appeared four or five years earlier, Belinsky would probably have welcomed it unreservedly. However by 1844 the overtly romantic nature of much of Odoyevsky's fiction, the underlying idealist premises and the almost Slavophile stress on the destiny of Russia were not to Belinsky's taste. However, Belinsky had always had a high regard for Odoyevsky's contribution to the development of Russian literature and Odoyevsky was the main background figure behind *Notes of the Fatherland*, on which journal Belinsky was principal critic. The result was therefore probably something of a compromise.

Belinsky by 1844 was pursuing the theme of formal evolution, or dialectical synthesis, while at the same time attempting to deny that there had been any such thing as romanticism in the 1820s:[11] 'This struggle of the old and new is known as the struggle of Romanticism with Classicism. If one is to be truthful, we had here neither Classicism nor Romanticism. There was only the struggle of intellectual movement with intellectual stagnation.'[12] As such he was reluctant to confront head-on the phenomenon of romanticism in Odoyevsky. Odoyevsky in his mature works was able to reach a poetic eloquence which, in Belinsky's view, could be compared to that of Jean Paul Richter: *The Brigadier* (*Brigadir*), *The Ball* (*Bal*) and *A Dead Man's Sneer* (*Nasmeshka mertvetsa*) are cited as the best examples. These stories are saved from being too fantastic and given a positive character by a 'restless and passionate humour'. A number of other stories are named as being of the same type, but not quite as good: *The Live Corpse* (*Zhivoy mertvets*) expresses the same idea as *The Brigadier* but lacks the earlier story's 'lyrical animation'; *Town without a Name* (*Gorod bez imeni*) is in the spirit of Odoyevsky's best works 'but its basic idea is somewhat one-sided'. This story, plus a number of others, are treated less enthusiastically than had been the case in Belinsky's earlier writings, although *Princess Mimi* is exalted as 'one of the best Russian *povesti* [stories]'. However, it is with the story *The Sylph* (*Sil'fida*) that Belinsky's criticism starts to bite: '*The Sylph*', a story which Belinsky had read 'with pleasure' in 1838,[13] 'belongs to those of Prince Odoyevsky's works in which he began to deviate decisively from his earlier direction in favour of some kind of strange fantasy'. From this point on, in Belinsky's view, Odoyevsky's works all possess two sides to them; while he remains in the realm of reality he is as impressive as before, but as soon as he descends to the fantastic the reader does not know what to make of him. Anything smacking of the fantastic Belinsky now sees as magical ravings which have no place in post-Enlightenment Europe. Similarly, the two stories now comprising *The Salamander* (*Salamandra*) are rated, the Finnish sections apart, 'incomprehensible'. The influence of Hoffmann (whom Belinsky had once ranked alongside Shakespeare and Goethe) was seen as the probable cause of this deviancy. Belinsky still enjoyed many of the stories of *Russian Nights*, but the 'frame-tale' device he found 'unnatural and forced'. He admitted that the conversations contained weighty ideas, but would have preferred them to have been assigned to a separate article. In the Epilogue, Faust, whom Belinsky takes to be the author himself, talks a great deal of sense, Belinsky admits, on the subject of poverty, the working class and indifference to truth and conviction. However, as a westerniser, Belinsky has to take strong exception to the suggestion that the West is dying and is appalled by both Faust's failure to see any progress in the sciences and a view of history as a mere chaos of facts.

The critical aspects of Belinsky's otherwise not unfavourable review of Odoyevsky's collected works had a considerable effect on that writer's subsequent reputation. While one has to agree with Karlinsky that 'Belinsky's review of *Russian Nights* inaugurated the tradition of minimising and dismissing the more original and profound aspects of Odoyevsky's writings', it would be unjust to lay too much blame at Belinsky's door for Odoyevsky's subsequent neglect; Belinsky's successors and interpreters were even more responsible and other factors were involved — not least Odoyevsky's early departure from the literary scene and failure to reprint his works.[14]

The only other serious review, by Valerian Maykov, also divided Odoyevsky's works into two categories: that of the mystical (which includes nearly all of *Russian Nights*) and that of '*povesti* of unquestionable literary worth and to which mysticism is alien'.[15] Mysticism has no place in literature (other than folk literature), which now requires 'the exposition of society and its development and of the spirit of the people' — in other words 'realism' (a term which Maykov, like Belinsky, does not use). However when Maykov turns to the works in which 'human life, our sufferings and our misfortunes' can be found (*Princess Zizi* and *Princess Mimi*), his tone immediately changes.

From 1845 until his death in 1869, Odoyevsky's name appeared only fleetingly in the pages of Russian literary criticism, but one critic who paid some attention to his work was Apollon Grigor'ev. Grigor'ev, like Odoyevsky, took his basic conception of art from Schelling; at the same time he considered himself, in certain senses at least, to be a follower of Belinsky.[16] In his sympathetic review of Gogol's *Selected Passages from Correspondence with Friends* (1847), Grigor'ev compares that 'apparent, for him dark, strength' pervading Odoyevsky's *Town without a Name* to Gogol's idea of evil.[17] Much more sympathetic to romantic mysticism than most of his predecessors and contemporaries, Grigor'ev nevertheless followed Belinsky and Maykov in his reading of much of Odoyevsky's work: it was in his evaluation that he differed. His *Moskvityanin* articles of 1852 contain several references to Odoyevsky:

> In the fine didactic stories of Odoyevsky [*A Dead Man's Sneer, Town without a Name, Apartment with Heat and Lighting* (*Kvartira s otopleniyem i osveshcheniyem*)] you will hear only a negative emotion [*pafos*], an emotion on a par with the bitter irony of Hamlet, with the sceptic's smile of sorrow, with the vague strivings of the mystic. You feel that hostility has not overpowered reality here, does not possess it in a manly way, and merely cries over it, merely promises something better in the misty boundless distance.[18]

In the character of Princess Mimi, Grigor'ev sees neither a living being nor a type but an idea, and a monstrous one at that, 'drawn out, like a mathematical computation, from exclusively melancholy and gloomy observations, a truly dialectically developed passion'.[19] He thus hints at the presence of an element of philosophical duality, divines an essential pessimism and expresses a certain dissatisfaction in the treatment of social reality.

A. Skabichevsky's 'Forty Years of Russian Criticism' (*Notes of the Fatherland*, 1870) described Odoyevsky as a 'well-known, but, unfortunately, little appreciated writer'.[20] The Populist critic took a somewhat impressionistic view of aesthetics and regarded Odoyevsky as a 'second-rate' (*vtorostepennyy*) artist, but of great historical importance as a man of ideas. Skabichevsky places great emphasis on the historical importance of Schellingianism in Russia, which philosophy, with its pantheistic and intuitive elements and stress on intellectual contemplation, he saw as 'a progressive step forward' for its day, as well as 'completely corresponding to that apotheosis of feeling and fantasy in which our romantic movement manifested itself in the 1820s'. Skabichevsky pointed out the mistake of attempting to see Odoyevsky as either a Slavophile or a westeriser (it was possible in the 1830s to be a mixture of both and Schellingianism could serve as a base for either persuasion) and commented that Belinsky had failed to appreciate all sides of

Odoyevsky because of standing too close to him in time. Yet Skabi-chevsky does not appear to have appreciated the extent of Odoyevsky's later drift towards positivism and was also puzzled, like most of his predecessors, by the form of *Russian Nights*.

Ch. Vetrinsky (1899) complained of the neglect of figures such as Odoyevsky, drew attention to the theme of moral death in Odoyevsky's work and suggested that *Sebastian Bach* may have been based on Odoy-evsky's own domestic life.[21] P. Mizinov considered that the personal and biographical elements in Odoyevsky's works had not yet been touched on and made an identification between the young Odoyevsky and Griboyedov's Chatsky (and less plausibly between Odoyevsky and Goncharov's Aduyev); Mizinov also stressed the possible influence of Odoyevsky on Gogol's *The Nose* (*Nos*) and *The Portrait* (*Portret*) and saw him as 'another Faust'.[22]

An original, if slightly extravagant, approach by N. A. Kotlyarevsky claimed Odoyevsky for the symbolist tradition: Odoyevsky's goddess was always wisdom (*mudrost'*) and as a writer he 'set himself the grand-iose, almost unfulfillable task . . . he wanted to let us see the unseeable, to speak of the inexpressible in concrete images'.[23] Kotlyarevsky held *Russian Nights* to be of immense importance, though regarding it as simply stories 'supplied with a special philosophical commentary', and correctly stated that Odoyevsky was trying to be at one and the same time 'poet, philosopher and publicist'. The reason that to many of his contemporaries his stories seemed hazy (*tumannyye*) was perhaps that 'the real story was written between the lines'. *Russian Nights* was 'permeated with romanticism and metaphysics' representing not merely 'the confession of a whole generation which has accomplished its task and is making way for new people', but signalling 'the long sleep of metaphysical thought'.

B. A. Lezin's 1907 study, quoting from unpublished sources, stresses the autobiographical and subjective qualities in Odoyevsky's work. Lezin regards *Russian Nights* as an 'author's confession' and Arist (Odoyevsky's early protagonist of the 1820s, in whom he also sees affinities with Chatsky) as a prototype of the later Faust.[24] He sees the embodiment of Odoyevsky's 'practical activity' in *Segeliel' or a Don Quixote of the 19th Century* (*Segeliel' ili Don Kikhot XIX veka*). The supposed 'death' of Faust, subsequent to the action of *Russian Nights*, Lezin sees as proof that Odoyevsky developed beyond his Faust stage. He considers the form of *Russian Nights* to have been borrowed from *The Decameron*, stresses the dominance in it of the idea of the infinite, Odoyevsky's use of antithesis and the theme of the inadequacy of language, while seeing its essential message as one of optimism and faith in the radiant future (*svetloye budushcheye*).

I. I. Zamotin saw Odoyevsky's view of art as, not a copy of nature, but the depiction of beauty of the spirit in material form, the representation of the infinite in the finite.[25] Life was seen as 'a synthesis of the elements of the ideal and the real'.[26] These ideas Odoyevsky was attempting to demonstrate in *Russian Nights*, which undervalued work, Zamotin felt, occupied an outstanding place in Russian literature of the 1830s. Its form Zamotin saw not so much as Hoffmannian as that of classical drama; with its dialogue and chorus figure it contained the inspiration of Plato as well as that of Schelling.[27]

R. V. Ivanov-Razumnik, stressing the impact of German philosophy on the intellectual development and literature of Russia, wrote of the 'link of continuity' between the circles of Odoyevsky (in the 1820s) and Stankevich.[28] Schelling, the essence of whose philosophy is 'romanticism of genius', Razumnik regarded as the undisputed 'philosophical ideologue of this remarkable current of the early nineteenth century'.

P. N. Sakulin's monumental study of 1913, by far the most ambitious and detailed work on Odoyevsky ever attempted, immediately became the essential reference work for all subsequent Odoyevsky scholarship; therein lies its main worth, although it will also yield perceptive observations to the reader of persistence. Sakulin's basic thesis is that Odoyevsky's career can be divided into three periods: the period of the *lyubomudry* and *Mnemozina* (Schellingianism); the period of 'philosophical-mystical idealism' fully expressed in *Russian Nights*; and, dating from the second half of the 1840s, that of 'scientific realism'[29] (by which Sakulin really means positivism). This labelling is now generally adjudged oversimplistic, and Sakulin's own apparent realisation of this may well have been a factor in his failure to complete his mammoth project. His traditional enough verdict on *Russian Nights* as 'the poetic monument of philosophical-mystical idealism' has also since been questioned.[30]

The first significant response to Sakulin's study was an article by Vasiliy Gippius.[31] Sakulin, in Gippius's view, 'is inclined to resolve too simply the question of Odoyevsky's ideological evolution' as 'inevitable'. Odoyevsky's romanticism is thereby presumed to be 'an unfortunate youthful aberration' by Sakulin, who is revealed as fundamentally hostile to romanticism. Sakulin fails to compare Odoyevsky with the Jena school of romanticism, and therefore the proximity seen between Odoyevsky and 'the epigone of romanticism', Hoffmann, loses conviction. Odoyevsky's romanticism should, Gippius believes, be approached 'from the point of view of romanticism', in which case it is not so much Odoyevsky's 'closeness to the tenets of romanticism' that convinces us that he will later renounce these tenets, as his 'secret schism from them'. The real key is the consistent underlying presence (the story between the lines suspected by Kotlyarevsky?) in Odoyevsky's fiction from *A Student's Diary* (*Dnevnik studenta*) to *Russian*

Nights of a pessimistic dualism, which Gippius credits Grigor'ev with having been the first to spot. He points to the influence on the *lyubomudry* of Spinoza and regards Schelling, too, not so much as having been faithfully followed by Odoyevsky as 'somehow accommodated to his dualistic disposition'. This dualism is epitomised in 'the hopeless schism of soul and flesh', the 'everyday living' (*vsyo zhivoye*) covered by a 'cold membrane' (*kholodnaya obolochka*) in *The Sylph* or the 'human clothing' (*chelovecheskaya odezhda*) in *Segeliel'*. Even the supposedly realistic *Princess Mimi* is not exempt: Gippius refers to the omitted prologue in which 'devils' are shown to be living in Mimi's cellar[32] and asks what Belinsky would have made of that. A lover, potential or actual, of the female sex is presented as either a Philistine (*meshchanka*) of this world or an enchantress (*volshebnitsa*) of the other (*The Salamander, Kosmorama* and *The Sylph*). *Russian Nights* Gippius sees as Odoyevsky's romantic 'universal novel', the search to make sense of the world through studying the links between various phenomena. The form he sees as closer to Tieck's *Phantasus* than to Hoffmann. He singles out the barbs against reason and the notion that 'science must be poetic' (corresponding to the idea of Novalis that 'all knowledge must be poeticised'). In the absence of any real faith 'all romantic dreams can turn out to be illusions' and thus it was with Odoyevsky, whose romanticism and Slavophilism were 'built on sand'. What started with Odoyevsky as doubt, Gippius argues, developed a new respect for 'experiment' (*opyt*) and turned less towards positivism than a 'moderate Kantianism'. An element of dualism was preserved in the division between the 'knowable' and the 'unknowable'. By the 1860s 'reason' had been restored to favour and a 'positivist phase' had been reached. Thus Gippius somewhat rearranged Sakulin's three-period chronology.

In pre-revolutionary criticism of Odoyevsky we can therefore distinguish two main strains. The first, inaugurated by Belinsky and Maykov and reflected in a more elaborate form by Sakulin, separates the 'romantic' and the 'realistic' elements in Odoyevsky's fiction, usually expressing a heavy preference for the latter. The second, originating with Grigor'ev, was developed by Kotlyarevsky and Gippius and begins from the premise that there is nothing wrong with romanticism anyway. Other commentators, from Skabichevsky onwards, occupied a more intermediate position, offering the occasional corrective insight. Views based on the Belinsky tendency were to hold almost total sway for the first fifty years of the Soviet period.

O. Tsekhnovitser's introduction to an edition of Odoyevsky's *Romantic Stories* (*Romanticheskiye povesti*), chosen it might appear with Belinsky's taste in mind, followed Sakulin's periodisation of Odoyevsky's evolution with no reference to Gippius. Explaining Odoyevsky's shortsightedness regarding social and political change in *The*

Year 4338, he writes: 'Odoyevsky was still exclusively in the power of Schellingianism, of philosophical-mystical idealism, and was far from that scientific realism [Sakulin's term] which he got to only in the 50s and 60s.'[33] Without doubting Tsekhnovitser's admiration for Odoyevsky, it may be said to have been unfortunate for Odoyevsky scholarship that some quotations contained in Tsekhnovitser's work (and in Sakulin's *Russian Literature and Socialism*)[34] were subsequently used selectively to brand Odoyevsky's type of romanticism as a wholly negative element in the development of Russian literature. There followed no further edition of Odoyevsky's fiction until 1959 and a meagre output of literary scholarship. In most of the latter, in any case, in keeping with the times Odoyevsky's 'realistic' stories were singled out for praise and his 'fantastic' works for condemnation.

B. Koz'min, in his introduction to Odoyevsky's diary, found it necessary to overstate Odoyevsky's position as a believer in the status quo and a 'supporter of serfdom' (though admitting some modification from the late 1840s), as well as his hostility to the revolutionary movement.[35] In V. Zhirmunsky's *Goethe in Russian Literature*, just four pages are devoted to the fascinating question of Goethe's impact upon Odoyevsky, whose use of epigraphs from Goethe is mentioned, but otherwise little point of contact is seen between their respective works. Odoyevsky's use of the name Faust is accorded just one sentence. Zhirmunsky regarded Odoyevsky as being 'in the camp of the Slavophiles' in the 1840s and therefore any further examination of the connection appeared superfluous.[36] V. Vinogradov, in his 'Lermontov's Prose Style', produced a quote to establish Odoyevsky as a 'conservative aristocrat' and considered his 'mystical idealism and consequent forms of fantastic depiction completely alien to Lermontov', although the latter was attracted to Odoyevsky's satirical style of psychological tale, particularly his use of the Hoffmannian 'device of the doll-automaton'.[37]

Typical was B. S. Meylakh's contention that Odoyevsky was 'like two distinct authors': 'the original and gifted artist' who exposed 'the world of empty, worthless society people'; but also the author of 'mystical-fantastic stories' (*Kosmorama, Segeliel', The Sylph*), on which lies the heavy influence of the idealist philosophy which contaminated Odoyevsky in his youth. Meylakh goes as far as to say: 'if this influence on Odoyevsky's work had remained constant, then his works would hold no interest even for the literary historian'. And yet, despite these defects, there are grounds for speaking of 'ambiguities in his world view' and progressive elements are to be found in the 'strongest' of his stories — *Princess Mimi* and *Princess Zizi*. *Russian Nights* is accorded just one paragraph, pointing to the anti-capitalist tendency of *Town without a Name*.[38]

D. Blagoy and Yu. Oksman, in 1952, placed Odoyevsky 'at the head of an ever intensifying opposition' to Pushkin, planning with Krayevsky to wrest political control of *The Contemporary*. This version of events, based on a reading of one short letter from Odoyevsky and Krayevsky to Pushkin, was refuted by R. B. Zaborova in 1956.[39]

By this time a rediscovery was taking place of Odoyevsky's role in the history of Russian music and of popular education with large selections of his work in these areas republished.[40] The first solid sign of a restoration to literary respectability, however, was the appearance in 1959 of the volume *Povesti i rasskazy*, which included works not republished since 1844. Despite her enthusiasm for Odoyevsky and her more tolerant manner, the editor, Yevgeniya Khin, does not deviate far from the 1950 views of Meylakh, which, crude oversimplification though they may be, can be traced back to Belinsky.[41] No mention is made of Gippius, a 'critique of capitalism' is again a main feature of *Russian Nights* and, true to the Belinsky—Meylakh axis, Khin maintains the split personality approach to Odoyevsky's writing: 'Odoyevsky the idealist, the romantic, constantly struggled with Odoyevsky the realist, the sensitive artist, the humanist and enlightener'. The latter played his part in 'progressive Russian romanticism' (as opposed to the 'passive, idealist romanticism' of such as Zhukovsky, 'devotees of a feudal-monarchist order, idealizing the Middle Ages and urging withdrawal to an irrational, mystical world'). In works such as *Kosmorama, The Salamander, Segeliel'* and *The Improvisor* (*Improvizator*) (all omitted from the collection), Odoyevsky trod the path of the German romantics. 'Odoyevsky in his best works took another path' — in such stories as *New Year* (*Novyy god*), *Princess Mimi, Katya or the Story of a Ward* (*Katya ili istoriya vospitanitsy*) and *Princess Zizi* (all included) — that of the 'struggle for a realistic depiction of contemporary Russian life', which Khin equates with 'Pushkin's . . . definition of true romanticism as the treatment of living reality'. The only break with the Belinsky—Meylakh tradition is the appropriation of *The Sylph* for the 'progressive' canon: justified as 'a retreat from illusory, idealist fantasy' in its 'irony over the "mystical ravings" of its hero', whose 'ties with the other world are motivated as a psychopathic phenomenon'. The story is 'a turning point in the writer's work', which is why 'Pushkin, who was critical of Odoyevsky's idealist predilections, nevertheless printed *The Sylph* in *The Contemporary*'. In Khin's view, Odoyevsky's 'true romanticism' dissolves into the new emergent realism. The overtly romantic mode, which Khin seems to believe should have been kept down by the progressive tendency, is thus depicted almost as an interloping Mr Golyadkin Junior!

Writing on *Sebastian Bach* in 1964, Ye. D. Chkatarashvili also viewed Odoyevsky's artistic practice as 'evolving towards realism, with the artist-experimentor in *Bach* managing to conquer the romantic theoretician-thinker in himself'.[42] Odoyevsky's view of art is seen by Chkatarashvili as essentially a reflection of reality (therefore departing from the romanticism of Tieck and Schlegel), but a reality containing much that is unknown and incomprehensible. Despite remaining a romantic, Odoyevsky was not isolated from reality. He distorted it and counterposed its hostile, fantastic side but still 'breathed the juices of this reality', reproducing it in *Russian Nights*.

It is, however, from the later 1960s that the 'modern period' of Odoyevsky scholarship can be said to date. Crucial was the work of Yuriy Mann, who provided the first sustained reading of *Russian Nights* as an artistic whole, the 'basic tone' of which was one of 'total and uncompromising disappointment'.[43] Odoyevsky's original idea had been 'to reduce all philosophical ideas to one denominator' and to compose 'a huge drama involving all the philosophers of the world'. Mann sees Hoffmann, Pogorel'sky, Goethe, Tieck and Plato in the genealogy of *Russian Nights*, but 'the principles of philosophical aesthetics and, in a wider sense, philosophical systematism of the 20s and early 30s' as the main influence on Odoyevsky's artistic design. Mann found himself less approving of the findings of Odoyevsky's ambitious enquiry than of the searches and rejections, which 'are crystallised in the very structure of his work'. The material is arranged in three layers: the 'oldest' stories, originally designed for inclusion in *House of Madmen* (*Dom sumasshedshikh*), investigating the lives of 'great' or 'mad' people (*bezumtsy*) plus the chain of novelettes left by 'Economist'; a transitional layer of 'unplanned fragments' (*The Last Suicide* (*Posledneye samoubiystvo*) and *Town without a Name*) reflecting 'collective madness' and originating from the intellectual 'journey' of the two deceased friends; and thirdly the overall framework – the deliberations of Faust, Viktor, Vyacheslav and Rostislav. Interconnections exist within the parts – 'each subsequent character shades in the weakness of the preceding one'; no real answers are provided, yet 'each answer in some way fills out the previous one'. Ample use is made of 'Odoyevsky's favourite device – the handing over of the narration to invented storytellers'. Thus, Mann argues, is achieved 'an impression of multiplicity', of the passing on of 'the spirit of the times'.

Mann distinguishes 'philosophical aesthetics' from 'general romanticism' and sees it as a line, inspired by German idealist philosophy, stretching from Odoyevsky and Venevitinov, through Nadezhdin, to Stankevich and Belinsky; as such it was the 'top layer' of romantic aesthetics.[44] It carried on a dual struggle in the 1820s: with classicism and with romanticism proper. Aesthetically it was closer to romanticism but could nevertheless accept elements of classicism, such as didacticism and civic feeling (*grazhdanstvennyy pafos*) in the early

Odoyevsky. But inherent in its formulations were 'inner difficulties and contradictions' which led it into crisis by the late 1820s, when, in Odoyevsky's testament, 'Schelling's philosophy ceased to satisfy the seekers of truth and they dispersed in various directions'. From this crisis in philosophical aesthetics, Mann considers, arose 'the unique architectonics of *Russian Nights*, which surmounted the romantic norms and carry the clear imprint of philosophical universalism'.[45]

Odoyevsky, by the completion of *Russian Nights*, had himself assimilated 'the idealist dialectic', by which Faust posits 'the unification of contradictions' as 'the so-called spirit of the times'.[46] Of the exponents of philosophical aestheticism close to Odoyevsky, such as Kireyevsky and Shevyryov, Odoyevsky was 'the only one who attempted to find a way out of the crisis by artistic practice', by 'an accumulation of new elements within old systems'. The complexity of *Russian Nights* was due, in Mann's view, to a combination of factors making the work, by 1844, seem 'out of step with the times': '. . . to the antiromantic movement of the time Odoyevsky reacted in romantic forms, restructuring and finding new possibilities in them. The inner stimulus of this restructuring was the philosophical task. Hence the broadening from romantic to philosophical universalism.'[47]

Such a radical re-evaluation of *Russian Nights* involved dissension from previous Odoyevsky criticism. The views of Belinsky, Maykov, Sakulin and Gippius are all faulted. *Russian Nights*, in Mann's view, cannot be satisfactorily accounted for in terms of the metaphysics stressed by Kotlyarevsky, the Schellingianism of Zamotin, the 'philosophical mysticism' of Sakulin or the Hoffmannian ideas suggested by Gippius. Mann is equally critical of aspects of Soviet criticism, contending that 'the view that the representatives of Russian philosophical aesthetics were political reactionaries is greatly exaggerated'. Social criticism may have been sublimated into 'abstract generalised platitudes', but still, this movement in its own way was a positive preparation for the future development of Russian thought — 'even sociological and political thought'.[48] Just as he discerns a dialectical process in Odoyevsky's fiction and in the movement whence it sprang, there can also be seen a dialectical process at work in Mann's criticism, which contains something of a synthesis of the critical approaches of Belinsky and Sakulin on the one hand, and of Grigor'ev and Gippius on the other, as well as ideas touched on earlier by Skabichevsky, Kotlyarevsky, Lezin, Zamotin and Ivanov-Razumnik and developed in more general terms by such recent commentators on the philosophy and aesthetics of the romantic period as Z. A. Kamensky and V. V. Vanslov.[49]

Ye. A. Maymin follows Mann in perceiving a basic consistency throughout Odoyevsky's work from the early 1820s to *Russian Nights*, thereby rejecting the 'two Odoyevskys' theory and disagreeing particularly with Khin's view that Odoyevsky moved away from romanticism in the second half of the 1830s. Mysticism in stories such as *The Sylph, The Salamander* and *Kosmorama* is seen as fulfilling the same function as the fantastic in *Motley Tales (Pyostryye skazki)*: that of a device 'to switch the narration to a higher wavelength' and introduce a 'philosophical ring' — in other words 'a property related to form rather than content'.[50] On the other hand, the 'realistic' stories (*Princess Mimi* and *Princess Zizi*) Maymin sees as 'in no way falling outside Odoyevsky's romantic system' given that 'a mercilessly truthful, critical attitude to reality' should by no means be considered the monopoly of realism, and, while Odoyevsky may have changed his artistic manner, 'he never changed his artistic faith'. *Russian Nights*, Maymin claims, is perhaps closest to F. Schlegel's definition of the novel as 'a Socratic dialogue of our time' and to his view of the fragment as 'the most truthful means of artistic expression'. However, the fragmentary nature of the work 'does not detract from its wholeness in terms of inner structure'; on the contrary, it complements 'the deep *musical* unity of all its parts'. The initial idea, 'the idea of happiness', combined with a key theme of the book, that of the poet and poetry, suggests to Maymin (here he follows Lezin, rather than Gippius and Mann) 'elements of a positive solution to the problems of human knowledge and possible human happiness'.

M. I. Medovoy approached Mann's position in regarding *Russian Nights* as 'an idiosyncratic balance sheet' of 'the most complicated ideological processes occurring at the end of the 30s — beginning of the 40s'.[51] He questioned the traditional identification of Odoyevsky with Faust: the other conversationalists are also mouthpieces for the author's ideas and, in any case, 'Odoyevsky thought more broadly and more freely than his protagonists'. M. S. Shtern also pays particular attention to the composition of *Russian Nights*, the interrelation of fragment, cycle and dialogue: 'the structure of the cycles reconstructs the macroworld of nature, history, civilization, and the microworld of separate human existence'. This is achieved, she believes (developing Maymin), by the 'musical—*leitmotif* character' of the composition: inner association, variation, repetition and the interplay and development of fundamental 'musical' themes of the book, reduced to key words or phrases in 'the numerous individual motifs linking the various cycles and fragments'.[52] According to B. F. Yegorov, the 'saturated intellectualism' of Odoyevsky's stories at times approaches the 'metalanguage' of the 'description of the process of creation itself', more normally associated with the twentieth-century art of, say, Thomas Mann.[53]

V. I. Sakharov describes Odoyevsky's so-called 'enigmatic' tales (*The*

Sylph, The Salamander, Kosmorama and *The Orlakh Peasant Girl (Orlakhskaya krest'yanka)*) as 'masterpieces of romantic prose'.[54] *The Salamander* had been a major butt of critical disapproval since Belinsky. The first stage in its 'rehabilitation' had been the 1971 article by a German scholar claiming it as the work of 'a progressive romantic, the heir of civic, instructional thought' and stressing the realistic descriptions of the Finnish landscape, folkloric elements, the historical content and Odoyevsky's preference for the methods of the natural sciences over mysticism and cabalism.[55] Sakharov calls *The Salamander* a 'composite' work, comprising history, philosophy and fiction in two parts of divergent genres and concerned with three epochs (those of Peter the Great, the post-Petrine aftermath and Odoyevsky's own), with the fantastic elements serving as merely an aid to this design. Sakharov emphasises the impact of Pushkin on *The Salamander*, pointing to parallels with *The Negro of Peter the Great* (*Arap Petra Velikogo*), *Poltava, The Bronze Horseman* (*Mednyy vsadnik*) and *The Queen of Spades* (*Pikovaya dama*).[56] However, M. A. Tur'yan stresses rather the prominence given to the primitive Finnish tribal culture: 'in its way a return to the "radiant condition" of humanity at the dawn of existence, a condition "which has now become incomprehensible to us"'. A distinction is made between 'rational mysticism' (the pseudo-scientific 'applied alchemy' of the old Count) and 'irrational mysticism' (the 'higher' psychic powers of El'sa-Salamandra) and the events of the second part are seen to arise from an imbalance between faith in rational and in instinctive modes of cognition. *The Salamander* is thus regarded by Tur'yan as primarily a philosophical tale involving the idea of *karma* and an unusually advanced treatment of the conscious and subconscious. Odoyevsky's method in *The Salamander* is considered as still essentially romantic, but as signifying 'a certain new phase in the history of Russian romanticism . . . which linked late romanticism with subsequent realist literature — including the novels and stories of Dostoyevsky and Turgenev, noted for their keen interest in the "psychological fantastic"'.[57]

The question of Hoffmann's influence was aired again by A. B. Botnikova, who sees comparisons between *The Retort* (*Retorta*) and *The Golden Pot* and the animated dolls in *Motley Tales* and *The Sandman*, but regards *Motley Tales* as essentially rationalistic and moral rather than romantic, with Odoyevsky's grotesque images being used for 'allegorical' rather than 'metaphorical' purposes. Themes of madness, the predicament of the artist and the use of musicians are common to both writers, particularly striking being the depictions of Piranesi and Cavalier Gluck (though Botnikova sees the former rather as a reflection of the frustrations of Odoyevsky's strivings for 'the systemization and generalization of philosophical knowledge'). However, Botnikova argues that Hoffmann is never more than a point of departure for Odoyevsky in the creation of 'his own aesthetic system'.[58] We return to this, and a number of other questions, in Section III.

II

We now turn to Odoyevsky's own conception of romanticism and to a survey of the main romantic features in his works. This is intended to place Odoyevsky's romanticism in a more European context, to thereby illuminate more clearly the nature of Odoyevsky's romanticism, and to provide a broader perspective from which to see Soviet views on the subject.

Although he wrote compulsively on almost every subject, including many which may be said to be related to romanticism, Odoyevsky wrote very little on romanticism itself. His essays on aesthetics of the 1820s, while strongly imbued with a romantic philosophy of a mainly Schellingian hue, are at the same time mainly concerned with polemics against the hitherto dominant classical aesthetic.[59] As Mersereau has said of the journalistic criticism of the period: 'the issues themselves were far from clear, and personal animosities often were more important in determining opinions than critical attitudes'.[60] Odoyevsky's published literary articles of the 1830s and 1840s are virtually devoid of theory and almost entirely polemical: this time against the dominant tendency of reactionary ignorance and bad taste propagated by the 'ruling triumvirate' of official Russian literature — Bulgarin, Grech and Senkovsky.[61] The apparent reluctance on Odoyevsky's part to engage in theoretical discussions of romanticism is due at least in part to the confusion over the use and understanding of the term 'romantic' at that time and to the idiosyncratic nature of the literary arguments of the 1820s and 1830s in Russia.[62]

Russian Nights, for example, although in content heavily, if by no means exclusively, romantic (by almost any definition of the term) uses the word only two or three times: most notably, perhaps, when Faust remarks on the apparent contradiction in Shevyryov's discovery (from Longinus) of 'romanticism in the era of ancient classicism'.[63] In *Princess Zizi*, in Sakulin's view, Odoyevsky is at pains to differentiate, through the characters in the story, 'true' from 'superficial' romanticism: genuine and deep idealism, as opposed to the pose of foreign imitation.[64]

The nearest thing to a consciously expressed view of romanticism is perhaps contained in Odoyevsky's fragmentary and only recently published article '*Classicism and Romanticism*', which appears to have been really directed against the French varieties of both literary modes.[65] The distinction is nevertheless drawn between the mathematical calculation and blatant imitation of writing in the classical mode and the intuitive originality and emotional profundity achievable through the romantic approach, with Beethoven cited as the exemplary instance.[66] For Hoffmann, too, Beethoven's music evoked 'that infinite yearning which is the essence of romanticism',[67] while the view of romanticism as primarily the revolt of emotion against the rules of neo-classicism is still prevalent in modern criticism.[68] Not that Odoyevsky believed, however, that there should be no restraints; in another fragment of the 1830s he wrote of the dangers of materials not being brought into: 'strict and natural order . . . the fruits of this chaos of ideas will manifest itself in mistakes in philosophy, monstrosities in the world of fine arts, crimes in the world of politics'.[69] This acceptance of certain necessities and consequent stress on method in romanticism was shared by Vyazemsky.[70]

The foregoing could scarcely be considered a satisfactory exposition of the nature or extent of Odoyevsky's romanticism. His real view of romanticism, therefore, has to be extrapolated from many writings of various periods, and in particular from his artistic works. While a comprehensive examination of all romantic elements in Odoyevsky would obviously be beyond the scope of a single essay, we can pick out a number of the more prominent features and attempt to relate them, in particular, to Germanic models.

The impact of German *Naturphilosophie* on Odoyevsky in the early 1820s has been well documented.[71] He worked on an unfinished translation of Oken[72] and attempted to explain Schelling's Transcendental Idealism and Philosophy of Identity in the pages of *Europe Herald* and *Mnemozina*. His '*Aphorisms from German Philosophy*', for example, argued such Schellingian points as the identity, only in dual form, of the material and the abstract, which in combination form the absolute.[73] In *Russian Nights* he later stressed the historical importance of Schelling as the 'Christopher Columbus of the soul'.[74] Thinkers prominent among the mentors of the German romantics, such as Jacob Boehme and Louis Claude de Saint-Martin,[75] were to be post-Schellingian influences on Odoyevsky.

India and Italy were of particular interest to the romantics[76] (especially India to Friedrich Schlegel).[77] Odoyevsky based a number of his apologues of the 1820s on Indian themes (mainly from the *Panchatantra*, through a French translation) and there was a mild vogue for eastern tales in Russia at that time.[78] Odoyevsky's main Italian interest was the figure of Giordano Bruno, on whom he wrote an unfinished and still unpublished novel.[79] Odoyevsky saw a line of development from the sixth-century B.C. Eleatic School of philosophy (precursors of the 'divine Plato'), stretching through the Neoplatonists and re-appearing unexpectedly in Bruno, to give birth to Spinoza and hence to the (German) 'new thinkers'.[80] Schelling revived Neoplatonism and derived his view of art as intellectual intuition from Bruno; echoes of Bruno and Spinoza are also present in Schelling's system of Identity, at the all-embracing 'point where all differences are reconciled'.[81] The propensity for synthesism, widespread in Odoyevsky's writing (and particularly irritating to Belinsky, who took it as reconciliation with the status quo),[82] is clearly stated by Faust in the Epilogue to *Russian Nights*: there is 'no opinion the contrary of which could not be estab-lished', the result being that 'epochs of contradiction end in what is known as syncretism'.[83] The struggle of ideas was, in Odoyevsky's view, necessary; but not the triumph of one or another — rather of something in between.[84] The chief aim of Novalis was to reconcile through symbol; Roger Cardinal terms Schelling 'a born synthesizer', while 'the simultaneous validity of conflicting ideas is indeed ʳthe very systole and diastole of Romantic truth', or, in another view, the 'one salient characteristic' of the romantic movement.[85]

Odoyevsky's article on the Eleatic School[86] was designed as part of a vast encyclopedic 'Dictionary of the History of Philosophy'. The scope and universality of *Russian Nights* have been noted, as we have seen, by many critics. Even in his later more positivistic years, Odoyev-sky was eagerly engaging on encyclopedic projects.[87] Most of Odoyevsky's more ambitious projects throughout his career remained unfinished, many never getting beyond the fragmentary stage.[88] This is totally in accord with the Germanic model of romanticism, which, in the words of Glyn Tegai Hughes, 'is both fragmentary and encyclo-paedic in its intentions'; Schlegel wrote of 'the textbook of universal-ity', and the encyclopedic projects of Novalis were 'to lay a foundation for all knowledge'.[89] Cardinal speaks of 'the astonishing number of unfinished Romantic works' and Marshall Brown of 'the conception of the romantic novel as a fragment whose completion is relegated to a mythically distant future'.[90] In Brown's view, romantic art is measured by its energy rather than its achievement (*tendenz* — the tension and striving for perfection — being all important) and there is a tendency to deliberately set goals which can never be reached.[91] Odoyevsky's single completed major project, *Russian Nights* is, we have seen, in its basic form a collection of fragments. The fragment in itself is seen as 'a new, revolutionary and still only partly accepted form', created by Novalis and Schlegel.[92] Novalis, 'this truly interdisciplinary thinker' (or 'scientific mystic', in Maeterlinck's words) was compiling a 'scientific Bible' of notes on such topics as 'moral astronomy', 'spiritual physics', 'poetic physiology' and 'musical chemistry'.[93] Odoyevsky's archive abounds in fragments and notes on a multitude of topics and combinations of topics: along with a treatise on 'Nature and Man', he was writing on such themes as 'Theosophical Physics', 'Physics — A Russian System' and 'The Science of Instinct'.[94] Thus from the philosophical basis of the identity of mind and world there arises the phenomenon of 'the Romantic scientist'.[95]

The theme of madness and obsession occurs in Odoyevsky, both in conjunction with fantastic elements (as in *The Sylph* and *The Salamander*) and in connection with the higher forms of spiritual activity of human life (the artistic figures depicted in *Russian Nights*). There is discussion of the thin dividing line between 'madness' and 'sanity' and of the similarity between the conditions of the madman and the poet (or any inventor of genius).[96] Schelling had written: 'people who do not carry a trace of madness in themselves are the people of empty, unproductive reason'.[97] For Hoffmann, madness had been a state of receptivity to knowledge not available to normal consciousness.[98] Faust's friends, the two seekers, ask:

> So is there not a thread passing through all the actions of the human soul and joining ordinary common sense to the derangement of concepts perceptible to madmen? On this ladder is the lofty condition of the poet, the inventor, not nearer to what is called madness than madness is to ordinary animal stupidity?[99]

'The thread', 'the ladder' and madness are, indeed, recurrent motifs for Odoyevsky.

Odoyevsky connects his investigations of 'madness' here with the breakdown of communication. The theme of the deficiency of language has long been noted as prominent in *Russian Nights*. Odoyevsky, in his 'Note to *Russian Nights*', written in the early 1860s, informs us that he arrived at this idea from 'a prolonged reading of Plato'; Goethe, incidentally, was also interested in such questions.[100] Such an attitude to language can be seen to fuse with certain notions of German romantic thought, such as the famous dictum of Novalis that 'the world must be romanticised . . .' (through the agency of the imagination and the magic utterances of the poet): 'in this way we will rediscover its original meaning'; this involves the two-way 'translation' of objects into thoughts and of thoughts into tangible form, arising once again from the concept of Identity (of mind and world) and the investigation of Nature in the spirit of 'Magic Idealism'.[101] Language is regarded as 'the prime agency in all dealings between consciousness and reality'.[102] Faust in *Russian Nights* insists on the presence of

> a quantum of poetry in every industrial enterprise [and the other way round] . . . the railways represent . . . a striving to destroy time and space, a feeling of human virtue and superiority over nature; in this feeling there is, perhaps, a recollection of man's former strength and of his former slave — nature . . .[103]

Odoyevsky's dual stress on the inadequacy of language yet the universal capacity of poetry (which 'enters into every action of man')[104] thus merges with ideas deriving from the *Naturphilosophie* of Schelling, the Magic Idealism of Novalis and the psychology of Schubert, Ritter and Carus. At the beginning of *The Apprentices at Sais*, Novalis presents the world as a system of 'signatures' (an idea from Boehme), referring to

> that marvellous secret writing that one finds everywhere, upon wings, egg-shells, in clouds, in snow, crystals and the structure of stones, on water when it freezes, on the inside and the outside of mountains, of plants, of animals, of human beings, in the constellations of the sky, on pieces of pitch or glass when touched or rubbed, in iron filings grouped around a magnet, and in the strange conjunctions of chance.[105]

In the introduction to *The Retort*, termed by one Soviet commentator 'a passionate defence of the romantic imagination',[106] Odoyevsky (or his surrogate, the purported narrator of *Motley Tales*, Gomozeyka) speaks warmly of the searches of medieval sages for, among other things 'the kind of language which a stone and a bird and all the elements would heed'.[107] Of the aesthetic process in pre-history, Novalis wrote (using a 'Fichtean myth of the fission of an originally unitary art'):

> The first art is hieroglyphistics. The art of communication, reflection, or language, and the art of representation and formation, or poetry are as yet One. Only later does this raw mass divide — then arises the art of naming, language in the proper sense — philosophy, and fine art, creative art, poetry in general.[108]

Russian Nights seems to posit a kind of inherited memory, preserved in legends, of a time when: 'man was indeed the king over nature; when every creature obeyed his voice, because he knew what to call it; when all the powers of nature, like humble slaves, prostrated themselves at man's feet . . .'[109] Elsewhere, introducing a group of stories and Indian legends, Odoyevsky employs similar terms of natural philosophy to describe the process of the birth of a legend, following the composition and continuation of a song:

> The first epoch of the development of the basic elements is complete; the poetic flowers fade, pinned to printed pages, but they fade because the fruit is ripening; all strengths of the organism are directed to it; the life-giving juice for the fruit is being produced in mysterious vessels; for it the wind blows, for it the leaves bathe in the cold dew, for it the sun's rays parch. The flower turns into a recollection; scholars support it with commentaries; its appearance inspires new poets — and the poem

continues, although under a different form; for its author is still the same — he has simply been born anew . . .[110]

In his *Psychological Notes* (1843), Odoyevsky talks of ancient music as a relic of 'a primordial, natural human language', which was 'known to man instinctively'.[111] At the beginning of *Sebastian Bach* we hear of 'a secret language, hitherto almost unknown, but common to all artists', and musical notes are referred to as 'hieroglyphics'.[112] Later in the story Albrecht recounts a potted mythic history of mankind and the birth of art, beginning at the carefree time when man had no need of *expression*, resting in its innocent cradle with an instinctive understanding of God, nature, the present and the future:

> But . . . the infant's cradle shook; the tender unfledged being, like a moth in a barely opened cocoon, was confronted by threatening and inquisitive nature: in vain the youthful Alcides strove to fetter its huge and diverse forms in his infantile babble; nature touched the world of ideas by the head and the coarse instinct of crystals by the heels, and challenged man to measure himself against it. Then were born the two constant and eternal but dangerous and perfidious allies of the soul of man: *thought* and *expression.*[113]

This provides, quite apart from anything else, the ironical spectacle of Bach, the towering genius of classical composition, being raised on romantic philosophy. The mythic imagery is analogous to that used by Hoffmann in *Meister Floh*, when Peregrinus, looking at Dörtje Elverdink through Master Flea's microscopic lens, sees through the network of nerves and silver threads beyond her thoughts: 'flowers that were being transformed into human beings, and then again human beings that flowed away into the earth to emerge glittering as jewels and minerals. And in among them moved all sorts of strange animals, which were transformed countless times and which spoke wondrous languages'.[114] Such vision is explained by Master Flea as follows:

> Since the time when Chaos condensed to formative matter — the World-Spirit has been forming all forms out of that available material, and from it dreams proceed with their images. These configurations are sketches of what has been or perhaps of what will be, sketches which the Mind quickly draws at its pleasure, when the tyrant named Body releases him from his slave's service.[115]

Odoyevsky would long have been familiar with Oken's conception of natural philosophy as 'the conjunction of empiricism and speculation'.[116] The mythic elements in Hoffmann's *Märchen*, reminiscent of Novalis, are said to derive from G. H. von Schubert, a student of the romantic physicist J. W. Ritter, who had been greatly influenced by Schelling's *Naturphilosophie*.[117] Schubert referred to the 'hieroglyphic language' of dreams connecting the inner world of the mind with outside events across time and accessible only to the 'hidden poet'.[118] Such studies of the subconscious were carried further by the painter and natural scientist C. G. Carus, who is now acknowledged as a predecessor of Jung.[119] Odoyevsky greatly admired the works of Carus (one of which he reviewed in *Notes of the Fatherland*) and once placed him on a level with Goethe, Leibniz and Lomonosov.[120]

Romantic literature is frequently concerned with striving or a quest; Heinrich von Ofterdingen, in Novalis's novel of that name, undertakes 'the quest for the Blue Flower, symbol of all man's longings in this world for something that transcends it'; when he finally plucks it he 'becomes a ringing tree, a stone'.[121] The long first sentence of *Russian Nights* outlines the nature of the quest, the 'wonderful task' (*chudnaya zadacha*) constantly engaged in by the human soul.[122] The hero in Novalis is hoping to discover 'a Romantic age, full of profundity, which underneath a simple clothing hides a higher shape'.[123] Odoyevsky goes on to speak of one layer beneath another as the covers are removed protecting 'the sacred secret (*zavetnaya tayna*) perhaps inaccessible to man in this life, but which he is permitted to approach'[124] (thus ultimate failure is prefigured from the start). Hughes says of the veiled goddess in *The Apprentices at Sais*: 'for Novalis, the veil conceals the profoundest secrets of the natural world'.[125] The motif of the veil in its various forms throughout Odoyevsky's writings attains the measure of a poetic and philosophical symbol. Symbols for Odoyevsky are connected with his ideas on expression and the 'primordial instinctual condition of man'; when this condition returns (through the agency of the ecstatic state of, for example, the poet), 'it seeks images for its inexpressible condition; not having language (for language is a presentiment of the epoch of reason), it uses an approximate language — i.e. symbols'.[126] Gippius noted the significance particularly of the phrase 'human clothing' in this respect;[127] other words used by Odoyevsky include 'cover' (*pokrov*), 'membrane' (*obolochka*), 'veil' or 'curtain' (*zavesa* and *pokryvalo*). These are frequently removed or peeled off to attain or reveal a further dimension of truth, essence or perception. Beneath every feeling, we are informed in *Russian Nights*, there hides another 'deeper and perhaps more disinterested', and behind that another and another until we reach 'the deepest recess of the human soul . . .', where there is 'neither time nor space'.[128] This is the place of the poet: 'the state of spirit, where time and space, past present and future do not exist';[129] and of the musician. The young Sebastian's nocturnal vision in the moonlit Gothic church at Eisenach, embracing in the indescribable edifice of the organ the unity of the mysteries of architecture and harmony, is a presentiment of this state:

> Angels of melody floated on its light clouds and vanished in
> mysterious embraces; in graceful geometric lines rose combina-
> tions of musical instruments; above the sanctuary ascended choirs
> of human voices; multicoloured veils of contra-sounds coiled and
> uncoiled before him and the chromatic scale streamed down a
> cornice like a playful bas-relief . . . Everything here lived a har-
> monious life, every irridescent motion sounded, every sound was
> fragrant — and an unseen voice pronounced distinctly the mysteri-
> ous words of religion and art . . .[130]

Novalis wrote in *Blütenstaub*: 'Is not the universe within us? . . . The
way of mystery leads inwards. Past and future, eternity and its realms,
these lie within us or nowhere', and in the words of Hughes was pre-
occupied with 'the attempt to spiritualise matter, to annihilate time
and space'.[131] Schubert and Carus were also concerned with states of
mind when 'boundaries between matter and spirit were blurred' and
'time and space become an indivisible unity'.[132]

Odoyevsky broaches the dislocation of time and space in a number
of stories including *The Sylph*, *The Salamander* and *The Live Corpse*.
However, the most startling treatment occurs in association with the
fantastic in the long-neglected story, *Kosmorama*. Sakulin regarded
Kosmorama as 'one of the best of Odoyevsky's mystical stories' (detec-
ting there the unseen hand of the English mystic, John Pordage); a
recent western writer calls it 'a Faustian drama of divine and infernal
powers struggling for the hero's soul', and notes the 'thread and links'
theory of moral responsibility.[133] Midway through the story (a purported manuscript acquired at an auction), which ends somewhat inconclu-
sively (a proposed continuation was never written), the face of the
protagonist is brushed by the hand of Count B-, the husband of his
intended mistress Eliza. The count has just returned from the dead,
with diabolical assistance, to take revenge on his 'faithful spouse'. The
touch of the dead immediately dissolves time and space for the protagonist:

> the walls, the earth, people appeared to me as light semi-shadows,
> through which I could clearly distinguish another world, other
> objects, other people . . . Every nerve in my body received the
> faculty of sight; my magic gaze embraced at one and the same
> time the past, the present, what had really been and what could
> have been.[134]

The vision includes all details of the count's past life plus the 'mysterious threads' which link these criminal events over several generations
with members of the protagonist's own family; and beyond that: 'at
this moment the whole history of our world from the beginning of

time was clear to me' through this 'external chain of events'; his gaze gradually moved up and down 'the magic ladder' of human history:

> I realised how important every thought is, every human word, how far their influence stretches, what a heavy respor.ibility for them lies on the soul, and what evil for all humanity can arise from the heart of one man who has exposed himself to the influence of unclean and hostile beings . . . I realised that 'man is the world' is not an empty play on words, thought up for amusement . . .[135]

While not seeking to regard Odoyevsky as a mere imitator of German romanticism or to deny the role of Russian traditions in his literary production, we would suggest that the foregoing discussion does indicate that the impact of German romanticism as a whole on the thought and fiction of Odoyevsky was more considerable than has generally been acknowledged and that it extended somewhat beyond merely the theory of Schelling and the practice of Hoffmann. However, there is one further literary principle employed by those whom the early Lukács termed 'the first theoreticians of the novel, the aesthetic philosophers of early Romanticism'[136] which should not be forgotten when considering Odoyevsky's romanticism. This is the principle of 'romantic irony', which acts in practice as an inbuilt defence mechanism enabling romantic fiction to combat potential criticism of its extravagances. As seen by F. Schlegel, this concept can involve 'ironic distance' or an element of self-parody: 'a stance whereby the artist becomes his own audience'; or a more complex notion of 'poetic reflection . . . as though in an infinite sequence of mirrors'; 'the aesthetic principle whereby a work incorporates its own critique'.[137] This is almost literally echoed at the beginning of *Russian Nights*: literary works of aesthetic pretensions 'must themselves be able to answer for themselves',[138] while the lengths to which Odoyevsky went in so many works to distance himself from his eventual reader through pseudonyms, narrators, sub-narrators, stories within stories and 'manuscripts' are obvious enough. The ironic treatment of romantic themes is slightly more ambiguous. Differing views exist regarding the presence of irony in *The Sylph*, but most commentators would now agree that Odoyevsky did not necessarily himself believe in the world of the sylph.[139] In the case of the *Motley Tales* cycle, *The New Jocko* (*Novyy Zhoko*) has been seen as a parody of the French frenetic writer Borel;[140] *Tale of a Dead Body* (*Skazka o myortvom tele* . . .) could be read as a playful advance on the predicaments of Peter Schlemihl and Erasmus Spikher (in works by Chamisso and Hoffmann respectively); while in *The Retort*, which bears a slight resemblance to *The Golden Pot*, the author's intentions may be parodistic as well as didactic. In fact it is possible to read *Motley Tales* as a whole as a parody on various forms of currently popular literature, including those using 'excessive' forms of romanticism. There is therefore no obvious reason to take the elements of Nature Philosophy, for instance, in the introduction to *The Retort*, very seriously. Nature description tends, as we have seen, to be couched in the imagery of Nature Philosophy; this is all the more noticeable given the virtually total absence of 'ordinary' descriptions of nature in Odoyevsky.[141]

Romantic irony has been described in short as an awareness by the author of the principles of romantic creation; and more fully as:

> Aesthetic distance, free play of the mind, relativizing, self-criticism within the actual work of art, the teasing and mystifying of potential readers, conscious experimenting with form and modes of expression, shifting tone, multiple reflections through tale within tale.[142]

Even the founding generation 'could never take its romanticism in deadly earnest', while Hoffmann's work is now frequently seen as filled with 'systematic irony'.[143] The elements of romantic irony listed above are clearly prominent in *Russian Nights* and elsewhere in Odoyevsky's romantic works.

Just as Odoyevsky's use of the imagery of Nature Philosophy can be seen to be largely contained within an ironical framework, so it could be said that in his fiction as a whole he avoids the more obscure and totally mystical excesses of the German romantics.[144] Despite his interest in the ideas of medieval science, he never shared the romantic yearning for the Middle Ages as such. It is often well-nigh impossible to gauge an author's interest or belief in particular concepts — as opposed to his employment of them for artistic purposes — and the dimension of irony does nothing to ease the problem in the case of many romantic writers. Hoffmann, for all his apparent aspirations towards a perfect artistic world, could write: 'The ideal — it is only a deceptive, pitiful dream'.[145] As we have seen, Gippius divined an essential pessimism in Odoyevsky's work and Mann has more recently stressed an overriding feeling of 'disappointment', while Maymin and Sakharov have argued for mysticism and the fantastic to be seen as essentially artistic devices. Some western commentators, too, have seen Odoyevsky as basically a rationalist; while this is certainly true of the later Odoyevsky, the evidence with regard to the 1830s remains contradictory.[146] For that matter Sakulin, who is commonly accused of overstressing Odoyevsky's philosophical-mystical idealism, denies that Odoyevsky was ever a whole-hearted Schellingian; Schelling was certainly an aesthetic influence, but it could not be said of Odoyevsky that 'he subordinated the whole world to an artistic formula'.[147]

Odoyevsky was in no way himself a 'romantic hero', a poet with a 'lyrical biography' in the sense in which Tomashevsky sees Byron, Pushkin or Lermontov.[148] O. Ilyinsky sees Odoyevsky as close to Goethe in the universality of his interests and the pursuit of natural knowledge, and it may well be that Goethe served as something of a model for Odoyevsky's all-round career.[149] Hoffmann, it should be recalled, was a musician and a lawyer as well as a writer, while Novalis was also a mining engineer. Mann sees Odoyevsky as the one exponent of Russian philosophical aesthetics to attempt a way out of a philosophical crisis by artistic means. This tactic certainly conformed with Schelling's belief that 'it is art alone which can succeed with universal validity in making objective what philosophy can only portray subjectively'.[150] Sakharov in fact argues, with justification, that this practice made Odoyevsky *more* of a romantic than hitherto.[151]

To conclude this survey of romanticism in the works of Odoyevsky, we tentatively postulate three possible levels of romanticism in a given work. The first, which alone has been sufficient to gain for many a writer the label 'romantic', involves the presence merely of superficial romantic themes and devices: Gothic elements, exotica, historical settings, mystification, with or without a touch of the supernatural. The second level would include the presence of some or all of the above features, plus elements of technical and formal innovation, resulting in a breakdown in classical authorial restraint, thus enabling emotions or the imagination to protrude more markedly. Most works of Russian romanticism would seem to belong in levels one or two. In the third category the presence of some or all of the elements of the first two levels would be accompanied by an identifiable underlying 'romantic' system or philosophy. Subdivisions within each level would, of course, exist: while according to this scheme Odoyevsky would certainly, through many works, qualify as a 'grade three' romantic he would probably figure lower on the scale than Hoffmann, and considerably lower than, say, Novalis.

III

Having attempted to assess the nature of Odoyevsky's romanticism, we now turn to the evaluation of romantic works. This inevitably depends on the attitude to romanticism which is adopted and, in turn, on which conception of romanticism is accepted; the variety of conceptions on offer has been considerable.

René Wellek separates the 'wider view' of romanticism (as 'a revolt against neo-classicism . . . centred on the expression and communication of emotion') from a 'more narrow sense' ('a dialectical and symbolist view' comprising 'a union of opposites, a system of symbols').[152] We have already encountered the view, with which Odoyevsky and Hoffmann apparently concurred, based on the primacy of emotion. That Odoyevsky, for one, practised romanticism more broadly than he defined it has, it is hoped, been amply demonstrated.[153] We have also mentioned synthesism in Schelling and Odoyevsky; the view of romantic literature as a synthesis of disparate elements (in particular of the sentimental and the fantastic) and a *mélange de genres* goes back to F. Schlegel. More recently a 'mixing of styles' also seems to be what Erich Auerbach understood by romanticism.[154]

The early Belinsky's essential criterion for judging poetry was a division between the 'ideal' and 'real'. Understanding classicism as 'the art of antiquity' and romanticism as 'the art of the Catholic European Middle Ages', it is scarcely surprising that he saw no meaningful debate between classicism and romanticism in Russia in the 1830s.[155] Already in the 1820s Ryleyev had held that there was no such thing as 'classical' or 'romantic' poetry, only 'old' and 'new'. In an essay of 1908 the young Lukács seemed to be expressing a similar view when he agreed with Stendhal that 'everything has at some point been Romantic and everything at some time becomes classical'.[156]

Belinsky by 1847 regarded romanticism as aloofness from social problems and therefore synonymous with conservatism.[157] Victor Hugo, in contrast, had defined romanticism as 'liberalism in literature'.[158] Much Russian and Soviet criticism, as we have seen, has followed the doctrine of 'two romanticisms'. This conception (implicit in his criticism of Odoyevsky) seemingly originated with Belinsky and takes various forms: 'old' and 'new' (from Ryleyev and Belinsky); 'active' and 'passive' (from Gorky)[159] and subsequently 'progressive' and 'reactionary'. The latter version of the dichotomy is traceable to 'Gorky and Lenin's sociologically grounded distinctions'.[160] However, it probably also owes something to the view of Lukács, some of whose works (such as *The Historical Novel*) were first published in Russian, but who is now very rarely cited in Soviet scholarship. Lukács distinguishes between a 'liberal Romanticism' which 'stands for the ideology of moderate progress' and 'Romantic reaction, the apologetic glorification of the Middle Ages'. Lukács appears to hold, however, that anyone of genuinely progressive or revolutionary views cannot have been a romantic, referring to 'politically and ideologically progressive writers who frequently, though unjustly, have been treated as Romantics'.[161] Odoyevsky, in the context of Tsarist Russia at least, would comfortably fit the 'liberal' category.

There is in any event a strong case for stressing the progressive side of romanticism (even in its narrower sense). While not politically engaged, even the arch-exponents of German romanticism were at first innovators in theory and practice and only in old age, in an adverse social and political climate, did those who lived long enough (or their 'epigones') embrace reaction. Kant, Fichte and Schelling all saw themselves as revolutionary philosophers (Hughes describes their movement as 'the cultural Maoism of the day') and Marx wrote of the 'honest thoughts of Schelling's youth'.[162] Novalis, himself a nobleman, criticised Goethe's *Wilhelm Meister* for its 'glorification of the hunt for the patent of nobility', complaining of its 'prosiness, Philistinism and snobbishness', while Cardinal cites the device of the mask in Jean Paul and Hoffmann as 'a revolutionary symbol of the disruption of the established order'.[163]

Hoffmann is anyway considered to be a special case. The hostility of the later Marx to romanticism seems to have excepted the writings of Hoffmann.[164] In the opinion of Lukács, only in Hoffmann and Balzac

> are the problems of the ugly new life of capitalism and the problems of the 'great world' dealt with in terms of the spirit of the new material. This new art and aesthetics thus grows out of the terrible and the grotesque, out of the distorted-sublime and the ghastly-comic.[165]

More recently James Trainer has written: '[Hoffmann's] deep interest in the occult was more scientific and methodical, and in his writings we find a great step forward in the direction of the psychological realism of the later nineteenth century'.[166] On Hoffmann's 'realism' Lukács writes: 'In Hoffmann, realism in detail goes hand in hand with a belief in the spectral quality of reality . . . Hoffmann's world is . . . an accurate enough reflection of conditions in the Germany of his time . . .'[167]

In an article of 1832 Ivan Kireyevsky characterised the dominant trend in literature exemplified by Scott and Goethe as, 'the reconciling of imagination with reality, and correctness of form with freedom of content' (tendencies erroneously labelled 'classicism' and 'romanticism').[168] The primacy of the imagination over the depiction of reality (conforming with the views of Schleiermacher, Schlegel and Novalis)[169] could almost stand as a further definition of romanticism, but never held full sway in Russia. The peculiar feature of Russian romanticism, in the view of Lidiya Ginzburg, is that 'the most abstract philosophical propositions relied on concrete facts from life and, conversely, any everyday and psychological fact was examined in the light of speculative categories'.[170] For this reason it was, as Botnikova points out, in the works of Hoffmann, 'the most realistic of the German romantics that Russian aesthetics saw its natural ally'.[171]

We have already noted the image of the ladder in Odoyevsky's work, but it has a somewhat wider significance in romantic literature than hitherto evident — a significance of which, it must appear, Odoyevsky was well aware. Eichendorff wrote that the poet 'only raises up the ladder from earth to heaven', while Hoffmann stated: 'I believe that the base of the heavenly ladder . . . must be firmly anchored in life . . .'.[172] Odoyevsky's *Kosmorama* includes what purports to be 'an apologue by Krummacher' concerning two men, one rich and one poor, who grow up in a deep cave, the only way out from which to the light above is by 'a very steep and narrow ladder'; the poor man, aspiring to the sunlight, takes the risk, climbs out and cannot believe the wonders of the new world; the rich man, satisfied already with his lot, remains in the cave.[173] The ladder here thus leads from a lower world to *this* world. The unfinished novel *Segeliel'*, with its ambitious three-stage design combining the descent to earth of a Lucifer figure, society and philosophy, was an artistic attempt 'to join heaven and earth'.[174] Furthermore it may be of significance that, like Goethe's *Faust*, *Segeliel'* begins in heaven and descends to earth, thus reversing the Eichendorff—Hoffmann model of a ladder stretching from reality to a higher world.

Modern elements in Odoyevsky's works have been noted in Soviet criticism by Mann, Yegorov and Tur'yan; even Meylakh, earlier so hostile to romanticism, has compared ideas in *Russian Nights* with 'paradoxicality' in Einstein.[175] In western writings attention has been drawn to Odoyevsky's anticipation of Jung (in his stress on the subconscious) and to his inclination towards existentialism.[176] A whole range of modern developments can be seen as prefigured by the German romantics.[177] Even some of what were formerly regarded as the more intuitive and eccentric speculations of the romantic thinkers can take on a new interest in the light of recent scientific theory.[178] We have already dealt with the awareness in Soviet criticism of a dialectical tendency in Odoyevsky and the principle of synthesism in his work. Lukács too admitted of the early nineteenth-century era of Nature Philosophy:

> It is a period in which mysticism is not merely a dead weight carried over from the theological past, but frequently, and very often in a manner difficult to distinguish, an idealistic haze which veils the still unknown future methods of dialectical thinking.[179]

Returning finally to Soviet criticism, we have seen a radical reappraisal of *Russian Nights* in the 1960s and 1970s, and a much more tolerant attitude to Odoyevsky's 'enigmatic stories', formerly dismissed by most critics as mystical rubbish, or extolled by the earlier few for their overt idealism. This situation is partly attributable to a more sophisticated reading of the texts concerned in the context of their philosophical and aesthetic background by a more sensitive brand of critic, and partly to a more sympathetic and discerning attitude to the phenomenon of Russian romanticism in general, and the part it played in the development of Russian literature. Typical in many ways of this growing trend are the contributions to the recent volume *A History of Romanticism in Russian Literature (1825–1840)*. V. Yu. Troitsky, writing on romantic prose of the 1830s, sees Odoyevsky's type of universalism in relation to man and the world as preparing the ground for 'that thoroughness in relation to character and circumstances which we observe in realism'; 'the development of romantic prose . . .', he declares, 'significantly enriched the fiction of the 30s' with its increase of pictures of everyday life and analysis and observation of society as such.[180] The fact that the contribution of romanticism is stressed in the context of natural and inexorable progress towards the emergence of realism remains, of course, significant. However, the problems attendant upon the analysis and evaluation of romantic literature have been faced more squarely than at any time since the 1920s — inescapably, because they were there to be faced — but the role of romanticism has at least now regained respectability. As the editors of *A History of Romanticism* recognise: 'Romanticism remained [in the 1830s] the only tendency which could respond to the ideological-artistic demands of its time.'[181]

Notes

1. See André von Gronicka, *The Russian Image of Goethe*, Philadelphia, 1968, pp. 119—24; Charles E. Passage, *The Russian Hoffmannists*, The Hague, 1963, pp. 89—114; and Norman W. Ingham, *E. T. A. Hoffmann's Reception in Russia*, Würzburg, 1974, pp. 177—93. To term Goethe a 'romantic' is, of course, to use the word in its wider sense; more will be said on this later.

2. John Mersereau Jr, 'The Chorus and Spear Carriers of Russian Romantic Fiction', in *Russian and Slavic Literature*, ed. Richard Freeborn, R. R. Milner-Gulland and Charles A. Ward, Cambridge, Mass., 1976, p. 38; Victor Terras, *Belinsky and Russian Literary Criticism*, Madison, 1974, p. 160; Donald Fanger, *The Creation of Nikolai Gogol*, Cambridge and London, 1979, p. 30.

3. Simon Karlinsky, 'A Hollow Shape: The Philosophical Tales of Prince Vladimir Odoevsky' (*Studies in Romanticism*, V, 3, Spring 1966, pp. 169—82).

4. 'A Man of Three Generations' was the title used by Ch. Vetrinsky ('Chelovek tryokh pokoleniy'), *V sorokovykh godakh: istoriko-literaturnyye ocherki i kharakteristiki*, Moscow, 1899, pp. 293—330.

5. *Sochineniya knyazya V. F. Odoyevskogo v tryokh chastyakh*, St Petersburg, 1844.

6. For example, Pogodin and Belinsky; see P. N. Sakulin, *Iz istorii russkogo idealizma. Knyaz' V. F. Odoyevsky: myslitel'-pisatel'*, I, Part 1, pp. 248—9 (hereafter Sakulin, *Iz istorii*).

7. See (on Pushkin) *A. S. Pushkin — Kritik*, Moscow, 1978, p. 448; (on Gogol) Vladimir Shenrok, 'N. V. Gogol' (*Russkaya starina*, 1902, 2, pp. 264—5).

8. V. G. Belinsky, *Polnoye sobraniye sochineniy*, Moscow-Leningrad, 1953—9, I, 1953, pp. 275—6. Hereafter *Pol. sob.*

9. Ibid., III, pp. 188, 382.

10. Ibid., VIII, pp. 297—323. This essay, entitled 'Sochineniya knyazya V. F. Odoyevskogo', is reprinted, with some cuts, in V. F. Odoyevsky, *Posledniy kvartet Betkhovena*, Moscow, 1982, pp. 344—69.

11. On Belinsky's evolution see Joe Andrew, *Writers and Society during the Rise of Russian Realism*, London, 1980, pp. 114—50; and Terras, op. cit., esp. pp. 32—42, 77—91 (and on romanticism, pp. 39, 202—3).

12. Belinsky, *Pol. sob.*, VIII, p. 297; subsequent quotations from this article, unless otherwise stated, are from pp. 306, 310—11, 313, 314, 315 and (on the Epilogue) 316—18.

13. Ibid., II, p. 356.

14. Karlinsky, op. cit., p. 170. In a later work, *The Sexual Labyrinth of Nikolai Gogol*, Cambridge and London, 1976 (p. 281), Karlinsky places the blame for the neglect of such writers as Odoyevsky squarely on Chernyshevsky. For an expanded examination of Belinsky's literary and personal relations with Odoyevsky, see Neil Cornwell, 'Belinsky and V. F. Odoyevsky' (*Slavonic and East European Review*, LXII, 1, 1984, pp. 6—24).

15. (Originally in *Finskiy vestnik*, 1, 1845). Valerian Maykov, *Kriticheskiye opyty (1845—1847)*, 2nd edn, St Petersburg, 1891, pp. 297—312 (quotes from pp. 297, 310—11).

16. D. L. Azizov, 'Filosofsko-esteticheskaya kontseptsiya Apollona Grigor'eva', in *Romantizm v russkoy i sovetskoy literature*, vyp. 6, Kazan, 1973, pp. 64 −91 (69); Terras, op. cit., pp. 214−22.

17. 'N. V. Gogol' i ego perepiska s druz'yami', *Sobraniye sochineniy Apollona Grigor'eva*, Moscow, 1916, vyp. 8, pp. 11−13.

18. 'Russkaya literatura v 1851 godu', *Sochineniya Apollona Grigor'eva*, St Petersburg, 1876, I, p. 18 (reprinted New York, 1970); also in Apollon Grigor'ev, *Literaturnaya kritika*, Moscow, 1967, p. 195.

19. *Sochineniya Apollona Grigor'eva*, op. cit., I, pp. 37−8; also in 'Russkaya literatura v seredine XIX veka', *Sobraniye sochineniy Apollona Grigor'eva*, Moscow, 1916, vyp. 9, pp. 42−3.

20. *Sochineniya A. Skabichevskogo v dvukh tomakh*, 2nd edn, St Petersburg, 1895, I, pp. 256−79 (quotations follow from pp. 258, 260 and 270−2).

21. Vetrinsky, op. cit., pp. 293−330.

22. P. Mizinov, *Istoriya i poeziya: istoriko-literaturnyye etyudy*, Moscow, 1900, pp. 421−91 (esp. pp. 424, 435, 488−91).

23. N. A. Kotlyarevsky, *Starinnyye portrety*, St Petersburg, 1907 (reprinted in Kn. Vladimir Odoyevsky, *Devyat' povestey*, New York, 1954, pp. 9−28, esp. 9−11, 12, 26−7, from which quotations follow).

24. B. A. Lezin, *Ocherki iz zhizni i literaturnoy deyatel'nosti knyazya Vladimira Fyodorovicha Odoyevskogo*, Khar'kov 1907 (see pp. 1, 55, 92, 103, 109, 107, 70−2, 131ff. and 67).

25. I. I. Zamotin, *Romantizm dvadtsatykh godov XIX stol. v russkoy literature*, St Petersburg, 1907, II, pp. 361−418 (410).

26. I. I. Zamotin, 'Literaturnaya techeniya i literaturnaya kritika 30−kh godov', in *Istoriya russkoy literatury XIX v.* (ed. D. N. Ovsyaniko-Kulikovsky), Moscow, 1908, I, pp. 277−330 (298−300).

27. Zamotin, *Romantizm dvadtsatykh godov*, pp. 400−1.

28. R. V. Ivanov-Razumnik, 'Obshchestvennyye i umstvennyye techeniya 30-kh godov', in *Istoriya russkoy literatury XIX v.*, op. cit., I, pp. 247−76 (249, 254).

29. Sakulin, *Iz istorii* (I, Parts 1, 2, Moscow, 1913) I, 1, p. 7. A useful summary of Sakulin's view of Odoyevsky can be found in his entry in *Entsiklopedicheskiy slovar'*, 7th edn, Moscow, 1916, pp. 504−9.

30. For an exposition of Sakulin's difficulties with Volume II see M. A. Tur'yan, 'Neokonchennyy trud P. N. Sakulina o V. F. Odoyevskom' (*Russkaya literatura*, 1974, 2, pp. 164−71).

31. Vasiliy Gippius, 'Uzkiy put'. Kn. V. F. Odoyevsky i romantizm' (*Russkaya mysl'*, 1914, 12, pp. 1−26). The following quotations are from pp. 1−2, 9, 22, 5−6, 12, 8, 13−18, 22−3 and 25−6.

32. See Sakulin, *Iz istorii*, I, 2, pp. 103−4.

33. Orest Tsekhnovitser, 'Predisloviye' (pp. 5−20) and 'Siluet: V. F. Odoyevsky (vstupitel'naya stat'ya)', in V. F. Odoyevsky, *Romanticheskiye povesti*, Leningrad, 1929 (reprinted Oxford, 1975, p. 18).

34. P. N. Sakulin, *Russkaya literatura i sotsializm*, Moscow, 1922, I, pp. 449−58.

35. '"Tekushchaya khronika i osobyye proisshestviya." Dnevnik V. F. Odoyevskogo 1859−1869 gg.', B. Koz'min, introduction ('Odoyevsky v 1860-e gody'), in *Literaturnoye nasledstvo* 22−4, Moscow, 1935 (p. 82).

36. V. Zhirmunsky, *Gete v russkoy literature*, Leningrad, 1937, pp. 189, 191–4; for a slightly more satisfactory discussion of the question see von Gronicka, op. cit.

37. Viktor Vinogradov, in *Literaturnoye nasledstvo* 43–4, Moscow, 1941, pp. 517–628 (522, 541, 550–2).

38. B. S. Meylakh, 'Russkaya povest' 20–30kh godov XIX veka', in *Russkiye povesti XIX veka 20kh–30kh godov*, Moscow-Leningrad, 1950, I, pp. v–xxxv (xxxi–xxxiv). By 1976, when Meylakh reviewed the 'Literaturnyye pamyatniki' edition of *Russkiye nochi*, his attitude was transformed: *Russkiye nochi* was a 'remarkable work'; more research was needed on its ideas (which at times reminded him of 'the latest arguments of Einstein and other twentieth-century scientists') and on Odoyevsky; *Russkiye nochi* was 'qualitatively a new genre' which remained to be investigated; and as for Odoyevsky's 'so-called mysticism, which was so exaggerated in the old studies', this was just a device, at least in his literary works – B. Meylakh, 'Pisatel' otkryvayemyy zanovo' (*Voprosy literatury*, 1976, 4, pp. 282–7).

39. (Blagoy and Oksman) *Literaturnoye nasledstvo*, Moscow, 1952, LVIII, pp. 23, 289–96; R. B. Zaborova, 'Neizdannyye stat'i V. F. Odoyevskogo o Pushkine', in *Pushkin: issledovaniya i materialy*, Moscow-Leningrad, 1956, I, pp. 313–42.

40. V. F. Odoyevsky, *Muzykal'no-literaturnoye naslediye*, Moscow, 1956, and *Izbrannyye pedagogicheskiye sochineniya*, Moscow, 1955, were the main publications (with copious introductions by G. Bernandt and V. Ya. Struminsky respectively).

41. Yevgeniya Khin, 'V. F. Odoyevsky' in V. F. Odoyevsky, *Povesti i rasskazy*, Moscow, 1959, pp. 3–38 (pp. 21, 4, 15–16, 25, 29).

42. Ye. D. Chkatarashvili, 'Biograficheskaya novella V. F. Odoyevskogo *Sebastiyan Bakh*', *Trudy Tbiliskogo gos. ped. instituta*, Tbilisi, 1964, XVIII, pp. 119–26.

43. Yuriy V. Mann, *Russkaya filosofskaya estetika (1820–30-e gody)*, Moscow, 1969 (Chapter 4), 'V. F. Odoyevsky i yego *Russkiye nochi*', pp. 104–48, and 'Conclusion', pp. 295–303; quotations are taken from this edition, see pp. 119, 113, 116–19, 122–3, 123–9, 130). A slightly shorter version of the same essay had appeared as 'Kniga iskaniy (V. F. Odoyevsky i yego *Russkiye nochi*)' in *Problemy romantizma: sbornik statey*, Moscow, 1967, pp. 320–59.

44. Zamotin had referred simply to 'romanticism' as a single entity, while Sakulin's term 'philosophical romanticism' displays a lack of precision in his view of the various layers of romantic aesthetics (see Mann, pp. 295–6).

45. Ibid., pp. 295–300. For a further account of the 'crisis of philosophical romanticism' see V. I. Sakharov, 'V. F. Odoyevsky i ranniy russkiy romantizm' (*Izvestiya Akademii Nauk SSSR. Seriya literatury i yazyka*, XXXII, 1973, pp. 405–18). For a detailed introduction to Russian aesthetics of the period see Z. A. Kamensky, 'Russkaya estetika pervoy treti XIX veka', in *Russkiye esteticheskiye traktaty pervoy treti XIX veka v dvukh tomakh*, Moscow, 1974, II, pp. 9–77 (hereafter *Traktaty*); and his book *Moskovskiy kruzhok lyubomudrov*, Moscow, 1980.

46. Mann, op. cit., pp. 142–3, 145.

47. Ibid., p. 146.

48. Ibid., pp. 141, 105—6, 296—7.

49. Z. A. Kamensky, 'F. Schelling v russkoy filosofii nachala 19 veka' (*Vestnik istorii mirovoy kul'tury*, 6, 1960, pp. 46—59) sees a strange opposition to this period between 'metaphysical materialism' and 'dialectical idealism'; V. V. Vanslov, *Estetika romantizma*, Moscow, 1966, is closer to traditional positivist and Soviet views in discerning two political shades of romanticism and consigning Odoyevsky to the more conservative (p. 25).

50. Ye. A. Maymin, 'Vladimir Odoyevsky i yego roman *Russkiye nochi*', in V. F. Odoyevsky, *Russkiye nochi*, Leningrad, 1975, pp. 247—76 (this essay appears to be a revised version of a section of Maymin's book, *O russkom romantizme*, Moscow, 1975, pp. 200—31, published a few months earlier), see pp. 257—8, 259, 262—3, 265—9.

51. M. I. Medovoy, 'Puti razvitiya filosofskoy prozy V. F. Odoyevskogo v seredine 1820—1840-kh godov' (Avtoreferat dissertatsii na soiskaniye uchonoy stepeni kandidata filologicheskikh nauk, L.G.P.I., Leningrad, 1971, pp. 15—16).

52. M. S. Shtern, 'Filosofsko-khodozhestvennoye svoyeobraziye prozy V. F. Odoyevskogo (ot apologov k *Russkim nocham*)' (Avtoreferat dissertatsii na soiskaniye uchonoy stepeni kandidata filologicheskikh nauk, L.G.P.I., Leningrad, 1979, pp. 7—9).

53. 'Ot redaktsii', *Russkiye nochi*, Leningrad, 1975, pp. 5—6 (hereafter *R.N.*, 1975).

54. V. I. Sakharov, 'Trudy i dni Vladimira Odoyevskogo', in Vladimir Odoyevsky, *Povesti*, Moscow, 1977, pp. 5—25 (16—17).

55. V. Feyerkherd, 'Romantizm i realizm v dilogii V. F. Odoyevskogo Salamandra', in *Problemy teorii i istorii literatury: sbornik statey posvyashchonnyy pamyati professora A. N. Sokolov*, Moscow, 1971, pp. 175—87 (187).

56. Sakharov, 'Trudy i dni . . .', op. cit., pp. 18—19; and V. I. Sakharov, 'Yeshcho o Pushkine i V. F. Odoyevskom', in *Pushkin: issledovaniya i materialy*, Leningrad, 1979, IX, pp. 224—30 (227—30).

57. M. A. Tur'yan, 'Evolyutsiya romanticheskikh motivov v povesti V. F. Odoyevskogo *Salamandra*', in *Russkiy romantizm*, Leningrad, 1978, pp. 187 —206 (195—6, 206). See also the same author's similar treatment of another neglected story: '*Igosha* V. F. Odoyevskogo (k probleme fol'klorizma)' (*Russkaya literatura*, 1, 1977, pp. 132—6). Some of Tur'yan's ideas expressed on these stories are similar to suggestions first made by Karlinsky ('A Hollow Shape . . .', op. cit., pp. 173—4, 178—9).

58. A. B. Botnikova, *E. T. A. Gofman i russkaya literatura*, Voronezh, 1977, pp. 79, 86, 88. She is critical of the western study by Passage, but does not appear to know the more reliable one by Ingham (see n. 1). For a full account of Russian and Soviet criticism of Odoyevsky, see Chapter 11 of N. J. Cornwell, 'The Life and Works of V. F. Odoyevsky (1804—1869)' (Ph.D. thesis, Queen's University of Belfast, 1983).

59. *Traktaty*, II, p. 605, n. 24; this volume includes several essays and fragments by Odoyevsky. See also Sakulin, *Iz istorii . . .*, I, 1, esp. pp. 270ff, 276ff.

60. John Mersereau Jr, *Baron Delvig's Northern Flowers 1825—1832: Literary Almanac of the Pushkin Pleiad*, Carbondale and Edwardsville, 1967, p. 40.

61. See for example 'Otvet na kritiku', in *R.N.*, 1975, pp. 231—4; and the earlier 'O vrazhde k prosveshcheniyu, zamechayemoy v noveyshey literature' (1836), *Sochineniya knyazya V. F. Odoyevskogo*, op. cit., 1844, (n. 5), III, pp. 360—72. The last mentioned article attacked the abuse and debasement of romantic methods, but without giving examples and without referring to romanticism as such. A number of Odoyevsky's critical articles have now been reprinted in the most recent selections of his works: see in particular V. F. Odoyevsky, *O literature i iskusstve*, Moscow, 1982.

62. For detailed discussions of this problem see Yu. Tynyanov, 'Arkhaisty i Pushkin' in his *Arkhaisty i novatory*, Leningrad, 1929 (reprinted Munich, 1967); and Sigrid McLaughlin, 'Russia: Romaniĉeskij — Romantiĉeskij — Romantizm' in *'Romantic' and its Cognates: The European History of a Word* (ed. Hans Eichner), Manchester, 1972.

63. *R.N.*, 1975, p. 173. For an expanded examination of this work see Neil Cornwell, 'V. F. Odoyevsky's *Russian Nights*: Genre, Reception and Romantic Poetics' (*Essays in Poetics*, VIII, 2, 1983, pp. 19—55).

64. See Sakulin, *Iz istorii*, I, 2, pp. 111—2.

65. *Traktaty*, II, pp. 181—2. Sakulin attributes this to the late 1830s (*Iz istorii*, I, 2, pp. 369—70).

66. It is interesting to note that the discussion of music in *Russkiye nochi*, following *Posledniy kvartet Betkhovena*, does not distinguish between 'romantic' and 'classical' forms when comparing the music of Beethoven with that of Mozart and Haydn.

67. Hans Eichner, 'Germany: Romantisch — Romantik — Romantiker', in *'Romantic' and its Cognates*, op. cit., p. 127.

68. See, for example, René Wellek's 'wider' conception of the romantic movement in his *A History of Modern Criticism: 1750—1950. The Romantic Age*, London, 1955, p. 3; and, applied to Russian literature, Oleg P. Ilyinsky, 'Some Fundamental Problems of Russian Romanticism (based on V. F. Odoyevsky's prose)' (Ph.D. thesis, New York University, 1970, p. v).

69. Sakulin, *Iz istorii*, I, 1, p. 463.

70. McLaughlin, op. cit., pp. 425—6.

71. See Sakulin, *Iz istorii* (e.g. I, 1, pp. 127ff); also V. I. Sakharov, 'O bytovanii shellingianskikh idey v russkoy literature', in *Kontekst 1977. Literaturno-teoreticheskiye issledovaniya*, Moscow, 1978, pp. 210—26; and the works quoted in n. 45 above.

72. Sakulin, *Iz istorii*, I, 1, pp. 135—6.

73. 'Aforizmy iz razlichnykh pisateley, po chasti sovremennogo germanskogo lyubomudriya', *Mnemozina*, 2, Moscow, 1824, pp. 73—84 (81).

74. *R.N.*, 1975, pp. 15—16.

75. Glyn Tegai Hughes, *Romantic German Literature*, London, 1979, pp. 5—6.

76. Eichner, op. cit., pp. 125—6.

77. Raymond Immerwahr, 'The Word Romantisch and its History', in *The Romantic Period in Germany* (ed. Siegbert Prawer), London, 1970, p. 50.

78. Sakulin, *Iz istorii*, I, 1, pp. 178—9 and 225.

79. For an examination of this work see M. I. Medovoy, 'Roman V. F. Odoyevskogo iz epokhi ital'yanskogo vozrozhdeniya', in *Uchonyye zapiski L.G.P.I.*, CDLX (Filologicheskiy sbornik), Leningrad, 1970, pp. 46—64.

80. Sakulin, *Iz istorii*, I, 1, pp. 141—2.

81. Wellek, op. cit., p. 75; Hughes, op. cit., p. 12.

82. Belinsky, *Pol. sob.*, VIII, p. 309 is the main example.

83. *R.N.*, 1975, p. 146.

84. 'Psikhologicheskiye zametki' (originally in *Sovremennik*, 1843), in *R.N.*, 1975 (p. 227).

85. Hughes, op. cit., p. 67; Roger Cardinal, *German Romantics in Context*, London, 1975, pp. 80 and 43; Immerwahr, op. cit., p. 34.

86. 'Sekta idealistiko-eleaticheskaya (otryvok iz 'Slovarya istorii filosofii')', *Mnemozina*, 4, Moscow, 1825, pp. 160—92.

87. On Odoyevsky's later writings see, for example, N. M. Mikhaylovskaya, 'Vladimir Fyodorovich Odoyevsky — predstavitel' russkogo prosveshchen-iya' (*Russkaya literatura*, 1, 1979, pp. 14—25).

88. Unfinished projects, to name just the main examples in the genres of fiction, include: *Iordan Bruno i Pyotr Aretino*; *Segeliel'.Don Kikhot XIX stoletiya*; *Dom sumasshedshikh*; *4338 god*; and the late *Samaryanin*. Fragments of some of these were published; all were ambitious attempts at novels or cycles, upon which the author expended very considerable time and energy.

89. Hughes, op. cit., pp. 4, 53, 67.

90. Cardinal, op. cit., p. 43; Marshall Brown, *The Shape of German Romanticism*, Ithaca and London, 1979, p. 121.

91. Brown, op. cit., pp. 46 and 56.

92. Hughes, op. cit., p. 78.

93. Cardinal, op. cit., p. 65.

94. Sakulin, *Iz istorii*, I, 1, pp. 462—3, 469ff. A short piece on the last-named topic, 'Nauka instinkta: otvet Rozhalinu' (1843) is one of the appendices in *R.N.*, 1975, pp. 198—203.

95. Cardinal, op. cit., p. 36.

96. *R.N.*, 1975, p. 25.

97. F. W. J. von Schelling, *Sämtliche Werke*, Stuttgart and Augsburg 1856—61, VII, p. 470 (quoted from Botnikova, op. cit., pp. 85, 199, n. 24).

98. See Botnikova, op. cit., p. 85; Cardinal, p. 99.

99. *R.N.*, 1975, p. 26.

100. 'Primechaniye k Russkim nocham', ibid., p. 191; Odoyevsky does not specify any source in Plato, but the *Cratylus* would seem a likely point of departure. In Goethe see for example 'Moritz as Etymologist' from *Travels in Italy*. Elsewhere Goethe claimed that 'writing is a misuse of language': 'Goethe in Sesenheim', in J. W. von Goethe, *The Sorrows of Young Werther and Selected Writings* (tr. Catherine Hutter), New York, 1962, p. 175.

101. Cardinal, op. cit., pp. 36—8 (the Novalis quote is on p. 38).

102. Ibid., p. 38.

103. *R.N.*, 1975, p. 35.

104. Loc. cit.

105. Quoted from Cardinal, p. 34. In another fragment ('Poetry and Philosophy') of 1830, Odoyevsky contrives to bring together a number of threads here touched upon in a single statement (the romantic — and Russian — view of the poet as prophet; the 'signature'/*signatura*; Plato; and the poeticisation of historical reality); on the function of the poet, he writes: 'At the minute

of inspiration he perceives the signature of the period of that time in which he lives and indicates the goal towards which humanity must strive, in order to be on the natural path and not on a perverted one. All other people only perform; hence the elements of poetry must, despite Plato, enter the political fabric of society. In the distinction between this idea and the thought of Plato, may be seen the distinction between the old society and the new', *Traktaty*, II, p. 178.

106. A. N. Nikolyukin, 'Tipologiya zhanra romanticheskoy novelly v vostochnoslavyanskikh literaturakh v sravnitel'nom otnoshenii' in *VII Mezhdunarodnyy s'yez slavistov. Slavyanskiye literatury*, Moscow, 1973, pp. 319–37 (331).

107. *Pyostryye skazki s krasnym slovtsom . . .*, St Petersburg, 1833, p. 4.

108. Novalis, *Schriften*, Stuttgart, 1960–75, II, pp. 571–2 (quoted from Brown, op. cit., p. 82).

109. *R.N.*, 1975, p. 24 (cf. p. 35 quoted above).

110. 'Neskol'ko slov (Opyty rasskaza o drevnikh i novykh predaniyakh)', *Sochineniya*, 1844, III, pp. 43–6. Mann also draws attention to this note in a more compositional connection (Mann, op. cit., p. 130).

111. *R.N.*, 1975, p. 227.

112. Ibid., pp. 103 and 109.

113. Ibid., p. 120. The practice of mythologising the history of mankind was, of course, continued in Russian literature by Dostoyevsky, particularly in *Son smeshnogo cheloveka*. For a discussion of Odoyevsky's possible impact on that story (via his story *Zhivoy mertvets* in particular) see Neil Cornwell, 'V. F. Odoyevsky's Ridiculous Dream About That?' (*Quinquereme – New Studies in Modern Languages*, II, 1, 2, 1979, pp. 75–86, and 246–55).

114. *Three Märchen of E. T. A. Hoffmann* (tr. Charles E. Passage), Columbia, S.C., 1971, p. 331. Cf. (noted by Passage, op. cit., n. 1 above, pp. 101–2) Kipriano's newly clairvoyant perception of his 'poor Charlotte' in Odoyevsky's *Improvizator* (*R.N.*, 1975, p. 94). Minerals held a considerable significance for the romantics – viz. Odoyevsky's reference to 'crystals' in the above passage from *Sebastiyan Bakh*; on the uses of *Kristall* in Hoffmann see Maria M. Tatar, *Spellbound: Studies on Mesmerism and Literature*, Princeton, 1978, Chapter 4.

115. *Three Märchen*, p. 350.

116. Brown, op. cit., p. 20.

117. See Hughes, pp. 118–19 and 123; Cardinal, p. 89.

118. Leonard J. Kent and Elizabeth C. Knight, Introduction to *Selected Writings of E. T. A. Hoffmann*, I: 'The Tales', Chicago, 1969, p. 13.

119. Hughes, pp. 16–17; Cardinal, pp. 125–33.

120. *Otechestvennyye zapiski*, 6, 1844; see *R.N.*, 1975, pp. 74, 183, 201, 286.

121. Siegbert Prawer, Introduction to *The Romantic Period in Germany*, op. cit., p. 9; Cardinal, p. 38.

122. *R.N.*, 1975, p. 7.

123. Paul Roubiczek, 'Some Aspects of German Philosophy in the Romantic Period', in *The Romantic Period in Germany*, op. cit., p. 314.

124. *R.N.*, 1975, p. 8.

125. Hughes, p. 68.

126. 'Nauka instinkta. Otvet Rozhalinu' (fragmenty), in *R.N.*, 1975, p. 199.
127. Gippius, op. cit. (n. 31), p. 8. This may be compared with Hoffmann's use of the 'botanical dressing gown' in *Datura fastuosa*.
128. *R.N.*, 1975, p. 34.
129. 'Nauka instinkta . . .', op. cit., in ibid., pp. 199—200.
130. *R.N.*, 1975, p. 113. The widespread use of synesthetic effects in romantic art is partly attributable, in Maria Tatar's view, to 'a firm belief in the existence of an internal sense that does not differentiate among the various modes of perception' (Tatar, op. cit., p. 46).
131. (Sixteenth fragment) quoted from Hughes, p. 65; Hughes, p. 66.
132. Ibid., p. 16; Cardinal, p. 132. Belief in a sixth (or 'inner') sense which allowed certain people at least 'to look into the past and future, to annul spatial limitations, and to enter into a perfect rapport with nature' was, according to Maria Tatar (op. cit., pp. 45—8, 73) common to the following thinkers: Mesmer, Baader, Ritter, Novalis, Fichte, Schelling and Schubert (the last named believed this faculty to reside in the solar plexus).
133. Sakulin, *Iz istorii* . . ., I, 2, pp. 82—90 (on Pordage, pp. 83—4); Jo Ann Hopkins Linburn, 'A Would-be Faust: Vladimir Fyodorovich Odoyevsky and his prose fiction, 1830—1845' (Ph.D. thesis, Columbia University, 1970, pp. 194, 197).
134. *Otechestvennyye zapiski*, 8, 1840, pp. 34—81 (61).
135. Ibid., pp. 62—4. This passage can be seen as an embellishment on ideas present in *Zhivoy mertvets* (*re* an analysis of which story see n. 113 above), dated a year earlier than *Kosmorama*.
136. Georg Lukács, *The Theory of the Novel* (tr. Anna Bostock), London, 1971, p. 74.
137. See Cardinal, pp. 48 and 51. For a more cautious view of the application of 'romantic irony' see Hughes, pp. 55—6.
138. *R.N.*, 1975, pp. 8—9.
139. For example Khin (in *Povesti i rasskazy*, op. cit., n. 41 above, p. 29) and Ingham (op. cit., n. 1 above, pp. 184—5).
140. Medovoy, 'Puti razvitiya filosofskoy prozy . . .', op. cit., n. 51 above, p. 9.
141. See also the passage on 'the decline of the planet', *R.N.*, 1975, pp. 23—4. Even when the fantastic 'other realm' is involved, as in *Sil'fida*, in Ingham's view (op. cit., p. 185) 'nature has no part in it'. The Finnish scenes in *Salamandra*, which have attracted some attention, were in fact written before Odoyevsky's visits to Finland (for a list of sources available to Odoyevsky, see Feyerkherd, op. cit., n. 55 above, p. 178).
142. Immerwahr (p. 35) and Prawer (p. 7), in *The Romantic Period in Germany*, op. cit.
143. Ibid. (Immerwahr), p. 59; on Hoffmann see Hughes, pp. 118—19.
144. This is not true of *all* his writings; he left scribblings of almost all imaginable kinds; suffice it to mention his 'New Mythology' of 'kardiads' and 'efirids', which Sakulin attributes to the influence of Pordage and sees as evidence of a serious interest in forms of mysticism way beyond Schelling (*Iz istorii*, I, 2, pp. 18—21).
145. *Werke*, 1871—3, V, p. 102 (quoted from Vanslov, op. cit., n. 49 above, p. 57).

146.	Ilyinsky sees Odoyevsky as the only follower of the line of German romanticism in Russian literature, and at the same time its sole representative of 'romantic rationalism' (op. cit., n. 68 above, pp. v and 179). Ingham (op. cit., pp. 191—2) also takes a rationalist view, based largely on the 'Letters to Countess Ye.P. R-y about ghosts, superstitious fears, deceptions of the senses, magic, cabbalism, alchemy and other mysterious sciences' (in *Sochineniya*, 1844, III, pp. 307—59); yet Odoyevsky was also addressing letters of an intensely mystical-religious nature to the same recipient — Countess Rostopchina (see Sakulin, *Iz istorii*, I, 1, pp. 453—7) — and to a mysterious 'NN' (Leningrad, State Public Library, fond 539, Opis I, pereplyot 94).

147.	Sakulin, *Iz istorii*, I, 1, pp. 150—1, 173—4.

148.	'A biography of a Romantic poet was more than a biography of an author and public figure. The Romantic poet *was* his own hero.' B. Tomashevsky, 'Literature and Biography', in *Readings in Russian Poetics* (ed. L. Matejka and K. Pomorska), Cambridge, Mass. and London, 1971, pp. 47—55 (49). It is, of course, possible to see *Russkiye nochi* as an 'intellectual autobiography', and autobiographical elements have been perceived in certain stories.

149.	Ilyinsky, op. cit., p. 4. Goethe himself seems more likely to have been a model for Odoyevsky's aspirations than Goethe's Faust, who was more a figure of artistic interest (for a heavy stress on Faust in both these respects see Linburn, op. cit., passim).

150.	Schelling, *Werke*, III, p. 629 (quoted in Brown, op. cit., pp. 82—3).

151.	Sakharov, 'V. F. Odoyevsky i ranniy russkiy romantizm', op. cit., n. 45 above, p. 417). For further discussion of romantic aspects and the origins of Odoyevsky's thought, see Chapter 2 ('The Thinker') in Cornwell, *V. F. Odoyevsky: His Life, Times and Milieu*, London, 1986.

152.	Wellek, op. cit., n. 68 above, p. 3. A somewhat vaguer view of the same distinction is given by Lukács: 'the physiognomy of Romanticism, in the proper, narrow sense, becomes blurred . . . unless one wishes to extend the concepts of Romanticism to embrace all great literature of the first third of the nineteenth century', *The Historical Novel* (tr. Hannah and Stanley Mitchell), London, 1962, p. 34.

153.	As early as 1825, A. A. Bestuzhev (Marlinsky) complained of the gap between theory and practice on the pages of *Mnemozina* ('Vzglyad na russkuyu slovesnost' v techeniye 1824 i nachale 1825 godov', in *Literaturno-kriticheskiye raboty dekabristov*, Moscow, 1978, p. 76). See also Sakharov, 'V. F. Odoyevsky i ranniy russkiy romantizm', op. cit., pp. 408—11.

154.	Immerwahr, op. cit., p. 52; Eichner, op. cit., n. 67 above, pp. 112—13; Erich Auerbach, *Mimesis: The Representation of Reality in Western Literature* (tr. Willard R. Trask), Princeton, 1968, p. 443.

155.	N. Mordovchenko, *Belinsky i russkaya literatura ego vremeni*, Moscow-Leningrad, 1950, p. 53; P. Berkov, 'Belinsky i klassitsizm', in *Literaturnoye nasledstvo*, LV, Moscow, 1948, pp. 151—76 (174). See Belinsky's statement quoted above from his Odoyevsky article.

156.	K. F. Ryleyev, 'Neskol'ko mysley o poezii: otryvok iz pis'ma k N.N.', in *Literaturno-kriticheskiye raboty dekabristov*, op. cit., pp. 218—22; Lukács, *Soul and Form* (tr. Anna Bostock), London, 1974, p. 79.

157. Sigrid McLaughlin summarises Belinsky's varying views of romanticism in *'Romantic' and its Cognates*, op. cit., see n. 62 above, pp. 444–9; see also n. 11 above.

158. From the introduction to *Ernani* (quoted from Vanslov, op. cit., p. 40).

159. Vanslov, p. 27.

160. McLaughlin, op. cit., pp. 456–8.

161. Lukács, *The Historical Novel*, pp. 63, 68 and 33 (he also refers on p. 68 to 'liberalish Romanticism'). At one point (pp. 33–4) he appears to be attempting to deny that Byron should be considered a romantic.

162. Hughes, op. cit., p. 9; Lukács, *Goethe and his Age* (tr. Robert Anchor), London, 1968, pp. 150 and 202.

163. See Wellek, op. cit., p. 88; Cardinal, op. cit., p. 31.

164. S. S. Prawer, *Karl Marx and World Literature*, Oxford, 1978, p. 397; Marx is known to have sent a copy of *Klein Zaches* to Engels in 1866 (ibid., p. 373).

165. Lukács, *Goethe and his Age*, op. cit., p. 243. For a fuller discussion of 'Romantic grotesque', see Mikhail Bakhtin, *Rabelais and his World* (tr. Helene Iswolsky), Cambridge, Mass. and London, 1968, pp. 36–45.

166. James Trainer, 'The Märchen', in *The Romantic Period in Germany*, p. 114.

167. Lukács, *The Meaning of Contemporary Realism* (tr. John and Necke Mander), London, 1963, p. 52.

168. 'Devyatnadtsatyy vek', *Polnoye sobraniye sochineniy I. V. Kireyevskogo v dvukh tomakh*, Moscow, 1911 (reprinted Farnborough, 1970, p. 90).

169. Schleiermacher held that 'imagination is the highest and most original part of man and everything outside it only reflection upon it' (quoted by Roubiczek, op. cit., in *The Romantic Period in Germany*, pp. 314–15); F. Schlegel that 'the imagination was an important source of genuine knowledge not attainable by other means' (quoted by Eichner, op. cit., in *'Romantic' and its Cognates*, p. 122); and Novalis, too, stressed 'the one universal strength, Imagination' (Cardinal, op. cit., p. 37).

170. Quoted by Botnikova, op. cit., n. 58 above, p. 184. Cf. Faust's statement in *Russkiye nochi* quoted above (see n. 103).

171. Botnikova, p. 184.

172. Brown, op. cit., p. 113; Trainer, op. cit., p. 114. On the tradition of 'steps' and 'ladders' in 'the process of psychic transformation' (from Jacob's ladder, Apuleius and the visions of Zosimos), see C. G. Jung, *Psychology and Alchemy* (tr. R. F. C. Hull), 2nd edn, London, 1980, pp. 55–7, 62.

173. *Otechestvennyye zapiski*, 8, 1840, p. 51. 'Krummacher' — presumably Friedrich Adolph Krummacher (1767–1845), author of *Parables* (1805). The ladder here, and the use of the adjective 'narrow' (*uzkiy*), is reminiscent of the phrase *uzkiy put'*, which recurs in Odoyevsky's writing — as noted by Gippius in the text and title of his 1914 article (see n. 31).

174. Sakulin, *Iz istorii*, I, 2, p. 52.

175. Mann, op. cit., p. 148; *R.N.*, 1975, pp. 5–6; Tur'yan, op. cit., in *Russkiy romantizm*, pp. 205–6; Meylakh, 'Pisatel' otkryvayemyy zanovo', op. cit., p. 285.

176. Karlinsky, op. cit., n. 3 above, pp. 173–4; Cornwell, op. cit., n. 113 above, pp. 81 and 252–3.

177. See, for example, Prawer, *The Romantic Period in Germany*, pp. 5–6.
178. For example, Oken's ideas (in *Über Licht und Wärme*) on the formation of the universe ('the periphery is the centre itself — placed everywhere', quoted from Brown, op. cit., p. 105) seems strikingly similar to modern cosmological theory.
179. Lukács, *Goethe and his Age*, p. 150.
180. V. Yu. Troitsky, 'Romantizm v russkoy literature 30-kh godov XIX v. Proza' in *Istoriya romantizma v russkoy literature: romantizm v russkoy literature 20–30-kh godov XIX v. (1825–1840)*, Moscow, 1979, pp. 108–72 (164, 168–9).
181. S. Ye. Shatalov and S. V. Turayev, introduction to ibid., p. 14.

Postscript

In the last five years a number of publications have appeared which reflect the evolving interest in romanticism both in Russia and the West. In the West the most notable development has been the increasing application to romantic texts of the deconstructive techniques of Paul de Man and Jacques Derrida. (See, for instance, Paul de Man and Tilottama Rajan. For a critical review of deconstructive techniques see L. J. Swingle, and for a general explication of theory Christopher Norris, esp. pp. 94, 132). Essential to this critical approach is an understanding that rhetoric inevitably subverts meaning. Sometimes, through the transcendence of romantic irony, the romantics themselves tragically proclaimed their awareness of this fact. Where they were apparently unaware, irony has had to await the deconstructionist's gloss, which discovers it in the text's self-contradictions and the flaws in its proclaimed intentions.

Such discovered irony corollarises easily into Marxist criticism, which, emphasising 'social structure as the primary unit of analysis', challenges 'the notion that people's actions and their reasons for their actions are transparent to them . . .' (Cheyney C. Ryan, pp. 90, 93). It remains to be seen whether deconstruction, like organic criticism before it a derivative of the romantic discourse which fascinates it, will come to exert any influence on critical approaches to Russian romanticism. There are good reasons for supposing not. Deconstruction is at its best when revealing the unconsciously subversive text beneath a purportedly intentional one. It needs to pit itself against a surface which denies subterfuge. The nineteenth-century Russian writer, both anticipating and reacting to the obstacle of censorship, incorporated his subversions more consciously than his western counterpart. For instance, the submerged political code detected in *The Tales of Belkin* by Andrej Kodjak is at odds with the superficial harmlessness of the work but its influence is essentially constructive, since if Kodjak's thesis is correct the surface text is deliberately contrived for the protection of the cryptic subtext which constitutes the true theme of the work.

Russian romanticism, as the title of this collection suggests, has always occupied a problematical position in the history of Russian literature and in relation to other European romantic movements. The comparatively late flowering of Russian literature deperiodised and synchronised the movements of neo-classicism, sentimentalism and romanticism and the latter was thus denied the period of almost undisputed hegemony which it had enjoyed in some European cultures. The more extreme manifestations of romanticism were thus comparatively rare in Russian literature: Yuriy Mann, for instance, argues that in Russian romantic narrative technique a fully developed scepticism about the fabula is very uncommon. Bounds are set beyond which the ironising process, so typical of late romanticism, may not go.

Another aspect of the Russian romantic problem is that writers such as Pushkin, Lermontov and Gogol moved from romanticism towards realism in the course of their creative careers. Russian critical theory has traditionally been at pains to find verbal formulae adequate to characterise a creative output capable of such a transition. Of erstwhile attempts (such as denying the existence of romanticism altogether) something has already been said in Chapter 1. In the case of a writer of Pushkin's stature the question of his commitment to romanticism continues to exercise Soviet scholars. In recent works both Ye. A. Maymin and N. V. Fridman have emphasised that for Pushkin the chief attraction of romanticism lay in its implied definitions of freedom: these Pushkin contrived to adapt and ultimately emancipate from their exclusively romantic context (Fridman, p. 25; Maymin, pp. 72ff). In the same way Fridman also considers Pushkin's interest in the unique and unusual as having an originally romantic inspiration, though it came to provide him with a passable bridge to realism.

Pushkin also provides Lotman, in his recent commentary on *Yevgeniy Onegin*, with an occasion to formulate some more general views on romanticism. Lotman suggests an original criterion for a romantic work: the fact that a text like *Onegin* requires a detailed explication of its realia in commentary form is proof that it is not a romantic work. 'From the point of view of commentary', writes Lotman, 'a poetic conception of a romantic text can be arrived at without detailed information about the everyday life (*byt*) of the epoch in which it was written'. A romantic work is, of its nature, 'abstracted from the real *byt* of the author and his readers'. Romantics, introducing *byt* into their text, always alienate it and 'purge it of realia' (Lotman (2), p. 8). Lotman offers three categories of such alienation: the exotic (geographically alien); the historical (temporally alien); the satirical. The last category is perhaps the most interesting because here *byt* is at its potentially most intrusive but is refracted by the use of satire. The same ideas are interpreted more personally in Lotman's biography of Pushkin. Here Pushkin's romanticism is presented as a form of fashionable cultural behaviour, 'bookish' in origin, whereby an artificial 'double of *byt* reality' is consciously manufactured by the aspiring romantic (Lotman (1), pp. 56, 58). For Lotman, Pushkin's romanticism was a phase which the poet felt socially obliged to put himself through without feeling total commitment. Victor Terras has also argued that romanticism was essentially uncongenial to Pushkin who consistently deromanticised the romantic *fabulas* he made use of. Unfortunately Terras defines romanticism along the line of Abrams' high romantic, biblical schema and so it is inevitable that few of Pushkin's works will accord with it (it suits Lermontov much better). A. D. P. Briggs addresses the same subject from a different angle in Chapter 2.

Recently a work ostensibly devoted to an aspect of German romanticism has offered a novel perspective on Russian romanticism, in particular on its problematical role in the works of Pushkin and Gogol. Virgil Nemoianu has adopted the German critical term *Biedermeier* to characterise a distinct form of 'tamed' romanticism which flourished in Europe between 1815 and 1848. It represents a narrowing of the wider perspectives and ambitions of earlier romanticism, with an insistence on the simplicity of everyday life and a strong idyllic orientation. Nemoianu believes that 'Russian literature skipped high romanticism and became Biedermeier' (Nemoianu, p. 138). Pushkin and Gogol exhibit strong *Biedermeier* characteristics. Both writers are concerned with the idyll. 'Many of Pushkin's best works have as their theme the defeat of romanticism by the Biedermeier', the death of Lensky providing a particularly striking example (Nemoianu, p. 142). Ultimately, *Biedermeier* itself is crushed: Pushkin exemplifies this in the fate of Eugene in *The Bronze Horseman*; Eugene, with his humble ambitions for domestic bliss, being a typical *Biedermeier* character. Gogol is, if anything, easier than Pushkin to assimilate to this paradigm since idyllic structures are crucial in his work. However, Nemoianu implies that Gogol's personal tragedy lay in his desire to retain high romantic, redemptive aims while making his artistic statements in the reduced and worldly terms of *Biedermeier* (Nemoianu, p. 147).

Biedermeierism is certainly an original formulation for the characterising features of many works produced in Russia during the romantic period. However, two other critics have recently addressed themselves to substantially the same phenomenon, in somewhat different contexts. Amalia Hanke, from an essentially philosophical standpoint, divides romantics into two categories. Some, like Blake and Coleridge, she calls 'transcendental idealists' (Amalia Hanke, pp. 7, 8): these are extreme subjectivists who assume, in epistemological terms, the complete construction of reality by the knowing subject. They claim a mystic, direct vision of the transcendental unity of all things, a vision comparatively uncluttered by concern for the natural world. To these she contrasts 'natural idealists' such as Wordsworth and Keats. These evince 'strong attachment to the phenomenal world' and are unable to deny its objective reality (Hanke, p. 8). Nature, however, is able to offer them occasional moments of intersection between time and eternity. Hanke's prognosis for this late romantic trend is pessimistic: the tendency is for the attachment to nature to dominate the artist's creativity to such a degree that the transcendental insights are lost altogether. These moments of insight are strongly reminiscent of Gogol's accesses of poetic inspiration which soar above the natural clutter of *Dead Souls* achieving their zenith in the *troika* passage which concludes Part 1.

The Soviet critic A. M. Gurevich has also detected something similar to Nemoianu's *Biedermeier* in Pushkin, though he identifies it structurally as a romantic subtext beneath a substantially realistic discourse. 'The world of Belkin' (*Belkinskiy mir*) in *The Tales of Belkin* has still much in common with a romantic idyll sealed off from reality. However, Gurevich's romantic subtext in Pushkin is considerably wider than *Biedermeier*, embracing as it does other romantic themes, notably that of revolt (in *The Bronze Horseman* and *The Captain's Daughter*). In this connection it might well be added that although such a concept as *Biedermeier* may be helpful as an approach to the alloyed romanticisms of Pushkin and Gogol, it is far less relevant, if at all, to the other, often disparate forms of romanticism represented by the other writers dealt with in the present collection: the philosophical romanticism of Venevitinov and Odoyevsky, the revolutionary romanticism of Bestuzhev-Marlinsky and the Byronism of Lermontov.

It is considerably easier to identify the diverse trends which comprise the romantic movement than to address oneself to romanticism as a whole. Traditionally, Soviet scholars have attempted to simplify the difficulty by formulating romanticism as two major trends (progressive/revolutionary and conservative/reactionary) locked in dialectical conflict. Lauren Leighton is probably correct in concluding that this formulation has persisted because it accords well with Leninist teaching (Leighton (1), p. 64). However, two recent theoretical articles in *Voprosy literatury* suggest that the time-honoured division may now have fallen into desuetude. D. Nalivayko and I. Terteryan concentrate on those questions which were not resolved in earlier debates on romanticism. Nalivayko asserts the essential unity of the romantic movement but sets out to list the major trends within it. Among these are inner (subjective) romanticism; outer (nature-oriented) romanticism; folkloric, Byronic, Gothic, Utopian, historical, religious and civic. Nalivayko insists upon organicism as a kind of unifying credo for the whole movement. Trends within the movement are essentially differing receptions of organicism. Central to Nalivayko's approach is that romanticism is a heterodox phenomenon with 'centrifugal tendencies' (Nalivayko, p. 164). The trends are often the focus for geographically or chronologically localised dissent from the main movement. The major trend opposing organicism (though it is originally posited by it) is artistic preoccupation with uniqueness and individuality. The dialectic between man as individual and man as part of an organic whole is central to the fate of romanticism: the first trend mutated into symbolism and expressionism, the second into realism. Nalivayko's use of the synchronic/diachronic model for approaching romanticism offers a potentially new perspective for Soviet romanticism theory and an interesting alternative to the *romantizm/romantika* distinction which is discussed in Chapter 1.

Responding to Nalivayko, Terteryan agrees that the old progressive/conservative dualism is now obsolete. He notes that the so-called reactionaries (Novalis, Hoffmann, Wordsworth) had often produced more radical critiques of their societies than the so-called revolutionaries. On the whole, however, he feels that Nalivayko's 'trends' are too schematic (failing, for instance, to account for the combination of more than one trend in a single creative career) and suggests 'tendency' as a preferable term. Terteryan's use of the word tendency, while denoting the same phenomenon as Nalivayko's trend, does have the virtue of preserving something of the uniqueness of individual creativity (artists can *have* tendencies but not trends). Terteryan, like Nalivayko, perceives romanticism dialectically, but it is a dialectic between the desire for truth and naturalness on the one hand and the demand for maximum expressiveness on the other, both being enjoined by romantic aesthetics. With the passing of the romantic period these two principles developed into different movements much as suggested by Nalivayko.

No doubt the Soviet discussion on the nature of romanticism will continue. The perennial concern with romanticism reflects the fact that, as Terry Eagleton suggests, many of our modern definitions of literature began to develop and take shape in the romantic era (Eagleton, p. 18). More than that, our modern critical modes, whether formalist, organicist, structuralist or deconstructive, were anticipated in significant ways by the romantics. Each new critical system, in trying its strength against the complex texts of the romantic period, is also, in a sense, returning to its critical origins. For these reasons the problem of romanticism appears to be eternally reformulable, as well as eternally relevant: it is 'the problem of the interrelationship of man with his history, his nation, his society, with nature and with himself' (Terteryan, p. 181).

Select bibliography

As well as references in the *Postscript* the following list contains significant works relevant to the study of Russian romanticism published since 1980.

Al'tshuller, Mark, *Predtechi slavyanofil'stva v russkoy literature*, Ann Arbor, Michigan, 1984.

Arndt, Walter, ed. and tr., *Alexander Pushkin: Collected Narrative and Lyrical Poetry*, Ann Arbor, Michigan, 1983.

Briggs, A. D. P., *Alexander Pushkin: A Critical Study*, London, 1983.

Cornwell, Neil, *V. F. Odoyevsky: His Life, Times and Milieu*, London, 1986.

Debreczeny, Paul, ed., *American Contributions to the Ninth International Congress of Slavists* (Kiev, September 1983), II (Literature, Poetics, History), Columbus, 1983.

Debreczeny, Paul, *The Other Pushkin: A Study of Alexander Pushkin's Prose Fiction*, Stanford, 1983.

Debreczeny, Paul, tr., *Pushkin: The Complete Prose Fiction*, Stanford, 1983.

de Man, Paul, *The Rhetoric of Romanticism*, New York, 1984.

Eagleton, Terry, *Literary Theory: An Introduction*, Oxford, 1983.

Fridman, N. V., *Romantizm v tvorchestve A. S. Pushkina*, Moscow, 1980.

Garrard, John, *Mikhail Lermontov*, Boston, 1982.

Gurevich, A. M., 'Tema malen'kogo cheloveka u Pushkina i yeyo romanticheskiy podtekst', *Izvestiya Akademii Nauk SSSR (Seriya literatury i yazyka)*, XLII, 5, 1983, pp. 433—43.

Hanke, Amalia, *Spatiotemporal Consciousness in English and German Romanticism*, European University Studies, Series 18, XXV, Berne, 1981.

Kartashova, I. V., 'O svoyeobrazii esteticheskogo ideala rannikh romantikov' in *Problemy romanticheskogo metoda i stilya*, ed. N. A. Gulyayev, et al., Kalinin, 1980, pp. 3—23.

Kodjak, Andrej, *Pushkin's I. P. Belkin*, Columbus, Ohio, 1979.

Leighton, Lauren G., 'The Great Soviet Debate Over Romanticism: 1957—1964', *Studies in Romanticism*, XXII, 1, 1983, pp. 41—64 [Leighton (1)].

Leighton, Lauren G., 'Romanticism' in *Handbook of Russian Literature*, ed. Victor Terras, 1985, pp. 372—6.

Liberman, Anatoly, tr., and commentary, *Mikhail Lermontov: Major Poetical Works*, London, 1983.

Lotman, Yu. M., *Aleksandr Sergeyevich Pushkin: Biografiya pisatelya*, Leningrad, 1981 [Lotman (1)].

Lotman, Yu. M., *Roman A. S. Pushkina 'Yevgeniy Onegin'*, Leningrad, 1980 [Lotman (2)].

McCarthy, Sheila M., 'The Legacy of N. I. Nadeždin's Critique of Romanticism', *Slavic and East European Journal*, XXVIII, 2, 1984, pp. 164—79.

Mann, Yu. V., 'K probleme romanticheskogo povestvovaniya', *Izvestiya Akademii Nauk SSSR (Seriya literatury i yazyka)*, XL, 3, 1981, pp. 211—24.

Manuylov, V. A., et al., eds, *Lermontovskaya Entsiklopediya*, Moscow, 1981.

Maymin, Ye. A., *Pushkin: Zhizn' i tvorchestvo*, Moscow, 1981.

Mersereau, John Jr, *Russian Romantic Fiction*, Ann Arbor, Michigan, 1983.

Nalivayko, D., 'Romantizm kak esteticheskaya sistema', *Voprosy literatury*, XI, 1982, pp. 156—94.

Nemoianu, Virgil, *The Taming of Romanticism: European Literature and the Age of Biedermeier*, Harvard and London, 1984.

Norris, Christopher, *Deconstruction: Theory and Practice*, London, 1982.

Offord, Derek, 'Druzhinin and "The Pushkin School" of Russian Literature' in *Poetry, Prose and Public Opinion: Aspects of Russia, 1850—1890*, ed. William Harrison and Avril Pyman, Letchworth, 1984.

Peace, R., *The Enigma of Gogol*, Cambridge, 1981.

Pratt, Sarah, *Russian Metaphysical Romanticism: The Poetry of Tiutchev and Boratynskii*, Stanford, 1984.

Rajan, Tilottama, *Dark Interpreter: The Discourse of Romanticism*, Ithaca and London, 1980.

Ryan, Cheyney C., 'The Fiends of Commerce: Romantic and Marxist Criticisms of Classical Political Economy', *History of Political Economy*, XIII, Spring 1981, pp. 80–94.

Rydel, Christine, ed., *The Ardis Anthology of Russian Romanticism*, Ann Arbor, Michigan, 1984.

Swingle, L. J., 'Classic and Romantic', *Modern Language Quarterly*, March 1983, pp. 81–91.

Terras, Victor, 'Pushkin and Romanticism', in *Alexander Pushkin, Symposium II*, ed. Andrej Kodjak and Krystyna Pomorska, Columbus, Ohio, 1980, pp. 49–59.

Terteryan, I., 'Romantizm kak tselostnoye yavleniye', *Voprosy literatury*, IV, 1983, pp. 151–81.

Tikhomirov, V. N., 'K voprosu o vzaymodeystvii prosvetitel'stva i romantizma I. A. Goncharova', in *Problemy romanticheskogo metoda i stilya*, ed. N. A. Gulyayev, et al., Kalinin, 1980, pp. 49–59.

Index